EYEWITNESS IDENTIFICATION

LAWRENCE TAYLOR, J.D.

Contemporary Litigation Series

Consulting Editors for the
CONTEMPORARY LITIGATION SERIES

Professor Stephen R. Saltzburg
University of Virginia Law School

Professor Kenneth R. Redden
University of Virginia Law School

EYEWITNESS IDENTIFICATION

LAWRENCE TAYLOR, J.D.

Associate Professor

Gonzaga University, School of Law

Formerly, Deputy Public Defender, Deputy District Attorney (Los Angeles) and Attorney General's Special Prosecutor (Montana)

THE MICHIE COMPANY
Law Publishers
CHARLOTTESVILLE, VIRGINIA

Library of Congress Card Number: 82-81703
ISBN 0-87215-423-8

For my son Christopher

TABLE OF CONTENTS

ACKNOWLEDGEMENTS

While this book has been the result of research based upon many legal and scientific sources, the author is particularly indebted to Professors Elizabeth Loftus and Daniel Yarmey for their kind cooperation in making available materials from their respective books, *Eyewitness Testimony* (Harvard Univ. 1979) and *The Psychology of Eyewitness Testimony* (Free Press/MacMillan 1979), both excellent scientific works deserving to be on any trial attorney's bookshelf.

I would also like to express my appreciation to Bancroft-Whitney and the Lawyers Cooperative Publishing Company for their permission to use certain materials written for them by me and published in *American Jurisprudence Proof of Facts 2d* volumes 18 and 19.

PREFACE

> "My conclusions have cost me some labor from the want of coincidence between accounts of the same occurrences by different eyewitnesses. . . ."
>
> Thucydides, *The History of the Pelopennesian War* (413 B.C.)

On April 15, 1920, two men were observed leaning against a residential fence in Braintree, Massachusetts, watching as a cashier and his bodyguard walked by carrying bags containing over $15,000 from a nearby factory. One of the leaning men suddenly jumped forward, pulled a gun and shot the bodyguard, then shot the cashier as he tried to run away. A car pulled up next to the bodies, and the gunman and his accomplice jumped in and were quickly spirited away.

Some time later, police arrested two men for the killings: Nicola Sacco and Bartolomeo Vanzetti. Witnesses to the shooting were repeatedly shown photographs of the two suspects and then brought in to identify the two men in their jail cells. On May 31, 1921, the trial of the Commonwealth of Massachusetts versus Sacco and Vanzetti began.

Four witnesses positively identified Vanzetti during their testimony. Yet, not a single one of them had been able to identify him originally; it was only after being repeatedly shown photographs of the immigrant fish peddler that they were finally able to confirm his role in the murders. One of these eyewitnesses had even told a friend that "all he could see was the gun and [then] he ducked."

The case against Vanzetti was strengthened with the introduction of evidence that he had been convicted of an attempted payroll robbery a year earlier. That conviction rested heavily upon the testimony of an eyewitness who told a detective hours after the crime that he had not been able to get a good look at the culprit's face. Vanzetti was arrested two weeks later, and the witness taken by the police station to look at him. At the preliminary hearing, the witness' description was amazingly thorough, and at the trial it grew even more complete in detail; he had now become quite sure that he had gotten a very good look at the culprit.

The case against Sacco was similar. Five eyewitnesses positively identified the Italian shoemaker at trial. Yet, one had earlier admitted that he had not seen enough to identify anyone. Another advised the police that she was unable to see the faces of either of the two men. A third had told three different individuals that he would be unable to make any identification. A fourth had testified at the preliminary hearing that she had not seen enough at the scene to be able to identify Sacco.

At the trial, one of the witnesses positively identified Sacco as the man in the back seat of the car and gave the following detailed description: "[He was] slightly taller than I am. He weighed possibly from 140 to 145 pounds. He was a muscular — he was an active man. I noticed particularly the left hand was a good sized hand, a hand that denoted strength. . . . He had a gray, what I thought was a shirt . . . the face was what we would call clear-cut, clean-cut face. Through here was a little narrow, just a little narrow. The forehead was high. The hair was brushed back and it was between, I should think, two inches and two and one-half inches in length, and had dark eyebrows, by the complexion was a white, a peculiar white that looked greenish." The witness based her observations upon having seen the killers in the car as it sped away; she was sixty to eighty feet from the car, and observed it for only two or three seconds.

The defense presented convincing alibi evidence. A merchant testified that he recalled Vanzetti buying cloth from him in Plymouth at the time of the killings, and a clerk from the Italian consulate in Boston clearly recalled Sacco using a family group photo in applying for a passport on that day.

On July 14, 1921, Sacco and Vanzetti were found guilty of murder. Six years later, both men were electrocuted at Charlestown Prison. Vanzetti's last words, as he was being strapped into the electric chair, were: "I wish to tell you that I am an innocent man. I never committed any crime but sometimes some sin. I wish to forgive some people for what they are now doing to me."

The Sacco-Vanzetti trial is only one of the more celebrated examples of questionable eyewitness identification; it is certainly not the most blatant. Cases in which faulty identification plays the central role in a criminal conviction are common — even accepted as a fact of judicial life. Clearly, the detection and exposition of such damning evidence remains one of the primary tasks of trial counsel. Yet, in perhaps no other area of the law does the performance of this role rest so heavily upon a deep understanding of both human psychology and legal procedures.

How can various witnesses perceive and recall an identical event so differently? How is it possible for an honest witness — convinced that he is right — to be so mistaken? What are the mental processes by which identification is made? How can these processes be affected by police identification procedures? What methods are available with which counsel can prevent — or at least expose — erroneous identification? What are the legal safeguards which apply to pretrial and trial identification?

These are some of the questions which will be answered in the following pages.

PART ONE

THE PSYCHOLOGY OF THE EYEWITNESS

§ 1. Reliability of Eyewitness Identification.

> "What is the worth of identification testimony even when uncontradicted? The identification of strangers is proverbially untrustworthy. The hazards of such testimony are established by a formidable number of instances in the records of English and American trials. These instances are recent — not due to the brutalities of ancient criminal procedure."
>
> Felix Frankfurter

The tragic irony of eyewitness testimony is that it is at the same time the most trusted of evidence and too often the least reliable. As famed author/attorney Erle Stanley Gardner once observed, "Any veteran attorney knows that circumstantial evidence is about the best evidence there is and that eyewitness identification evidence is just about the worst."[1] This fact of judicial life has been borne out repeatedly in the courts — sometimes at the expense of innocent accused — as well as in hundreds of psychological tests. Yet, the average juror continues to place a great

1. Buckhout, R., 23 Scientific American 231 (1974).

amount of faith in the unerring ability of his fellow man to identify one individual from among many.

It has been aptly stated by a noted expert in the field:

> Eyewitness testimony is unreliable. Research and courtroom experience provide ample evidence that an eyewitness to a crime is being asked to be something and to do something that a normal human being was not created to be or do ... to play the role of tape recorder on whose tape the events of the crime have left an impression.... It reflects a 19th century view of man as perceiver.... Neither perception nor memory is a copying process. Perception and memory are decision-making processes affected by the totality of a person's abilities, background, attitudes, motives and beliefs, by the environment, and by the way his recollection is eventually tested.[2]

The following materials will provide trial counsel with a basic understanding to be considered not only for the purpose of understanding the underlying concepts, but also for their potential use in trial — as illustration in argument, as experimentation in court, or as material for cross-examination.

§ 1-1. The Effect of Eyewitness Testimony.

It was long ago observed in field studies that eyewitness identification evidence — no matter how unbelievable — is "taken by the average juror as absolute proof."[3] The unreliability of such evidence is now widely accepted among lawyers and psychologists, yet the man in the street continues to embrace it as determinative. While a juror may display a healthy skepticism when confronted with, say, fingerprint evidence or testimony establishing an alibi, this

---

2. Gardner, D.S., 50 Journal of Criminal Law, Criminology, and Police Science 20 (1959).

3. Wilder, L., et al., *Personal Identification* (1918).

doubt strangely disappears in the face of a witness pointing his finger at the defendant.

For those who question the tremendous impact of eyewitness testimony on the outcome of a trial, consider a study conducted in England. Headed by the renowned criminal jurist Lord Patrick Devlin, a committee studied all trials in England and Wales that had taken place in 1973 and which involved the use of a lineup — *i.e.*, where identification was a significant factor. They found 850 individuals chosen from lineups, of whom 82 percent were subsequently convicted by juries. In 347 of these 850 cases the *only* incriminating evidence was the identification. Yet the conviction rate among these 347 was a full 74 percent. This is all the more interesting when a further statistic comes to light: In roughly *half* of these trials, there was only one eyewitness. Clearly the Devlin Report [4] indicates that evidence of eyewitness identification has an overwhelming influence on juries.

What lawyers have observed in the courts, scientists have been able to confirm in psychological studies. Professor Elizabeth Loftus, perhaps the leading expert today on the psychology of the eyewitness, has conducted a number of experiments to determine the impact of eyewitness testimony on a trier of fact. In one of these,[5] Loftus presented a trial situation to 150 subject-jurors. Each of these "jurors" was told the following uncontested facts about the crime: The owner of a grocery store was confronted by a robber who demanded money. The grocer took $110 from the cash register and handed it to the robber, who grabbed the money and began to walk away. The robber then stopped, turned, and fired two shots at the grocer and his young granddaughter

4. Devlin, P., et al., *Report to the Secretary of State for the Home Department of the Departmental Committee on Evidence of Identification in Criminal Cases* (1976).

5. Loftus, E.F., 8 Psychology Today 116 (1974).

who was also standing behind the counter; both died instantly. The police arrested the defendant two-and-a-half hours later.

All 150 "jurors" were then presented with additional evidence in the form of arguments from the attorneys. The prosecution disclosed that the robber had been seen running into the apartment house in which the defendant lived; a search of the defendant's room disclosed $123 in cash; ammonia used to clean the grocery store's floor was found on his shoes; and paraffin tests indicated there was a possibility he had fired a gun that day. The defense pointed out that the defendant had taken the stand and denied guilt; the ammonia could have come from other places since he worked as a delivery man; and he had never fired a gun in his life. Fifty of the 150 "jurors" were then polled. Of these only 18 percent voted for conviction.

Now, Professor Loftus added an additional bit of prosecution evidence for the remaining 100 jurors: A store clerk had testified that he saw the defendant shoot the grocer and his granddaughter. Fifty of these 100 were now polled, and the conviction rate jumped from 18 percent to 72 percent.

Finally — and most interestingly — Loftus added the following relevant defense evidence: The eyewitness had been discredited by evidence that his uncorrected vision was only 20/400, that he had not been wearing his glasses when the robbery took place, and that he could not possibly have seen the robber's face from where he stood at the time. The last fifty jurors were then polled. Amazingly, 68 percent still voted for conviction — a drop of only four percent from the jurors who had heard the eyewitness testimony before it had supposedly been "discredited." Clearly, there existed an almost overwhelming faith in such testimony regardless of the circumstances.

In an experiment conducted by psychologists at Ohio

State University,[6] even more dramatic results were obtained. Subjects were broken down into two groups: witnesses and jurors. The "witnesses" were seated in a room. After a period of time, an individual entered the room, spied a calculator that had been left on a table, said she wanted it, picked it up and placed it in her purse and left. Thirty seconds later, the witnesses were given questionnaires and asked to give a description of the "thief," and then to pick her picture out of a set of six.

The "jurors" were then told about the "theft" and the identifications, and asked to observe one of the witnesses being cross-examined for the purpose of deciding whether the witness was correct in his or her identification. Half of the "jurors" then watched a witness testify correctly, and half observed a witness who had been completely wrong in his identification of the "thief."

The results were that roughly 80 percent of the jurors believed the eyewitness was correct in his or her identification. Incredibly enough, however, this 80 percent figure applied to *both* sets of jurors! In other words, the study indicated that the *accuracy* of identification is irrelevant: Jurors are just as likely to accept erroneous eyewitness evidence as they are likely to accept accurate eyewitness evidence.

If there is any trial lawyer who still has confidence in a jury's collective ability to accord eyewitness testimony its proper weight, he should consider the case of Harry Cashin.[7] The nineteen-year-old Cashin was brought to police headquarters three hours after a violent robbery in which a gun battle resulted in one of the robbers and a police officer being killed; a second robber escaped but was probably wounded in the process. Cashin was taken to

6. Wells, G.L., 12 Journal of Personality and Social Psychology 1546 (1978).

7. People v. Cashin, 259 N.Y. 434, 182 N.E. 74 (1932).

headquarters primarily because he had been a previous employee of the dead bandit, and it was hoped he would be able to give the police information about the dead robber's friends and acquaintances. Every other witness to the robbery was at the police station at the same time as Cashin; none identified him. Two months later, a prostitute picked Cashin out as the second robber.

At the conclusion of the trial, the prosecution's sole evidence was the prostitute's identification. The defense, on the other hand, had established that the prostitute had earlier sworn that she absolutely could *not* identify Cashin. Further, he did not resemble the description given by the other witnesses who had observed the crime and, in fact, every witness but the prostitute refused to identify Cashin as the culprit. Added to this was the fact that the escaped robber had probably been wounded, while Cashin was untouched three hours after the incident. Even more convincing, a cab driver identified the dead robber as one of two men he had driven to the scene of the crime; he testified that Cashin was definitely not the other man. Finally, Cashin had a solid alibi established by two witnesses.

The jury found Harry Cashin guilty of murder in the first degree.

Fortunately, Cashin's conviction was later overturned "in the interest of justice." But the lesson remains for all trial lawyers: Any eyewitness identification, no matter how apparent its untrustworthiness and no matter how contradicted by credible evidence, represents a very real danger to the client facing a jury.

§ 1-2. The Causes of False Identification.

Why is eyewitness identification such an inherently unreliable form of evidence? Why, despite the tremendous credence placed on such testimony by the average juror, is such evidence so commonly found to be in error?

There are basically four reasons for incorrect identification:

1. The witness is lying;
2. Perception of the event was impaired;
3. The witness' memory is faulty; or
4. Subsequent suggestive factors have influenced identification.

In most cases, a combination of two or more of these factors will be operating to produce a false identification. It is, of course, trial counsel's task to isolate the causes and expose them through the process of cross-examination.

There is always the possibility that the eyewitness may be lying in his testimony. With any witness, counsel must consider the motives for committing perjury: hatred for the defendant, a desire for revenge, or perhaps monetary or other gain. The motive for lying may be subtle. The desire to help, for example, can be a strong incentive. Feeling an urge to help solve the crime or bring a criminal to justice by rendering assistance to authority figures, the witness is compelled to identify someone — *anyone.* A sense of frustration from living in a world of seemingly unpunished crime and violence may give the witness further incentive to identify someone; his impotence in the face of years of crime is solved by finally punishing one of "them." Such individuals can become convinced that they are correct in their identification, thus crossing the line from perjury into erroneous testimony.

Yet another consideration is the witness who craves attention, wants to be liked, and needs to feel important. Inability to positively identify a suspect will mean to him that he will not receive the attention he needs. By pointing to the suspect, he will become the "star witness," the center of attention, and needed by the father-figure police or prosecutor. He, too, may come to believe that he is telling the truth.

Related to this is the rare case involving fantasy. Certain individuals will create fictitious people or imaginary events to satisfy their own psychological needs. This is most common among juvenile witnesses, and can take a particularly insidious form when the client is imagined — for whatever reason — to have been a participant in a real or fantasized crime.

Whatever the motive, it must be clearly brought out for the jurors to see. Counsel must attack the substance of the testimony itself — usually through establishing inconsistency either externally (with other testimony, evidence or known facts) or internally (with other segments of the witness' own testimony).

In the vast majority of cases, however, the faulty identification will be made by an honest witness — one who sincerely believes he is being both truthful and accurate, and has no reason to fabricate. These are the most difficult situations to handle because the witness is not trying to hide anything and the reasons for the misidentification are usually buried deep within his mind. Perhaps the witness had faulty vision at the time of observing the events or environmental conditions at the scene — lighting, distance, amount of time for observation — impaired perception; or perhaps the witness' memory is faulty, becoming more so with the passage of time.

In short, most eyewitnesses err because the human being is a fallible creation. His physiological equipment is imperfect: He does not always see what is there, and he does not always remember what he believes he has seen. Aggravating this fallibility as a human being, he is very subject to suggestive influences subsequent to the observation. What he recalls having seen may, in fact, be a product of another mind altogether.

To understand the complex procedures of the human mind as it relates to the eyewitness, picture identification as a three-stage process. The first stage consists of the *acquisition* of data; in this stage an event is perceived and information about it is stored in the witness' memory. The second stage involves the *retention* of that information; what has been observed is stored in the memory for future use. The third stage constitutes the *retrieval* phase of identification; the memory is scanned and relevant information is pulled out and communicated.

Each of these stages is critical to the eventual identification of a criminal suspect, and each of these stages can be affected by both internal and external factors. The information may simply not have been perceived in the first place, resulting in a failure at the acquisition stage. It may have been perceived accurately, but then lost or distorted during the retention stage, or it may become lost or interfered with during the retrieval stage.

Let us take a look at examples of how information at each stage can be adversely affected. The first stage is the acquisitive phase — or, to put it another way, the perception of objects and events. The ability of a witness to accurately observe is affected by a number of different considerations, among them his cultural expectations. There is a widely held belief among Americans, for example, that fat people are jolly, that Mexicans are lazy, and that Asians are industrious and neat. These stereotypes can have a profound influence on what an individual observes; for what he observes is influenced by what he *expects* to observe.

This is illustrated by a simple experiment conducted by two psychologists.[8] They showed subjects a drawing of two men talking to each other in a subway train. One of the men, wearing a neat business suit, was black; the other, wearing work clothes and holding a straight razor at his side, was white. The subject viewed the drawing briefly,

8. Allport, G., et al., *The Psychology of Rumor* (Henry Holt 1947).

then was required to tell a second subject all about it; the second subject then told a third and so on for six or seven subjects. Over forty groups of subjects were used, including blacks *and* whites. The results were dramatic. In over half of the subject groups, the final subject reported that the *black* man held the straight razor. In many cases, he was described as "threatening the white man with it" or "brandishing it wildly." Clearly a stereotype expectation — among blacks as well as whites — colored the perceptions of both those who perceived by observing the drawing and those who perceived by listening to the descriptions of others.

The retentive stage is also a fertile area for distortion of identification. Once stored in the memory, information can become lost — *i.e.,* forgotten. Also, contrary to common belief, once information is incorporated into the memory it *can* still be altered by intervening information.

As an example of this latter phenomenon, consider an experiment conducted by Professor Loftus.[9] Forty subjects were shown a film of a class being disrupted by *eight* demonstrators. At the end of the film the subjects were given questionnaires to answer about the film. Twenty of them were asked, "Was the leader of the *four* demonstrators who entered the classroom a male?" The remaining twenty were asked, "Was the leader of the *twelve* demonstrators who entered the classroom a male?" One week later all forty subjects were given a new questionnaire to answer — including the question, "How many demonstrators did you see entering the classroom?" The results were interesting. For those who had been given the "four" question the average answer was 6.4 demonstrators, while for the subjects who had been given the "twelve" question the average was 8.9. Obviously the intervening effect of the question on the subjects' memories was considerable; the subjects actually

9. Loftus, E.F., 7 Cognitive Psychology 560 (1975).

acquired additional information — or had existing information altered — during the retentive stage.

The relevance of this experiment should not be lost on criminal lawyers. Police questioning or newspaper accounts can have a tremendous impact on the witness' "memory."

Finally, the retrieval stage should be clearly understood as critical to eyewitness identification in criminal cases. It is during this phase that the information is recalled from memory — usually in reply to police questioning. Just as such questioning can implant new information during the memory stage, so it can also have a significant effect during the recall phase.

Again, an experiment was conducted to show how even the wording of a question can affect the answer given by a witness.[10] Subjects were shown a film about sports and were then asked a series of questions about the film after being advised that they should make every effort to be as accurate as possible. Half of the subjects were asked one form of a question, while the others were asked another form of a question. For example, half were asked, "How *long* was the movie?"; the other half were asked, "How *short* was the movie?" Those asked the former replied with an average answer of 130 minutes, while those asked the latter had an average answer of 100 minutes. Similarly, half were asked, "How *tall* was the basketball player?" while the other half were asked, "How *short* was the basketball player?" Again the results were clear. Those answering how tall the player was replied with an average answer of 79 inches; the subjects asked how short he was gave an average answer of 69 inches. The practical application of such psychological experimentation should not be lost upon counsel in a criminal case involving police questioning of eyewitnesses.

Given such subtle workings of the human mind, how does

---

10. Harris, R.J., 97 Journal of Experimental Psychology 399 (1973).

counsel determine when he is dealing with an accurate witness and when he is confronting an honestly mistaken one? Of course we cannot go into the witness' mind, but we can attempt to determine as far as possible the potentially suggestive influences that have acted upon the witness. For this reason alone it is important to have counsel present at any pre-trial identification procedure, such as lineups, photographic displays, or the questioning of witnesses. If counsel was not present, he should make every effort to obtain tape recordings or other evidence of exactly how identification was elicited from the eyewitness; often the only evidence will be the faulty recall of the witness, the self-serving testimony of the officer, or the highly edited version contained in police reports.

Lacking specific evidence of suggestive identification procedures, counsel can still look for the possibility of circumstantial signs of an erroneous identification. The following considerations indicating the probable unreliability of eyewitness identification testimony have been suggested by William J. Bryan, Jr., M.D.: [11]

1. The witness originally stated that he would be unable to identify anyone.
2. The identifying witness knew the defendant prior to the crime, but made no accusation against him when questioned by the police.
3. A serious discrepancy existed between the identifying witness' original description of the perpetrator of the crime and the actual description of the defendant.
4. Before identifying the defendant at trial, the witness erroneously identified some other person.
5. Other witnesses to the crime failed to identify the defendant.
6. Prior to the trial, the witness saw the defendant but failed to identify him.

---

11. Bryan, 10 Calif. Trial Lawyers Journal (2) 50 (1971).

7. Before the crime was committed, the witness had a very limited opportunity to see the defendant.
8. The witness and the person identified were of different racial groups.
9. During his original observation of the perpetrator of the crime, the witness was unaware that a crime situation was involved.
10. Identification contained inaccuracies about the person identified.
11. Witnesses differed as to identification of the defendant.
12. Witnesses placed the defendant in two different situations at the same time.
13. A considerable period of time elapsed between the witness' view of the criminal and his identification of the defendant.
14. The crime was committed by a number of persons.
15. The witness failed to make a positive trial identification.

§ 1-3. Individual Witness Capability.

Different witnesses vary tremendously in their individual abilities to observe, remember and recall. Circumstantial factors can, of course, be important in whether an individual is a good witness concerning a given incident: He may have been preoccupied with other matters, suffering from a headache, or simply not paying attention. But assuming equal attention and diverting influences, some people are simply better witnesses. What are the characteristics of a "good" witness? Is it possible to determine whether a given individual is a "good" or "bad" witness?

The day is coming when a witness can be psychologically tested and rated as to the reliability of his testimony, and his evidence weighed accordingly. In fact, such a test already exists — a test which counsel might consider employing with a progressive and cooperative court. Dr. Robert Buckhout, Associate Professor of Psychology and Director of the Center for Responsive Psychology at the

Brooklyn College for the City University of New York, describes a recently developed test using "signal detection theory" as "a means of coping with the fact that an observer's attitude interferes with his detection, processing and reporting of sensory stimuli."

In this test, the subject is given a stimulus (sight, sound or whatever) and asked to reply "yes" or "no" to a question concerning it; some stimuli are purposely false. For example, an auditory signal is sent in the midst of confusing noise; sometimes only the noise is sent. Is a signal heard? The tester then counts the correct "yes" answers ("hits") and the incorrect "yes" answers ("false alarms"). A cautious person will have very few "false alarms" and a high proportion of "hits"; a less cautious person will have more "hits," but at the cost of a large number of "false alarms." From the test information is drafted a "witness sensitivity curve" — a theoretical indication of the propensity for that person to give a "false alarm" (that is, to mistakenly identify a suspect).

Until the day that such testing becomes a proven and legally accepted procedure, counsel will have to rely upon his own assessment of an individual's abilities as a witness. Yet, there are certain characteristics about which general conclusions can be drawn. These involve the witness' age, sex, race, training and general anxiety level.

§ 1-3.1. Age.

Age can clearly be a factor in a person's ability to perceive an event and later recall it accurately. Generally speaking, psychologists have shown through repeated experiments that there is an improvement of eyewitness capability up to the ages of about fifteen or twenty, and that a decline begins at about the age of sixty. This is, of course, a generality; there is no end of examples of eighty-year-olds who can observe and recall with remarkable clarity.

The generality is most accurately applied to children. A child is constantly in a process of development, and his ability to observe, identify an object in his mind, relate it to his environment, remember it, later recall it, and match it with another object — *e.g.*, identify a suspect as the perpetrator seen earlier — will vary according to his stage of development. This is most apparent in the ability to recognize faces, illustrated in an experiment [12] in which a group of seventeen-year-olds and a group of twelve-year-olds were shown slides of faces and later asked to match them with other slides of faces; the older group had a higher percentage of correct identifications. Similar experiments have shown that a group of twelve- to fourteen-year-olds will identify better than six- to nine-year-olds,[13] and that eleven-year-olds will outperform eight-year-olds — who will, in turn, do better than five-year-olds.[14]

As with recognition ability, memory in the child improves with age. Jean Piaget, a prominent Swiss psychologist considered to be the primary authority on cognitive development in children, has shown that memory develops as it interacts with the development of other cognitive skills, such as the ability to group materials that must be remembered into categories; an object will be more easily remembered, as in the above example, because the child will learn that it belongs in the category of men's faces. He illustrated this memory ability very clearly in an experiment [15] in which children were shown a row of ten sticks of different lengths arranged in parallel and asked to remember them. A week later the children were asked to reproduce the sticks by drawing them; eight months later

12. Ellis, H., et al., 123 Journal of Genetic Psychology 173 (1973).
13. Goldstein, A., et al., 35 Child Development 129 (1964).
14. Kagan, J., et al., 44 Child Development 221 (1973).
15. Piaget, J., et al., *Memoire et Intelligence* (Presses Universitarres de France 1968).

they were again asked to draw the array of sticks from memory. Interestingly, the second sets of drawings were considerably more accurate than the first; the normal deterioration of a remembered event with the passage of time was much more than compensated for by the improvement of the children's memory.

The selective attention of children is another factor in their abilities as eyewitnesses. A child has a marked tendency — diminishing as he grows older — to favor certain stimuli and to ignore others. The isolation of an object will attract the child's attention more so than it would an adult's attention, as will the movement or novelty of the object. As the child matures, he gradually gains control over this perceptual process and he can focus his attention on features which are more closely related to his needs and purposes. In other words, a child called as a witness will display markedly poorer ability to concentrate on the relevant aspects of an observation while attending to the irrelevant; he will remember clearly the shiny gun in the man's hand, but nothing of the man himself.

In addition to his immature abilities of perception and memory, the child is dangerously susceptible to suggestive influences. As one expert has observed after considerable study, "Create, if you will, an idea of what the child is to hear or see, and the child is very likely to hear or see what you desire." [16] This has been borne out in numerous experiments, one of the simplest and most dramatic of which involved a psychologist asking a group of seven-year-olds what was the color of a particular teacher's beard.[17] Sixteen of the eighteen children replied that it was black, while the remaining two simply did not answer. In fact, the teacher did not even *have* a beard! Similarly, a teacher visited a classroom and talked to the children with

---

16. Brown, M.R., *Legal Psychology* (Bobbs-Merrill 1926).

17. Varendonck, J., 11 Archives de Psychologie 129 (1911).

his hat on for five minutes; later they were asked in which hand the teacher had held his hat; seventeen said the right, seven said the left, and only three recalled that he had never taken it off.

The psychological experts are fairly uniform in their assessment of children as eyewitnesses. As one scientist has observed, "Children are the most dangerous of all witness." [18] As an explanation, he stated: "First, the child does not distribute his attention the same way as the adult . . . secondly, the child is uncritical in filling out gaps in his memory and uses freely material supplied through custom, through his own imagination or through suggestion." [19]

Oddly enough, the courts permit leading questions to be asked of children. Yet, the child constitutes the most suggestible type of witness, and a leading form of questioning can serve to practically put answers in his mouth. The child is both suggestible and anxious to please the adults around him. Thus, whatever the adult police officer or lawyer questioning him infers in his question, the child will tend to affirm. This was dramatically illustrated in a recent test in which twenty-two eight-year-olds were questioned after returning to class from recess.[20] They were asked, "When you were standing in line in the yard, a man came up to you, didn't he? You surely know who it was. Write his name on your paper." No man had, in fact, been in the yard, but seven of the children wrote down a man's name. The psychologist then asked, "Was it not Mr. Jones?" Incredibly, *seventeen* of the twenty-two children replied that it was; when asked to describe him, the children wrote down *detailed descriptions* of the fictitious man's appearance and dress.

What of the effect of age on the senior citizen as an

---

18. Whipple, G.M., 8 Psychological Bulletin 307 (1911).

19. Whipple, G.M., 9 Psychological Bulletin 264 (1912).

20. Varendonck, J., 11 Archives de Psychologie 129 (1911).

eyewitness? Clearly, the perceptive and memory abilities will degenerate with advancing years. But while the common attitude has been that intellectual abilities also decline, it now appears that this is not necessarily so — and, in fact, intellectual abilities may, under favorable circumstances, actually improve with old age.

With the advancement of age, individuals require greater stimulus intensity to accurately perceive — brighter lights, louder sounds, stronger smells. To a certain degree this is compensated for by the individual, but this compensation is limited. Physiological changes such as decreased pupil diameter, altered structure and function of the optic nerve, lens and retina, and auditory insensitivity cannot be fully compensated for. After forty years of age, the individual's ability to see detail begins to decline;[21] he becomes increasingly farsighted, and after sixty years of age his ability to discriminate between blues, greens and violets becomes markedly impaired.[22] The older witness also has greater difficulty adapting to light changes. In one experiment, for example, it was found that after walking from light into a dark room, young people (late teens) were five times more sensitive to light than old (eighties) people.[23]

§ 1-3.2. Sex.

Are men better witnesses than women, or vice versa? Numerous psychological experiments have been conducted to determine whether one sex performs generally better than the other when it comes to perception and memory. To date, the results can best be summarized as inconclusive. Some tests indicate that females make better witnesses,[24]

21. Bischof, L.J., *Adult Psychology* (Harper and Row 1976).

22. Gilbert, J.G., 12 Journal of Gerontology 210 (1957).

23. MacFarland, *Theory and Methods of Research on Aging* (West Virginia University Press 1968).

24. Ellis, H., et al., 123 Journal of Genetic Psychology 173 (1973).

while others seem to establish that men are superior.[25] Still others have shown that there is absolutely no difference in the relative eyewitness abilities of the sexes.[26]

The most likely answer to the question seems to be that men will outperform women when they are dealing with male-oriented matters, and the reverse when confronted with female-oriented items. Women, for example, will tend to be more accurate in describing a suspect's clothing, where men will be more observant of the gun he is holding.

§ 1-3.3. Race.

There is no proven difference in the relative eyewitness abilities between members of different races. However, there is a very real difference in the general ability of a member of one race to identify a member of another race as opposed to one of his own race. It has been fairly well established that individuals are better at recognizing suspects who are members of their own racial group.

The classic study in this area involved the testing of white students from the University of Illinois and black students from Howard University.[27] Each student was shown photographs of ten white individuals and ten black for about a second-and-a-half each, and later asked to select them from photographs of forty whites and forty blacks. The results indicated that the subjects were clearly better able to identify members of their own race.

This study was later duplicated with the addition of Asian students.[28] Again blacks had greater difficulty recognizing faces of whites and Asians. Interestingly, how-

25. Clifford, B.R., et al., 63 Journal of Applied Psychology 352 (1978).

26. McKelvie, S., 28 Quarterly Journal of Experimental Psychology 459 (1976).

27. Malpaas, R., et al., 13 Journal of Personality and Social Psychology 330 (1969).

28. Luce, T.S., 8 Psychology Today 106 (1974).

ever, whites and Asians had relatively little problem in identifying members of each other's race — though both had trouble identifying blacks.

Is this difference the result of cultural causes? In other words, do blacks and whites have less trouble identifying members of their own race because they have not generally associated with — and so are not as familiar with — members of other races? Does racial prejudice play a role, or is there some innate reason for the difference?

Recent studies[29] seem to indicate that, contrary to popular belief, highly prejudiced persons were no more accurate in cross-racial identification than were their more egalitarian co-subjects. Further, the amount of interracial experience of the subject did not seem to have any significant relationship to his ability to identify a member of the opposite race. Apparently, then, this cross-racial identification factor is due to a deeper reason — one the psychologists have not yet been able to explain.

§ 1-3.4. Training.

Juries tend to place greater credibility on the eyewitness testimony of police officers because they are considered to be "trained observers." Because of his or her training and experience, it is felt the officer is more likely to be accurate in his or her identification than would be a lay witness. Is this borne out by scientific studies?

An interesting experiment was conducted in 1975, in which a motion picture of a street scene was shown to twenty-four police officers and 156 civilians.[30] The subjects were told to look for, among other things, any criminal conduct such as petty theft. The results showed that there was no appreciable difference between police and civilians in reporting actual cases of petty theft in the film. However,

29. Brigham, J.C., et al., 8 Journal of Applied Psychology 306 (1978).

30. Tickner, A.H., et al., 18 Egronomics 35 (1975).

the police observers wrote down more *false* reports of theft than did the civilians.

Apparently, training does not necessarily improve an individual's ability to perceive and remember events and faces. This was even more clearly illustrated in a study by three British psychologists of individuals attending a course specifically designed to improve the ability to recognize faces.[31] After three days of intensive training involving lectures, audio-visual materials, case histories, demonstrations and field exercises, the individuals were tested with the full expectation of finding a significant change in cognitive ability. To the psychologists' surprise, the subjects were found to have achieved absolutely no improvement in their capacity for remembering faces.

§ 1-3.5. Anxiety Level.

Every individual is suffering from his own general level of anxiety caused by the stresses of daily life. In well-adjusted individuals, this level will be relatively low but nonetheless existent; in the more troubled members of the population, anxiety can rise to crippling proportions. Does this anxiety level — *i.e.,* the individual's ability to deal with his surroundings — have an effect on his ability to perceive and remember? In other words, can the general level of anxiety determine to some degree how effective an eyewitness an individual is?

Professor Loftus recently conducted an experiment to answer this question.[32] She administered a test of anxiety level (the Multiple Affect Adjective Checklist) to eighty-four college students, as well as a test designed to determine stress experienced from undesirable life changes in the previous year (the Life Experiences Survey); each student was then given a score roughly indicative of his

31. Loftus, E.F., *Eyewitness Testimony* (Harvard Univ. Press 1979).

32. *Id.*

anxiety and life stress levels. They were then tested for their ability to perceive a complex event and later recall it by being shown a film involving the theft of a wallet and subsequently being asked questions concerning details of the incident. Finally, Professor Loftus gave the students a test intended to determine the degree to which an individual was preoccupied by irrelevant thoughts. After correlating the results, it was found that those students who suffered from greater anxiety levels and higher degrees of preoccupation tended to perform more poorly on the eyewitness test involving the wallet theft. Those students registering higher life stress levels, however, performed only slightly poorer on the eyewitness test than did students with lower life stress.

The results of this test were confirmed in an experiment conducted by another psychologist in which facial recognition was clearly shown to be impaired by increased levels of anxiety.[33]

It would seem apparent, then, that the eyewitness who is suffering from anxiety is less capable of accuracy than his more well-adjusted counterpart. Of course, an eyewitness is usually testifying to his observation of a criminal event — an event which will usually cause anxiety and stress in observers. How to recognize that anxiety, how to bring it out for a jury, and how to explain its significance within the present legal rules remains a problem for trial counsel. Certainly the testimony of psychological experts would be helpful if permitted — particularly where the expert has had an opportunity to examine the witness or at least observe his testimony.

33. Mueller, J.H., et al., 11 Bulletin of the Psychonomic Society 313 (1978).

§ 2. Perception.

> "Truth, like light, blinds. Falsehood, on contrary, is a beautiful twilight that enhances every object."
>
> Albert Camus

The potential eyewitness is surrounded by a vast world of stimuli — sights, sounds, smells — which are available for his senses to detect and commit to memory. Which of these stimuli will be selected for detection, and how accurately they will be perceived, are determined by a number of widely varying and often subtle factors. It becomes trial counsel's task, when confronted by an eyewitness who has identified his client, to find out exactly what physiological and psychological factors are contributing to the erroneous identification.

The perceptual process begins with the detection of some form of physical energy (light, sound) which reaches an intensity level sufficient to overcome the sensory threshold. Once excited, the sensory system transmits impulses to the brain. Individuals vary, of course, in their ability to detect energy signals of varying strengths; what one person will be physically capable of seeing or hearing, another's sensory system will fail to detect. More importantly, this sensory threshold will vary in a person from one time to the next according to such factors as his physical condition, emotional state, and motivational attitude.

These nonphysical considerations are much more important in the perceptual process than might be imagined.

Seeing a knife in a man's hand, for example, is not simply determined by the object registering as light waves on the eye's lens and being transmitted by way of the optic nerve to the brain for recognition and memory storage. Perception and recognition, according to the widely held theory of signal detection,[1] is actually a combination of sensory stimulation and decision making. Two witnesses may both observe an object in a gang member's hand; one may "see" a knife because he expects it to be there, while the other may observe what is actually present — a screwdriver. To the extent that an individual is impulsive or suggestive in this decision-making process, he may tend to observe things that are simply not there. To a certain degree, psychologists today are increasingly successful in their ability to determine the attitude or motivation of an individual and, thus, his probable relative value as a witness.

The problem of perception is complicated by the fact that many perceptions are ambiguous: What is observed is unclear, due possibly to distance, movement, poor eyesight or lack of viewing time. In such situations — few observations by eyewitnesses are not ambiguous to some extent — perception becomes heavily influenced by the witness' own feelings, needs and moral values. An obvious example would be that food is more quickly perceived and appears more attractive to a hungry man than to one who has recently finished a heavy dinner.

Applying this to a situation involving an eyewitness to a crime, most individuals will react to a criminal incident with some degree of fear and anxiety. Some observers would react with what Freud termed a "perceptual defense" by simply not perceiving the threatening stimuli to their eyes, or having seen them, do not remember them. Recent experiments [2] have shown that witnesses apparently have

---

1. Green, D.M. & Swets, J., *Signal Detection Theory and Psychophysics* (Wiley 1966).

2. Suedfeld, P., et al., 5 Bulletin of the Psychonomic Society 30 (1975).

multiple levels of perceptually processing the various situations to which they are exposed. When observing a high-stress situation such as a crime, some witnesses will defend themselves psychologically by rejecting the stimuli. Others, however, will concentrate on the stimuli to the point that other stimuli are not perceived — often long past the point when the crime is over. An example of this narrowing reaction would be the commonly encountered fixation of a witness' attention on the gun in a robber's hand to the exclusion of seeing the man himself.

Added to this, the existence of fear and anxiety in the eyewitness to a criminal event commonly results in other observable phenomenon. It has been repeatedly established, for example, that such eyewitnesses will significantly overestimate distances [3] and time [4] and, in fact, as stress increases so will estimates of distance and time. Similarly, increased stress has been clinically shown to increase the inaccuracy and recklessness of identification.[5]

Certainly, visual acuity must be considered in the course of cross-examining an eyewitness. But just as certain, counsel must consider the less obvious, and probably more relevant, psychological considerations that contributed to what was perceived.

§ 2-1. The Physiological Factor: Sight.

The fitness of the witness' sensory system is, of course, the first factor counsel will consider in determining the accuracy of an identification. In some cases, this will involve the witness' hearing, such as with voice identification. In the vast majority of cases, however, the relevant sensory mechanism in question will relate to the witness' sight.

The first consideration is the visual acuity of the

---

3. Werner, H. & Wapner, S., 24 Journal of Personality 153 (1955).
4. Beier, E.G., 65 Psychological Monographs 326 (1951).
5. Postman, L. & Bruner, J.S., 55 Psychological Review 314 (1948).

eyewitness. If a witness wears glasses during his testimony, his vision should automatically be questioned. He should be asked if he was wearing glasses at the time of the observation, as well as what his vision is — both corrected and uncorrected. The purpose for the glasses must be determined, whether for astigmatism, myopia, presbyopia, etc. But even if he was wearing glasses at the time and thereby had vision corrected to 20/20, there should be inquiry into when the last optical examination took place. Often an individual will wear the same set of glasses for years without getting an updated examination, despite the fact that the condition of his eyes has probably changed.

If the witness is not wearing glasses, the subject of his vision should nevertheless be looked into. When was the last time he had his eyes checked? Does his motor vehicle operator's license require that he wear corrective lenses when he is driving? Is there a night blindness problem? Of course, there is always the danger of emphasizing the excellence of a witness' vision to a jury; prior knowledge from investigation or discovery proceedings can prove invaluable.

Deficiencies in depth perception are commonly found among eyewitnesses. Such problems are often undetected, and yet they can result in serious identification and description errors. Nearsightedness (myopia) and farsightedness (hyperopia) will render testimony concerning distant or close observations unreliable. Yet depth perception problems are not always caused by physiological shortcomings. There are many factors of which counsel should be aware which will distort perception of depth in the mind of the observer. Lighting and the existence of shadows, for example, will emphasize the appearance of depth. Similarly, relative size of the observed object will affect perception. Larger objects are seen as closer, detailed ones appear to be more near the witness, and if one object is higher than another it will be perceived as being farther away. If one object partially blocks or covers another, it will be seen as being much closer than it may be. Linear perspective will also influence what is perceived. The greater the convergence of lines such as railroad tracks, the greater the impression of distance. Movement parallax can also be a factor. When a witness moves his head to one side, such as when he is scanning or turning, distant objects will tend to be perceived as moving in the same direction, while closer objects appear to move in the opposite direction.

Darkness adaptation is a function of chemical activity in the retina and can take thirty minutes or longer to accomplish. A change from light to darkness, or vice versa, can cause a momentary blindness. Exactly how long this blindness lasts, and the ability to eventually adjust to darkness, varies from individual to individual. As has been discussed earlier (§ 1-3.1), darkness adaptation is markedly reduced among older people. Counsel should question any observation that took place shortly after a change in lighting conditions.

Color blindness is another ever-present possibility in dealing with an eyewitness. Contrary to common belief, almost every person is "color blind" to some degree. We all vary in our ability to differentiate among similar colors: different shades of red may appear identical even though they are clearly distinguishable from greens and blues. This common condition is perhaps more accurately termed "color weakness." True color blindness occurs where significantly different segments of the spectrum cannot be told apart: some individuals are blue-yellow blind, while others may be unable to discern reds from greens. What makes identification of such individuals difficult, however, is the fact that many of them will be completely unaware of their problem; the witness will have learned without realizing it to differentiate colors by their brightness — a method which can often work, but which can also result in significant errors in the description of, for example, a suspect's eye, hair or clothing color.

Whether a given eyewitness is suffering from visual defects which would affect his description or identification is not always a simple matter for trial counsel to determine. Simply asking the witness is an unsatisfactory solution; rarely will he admit or even know of certain problems. If the testimony is critical and if the court is receptive or the prosecutor is willing, counsel might consider having an optical or opthalmological examination of the witness conducted, preferably as a part of pretrial discovery. At the very least, counsel should attempt to question the witness concerning any visual problems; it would be better if counsel could obtain test cards from an optician or opthalmologist to use in his pretrial questioning.

§ 2-2. The Environmental Factor: Conditions of Observation.

The conditions existing at the time of the incident will usually provide ample opportunity for cross-examination as to the witness' ability to accurately observe and identify an individual. The most readily apparent of these is the amount of time the witness had to observe. In most cases, the witness will have little time — perhaps only a few seconds. This minimal amount of time should, of course, be emphasized in trial, particularly in the context of this short period being further reduced, in effect, by distractions and excitement. While there is the argument that the image of an individual's face can be "burned" into the witness' memory in a split second, this appears to be refuted by scientific experimentation; certainly, the average person requires much more than this for a later detailed and reliable description and identification. An effective tactic of cross-examination in this area is to define the time period, then break it down by what was observed — in effect, steadily whittling the period down to a matter of only a second or two during which the face and possibly clothing and build was actually observed without distraction.

That the amount of exposure time is important to the reliability of a subsequent identification has been illustrated by psychologists. In one experiment,[6] a set of four faces were shown to one group for ten seconds and to another for thirty-two seconds. Eight minutes later, both groups were asked to identify the four faces from a set of 150. The results showed that the group having a longer observation period (eight seconds per face, rather than two-and-a-half) was considerably more accurate. Interestingly, the experimenters also asked the subjects what facial features they considered most important in their identification. Of 128 subjects, seventy-three replied "general facial structure," followed by eyes (66), nose (53) and skin (33); the least mentioned were hair (28) and ears (19).

Line of sight is another area that should be investigated. Quite often the witness will not have an unobstructed view of the suspect for various reasons: the suspect may be moving around interceding objects, the witness himself may be in motion behind such objects (possibly in an attempt to hide or get a better view), or the objects themselves may move in between the observer and the observed. In a hit-and-run case, for example, other cars (both parked and in motion) may temporarily block the eyewitness' view. At a bank robbery, other people may be moving across the witness' line of sight. Besides the distracting effect of such factors, there is the added effect of blocking vision. Often the witness will honestly not recall seemingly trivial matters, and a careful reconstruction of the scene through investigation and/or detailed cross-examination of the witness, as well as of other witnesses, will be necessary.

Lighting can be a critical factor. The majority of serious

6. Laughery, K.R., et al., 55 Journal of Applied Psychology 477 (1971).

crimes occur in the nighttime, and the effect of poor lighting should be obvious. The type, direction and strength of lighting at the scene should be established. The simple answer from a witness that "there was plenty of lighting from the street lamps" is not enough. The overhead lighting may not have illuminated the face; it may have been too far away; it may have created shadows; the lights may have merely outlined the subject, or even proved blinding to the witness. Obviously, weather conditions such as rain, snow or fog would be similarly relevant.

The type of thing being observed will also have an effect on a witness' ability to later describe or identify. The universal tendency to have one's attention caught more by one type of object than another is referred to by psychologists as "detail saliency." It is perhaps best illustrated and established by an experiment in which 151 male subjects were shown a two-minute movie depicting a number of individuals involved in an altercation between a man and a woman.[7] Each subject was thereafter asked to describe the entire incident as accurately and completely as possible. It was determined there were approximately 900 possible facts or items in the film that could have been mentioned. Yet some were mentioned by nearly everyone while others were mentioned by none; these "highly salient" items were also more accurately described. A greater degree of salience appeared to result when the observed event or item was large, visible for a long time, bright or well-lit, mobile, colorful, unusual or interesting in some respect; low salience occurred when the object or event was poorly lit, routine, uninteresting or generally insignificant.

The nature of the item or event being observed may have another effect on perception. The speed of a moving object, for example, is almost always seriously misjudged by witnesses. In one experiment involving a large group of air

7. Marshall, K.H. & Oskamp, S., 84 Harv. L. Rev. 1620 (1971).

force personnel who knew in advance that they were going to be asked about the speed of a car, testimony as to its speed ranged all the way from ten to fifty miles per hour.[8] Yet the car was travelling at only *twelve* miles per hour!

Time, as mentioned previously, is another notorious source of erroneous testimony. Invariably, the observer will overestimate the amount of time taken by an event, particularly if it involves a number of things happening, an interesting subject, or excitement. In one well-known experiment, a classroom filled with 141 college students witnessed an assault by a student on the professor.[9] Afterwards the students were told the "assault" had been staged and were then given questionnaires about the incident to complete. The "assault" had lasted only thirty-four seconds but, asked to recall the amount of time it had taken, the average answer was *eighty-one* seconds — over twice the actual amount of time involved.

This overestimation of time is most pronounced when the witness is experiencing stress or anxiety, as when he is watching a crime take place.[10] But time is not the only thing distorted by the effects of stress or anxiety; the accuracy of other observations will suffer as well. In a recent experiment, scientists showed a film about policemen searching a suspect to a group of subjects; a second film was shown to another group, identical but for the presence of some violent conduct by the officer in the middle of the film.[11] The results clearly indicated that the ability of the first group of subjects to accurately recall the events they had witnessed was significantly greater than that of the second group. The existence of violence had substantially

---

8. Marshall, J., *Law and Psychology in Conflict* (Anchor 1969).

9. Buckhout, R., 4 Criminal Defense 5 (1977).

10. Sarason, I.G. & Stoops, R., 46 Journal of Consulting and Clinical Psychology 102 (1978).

11. Clifford, B.R. & Scott, J., 63 Journal of Applied Psychology 352 (1978).

reduced the ability of the second group of subjects to accurately observe and recall, even as to nonviolent events at the beginning and end of the film. Such conclusions should be kept in mind by counsel — and possibly shared with a jury — when dealing with an eyewitness to a criminal incident.

§ 2-3. The Human Factor: Emotions and Attitudes.

As has been discussed, stress and anxiety can have a significant effect on a witness' ability to accurately perceive. In fact, any emotional arousal can have an impact on identification capability. This is so well established among psychologists that it has been "codified" as the Terkes-Dodson Law: Emotional arousal will increase learning and performance to a certain degree, beyond which there is a decrease.[12] In other words, a little excitement will sharpen perception, but fear will dull it. Theoretically, every individual has his own performance curve, but it will follow a general pattern.

The reason for this impairment has been theorized to be a narrowing of attention when confronted by danger or stress. Much like the secretion of adrenalin, this is nature's way of arming the animal to deal with threats. Unfortunately, this focusing of attention decreases perceptual scope and acuity. This phenomenon is most commonly encountered by criminal lawyers where a crime involving a weapon results in what is called "weapon focus": The witness tends to concentrate his attention on the barrel of the gun or the blade of the knife, to the exclusion of everything else.

This phenomenon is not a figment of the lawyer's imagination but has been repeatedly documented by

12. Hilgard, E.R., et al., *Introduction to Psychology,* (6th ed. Harcourt, Brace, Jovanovich 1975).

experimentation. In one such experiment,[13] for example, psychologists staged an incident for a series of subjects wherein the isolated subject, while waiting in an anteroom to be interviewed by the psychologist, witnessed one of two events. Half of them heard a normal conversation in the next room, followed by a person walking in from that room holding a pen in his hand covered with grease; the other half heard an angry conversation in the next room, complete with the sound of chairs crashing, followed by the same person bolting into the room with a letter opener in his hand covered with blood. In both cases, the person was observed for four seconds before returning to the room next door. Each subject was immediately questioned concerning a description of the person and was shown a set of fifty photographs from which he was to be selected; the description and identification process was repeated a week later. In almost every case involving the letter opener, the subject described some type of weapon, whether accurately or inaccurately; few of the other group were able to describe or even recall the pen. Most importantly, the group confronted with the bloody letter opener had significantly lower accuracy rate when it came to identifying the actor from the set of photographs.

Personal expectations will also influence observations. Whether from ingrained prejudices or culturally imposed expectation, perception is distorted to fit what the witness expects to see. One such example has already been discussed (§ 1-3.3) where, when shown a drawing of a white man holding a straight razor while talking to a black, both white and black subjects tended to describe the black as holding the razor. Obviously this is reflective of a commonly held racial stereotype: Many people expect blacks to be

13. Johnson, C. & Scott, B., "Eyewitness Testimony and Suspect Identification as a Function of Arousal" (Paper presented at the American Psychological Association, Washington, D.C. 1976).

violent and when confronted with a weapon situation, "see" it in the black's hand.

These expectations can take far more subtle forms, however. A witness who looks at a photograph of a drugstore located in the middle of a block will remember it as being on the corner — *i.e.,* the well-known "corner drugstore." This was shown in an experiment [14] where subjects were shown twelve playing cards — all aces in all four suits. Included were five aces of spades, but two of them had been colored red. As a result, most of the subjects reported having seen three aces of spades; having seen the red, they had automatically rejected it as being a spade. Interestingly, some subjects reported having seen a *purple* ace of spades — a mixture of what was expected and what was actually seen. In fact, some subjects responded to being confronted with what was contrary to expectations by becoming upset and saying such things as, "My God! I'm not even sure now what a spade looks like!" or "I don't know what color it is now or whether it's a spade or a heart!"

This expectation in a witness need not be deeply ingrained. The police can inject such expectations when presenting a lineup or photographic displays to an eyewitness for identification. To illustrate this short-term expectation effect, consider an experiment [15] where 256 students viewed a film about the disruption of a speech by a political dissident. Although all subjects viewed the same film, half were previously told they would be seeing a threatening, angry radical, while the other half were advised they would see a polite student concerned about free speech. The result: After viewing the film, the former group described the dissident as an angry radical, and held stronger views about the impropriety of his conduct. This

14. Bruner, J.S. & Postman, L., 18 Journal of Personality 206 (1949).

15. Peterson, M.A., "Witnesses: Memory of Social Events" (Doctoral dissertation, U.C.L.A. 1976).

group also tended to recall more details about the filmed incident that coincided with their preconceptions.

Yet another experiment [16] which illustrates this effect of advance knowledge upon perception involved a group of students who were unknowingly subjected to a staged incident. The teacher left the room, mentioning as he did that the brown paper bag on the table contained a calculator. A second group was told the bag contained a carton of cigarettes. In each case, an actor entered the room, took the bag, dropped it, picked it up, then ran out. All students were then asked the value of the stolen merchandise, and shown six photographs for identification of the culprit. Only nineteen percent of the "cigarette" students were able to correctly pick out the actor, but *fifty-six percent* of the "calculator" students were able to do so. Obviously the cost of the object, and the seriousness of the crime, caused increased perception. To put it more generally, prior knowledge resulted in changed perception of an identical event.

§ 2-4. Perceiving People.

As has already been seen, any identification can be complicated by numerous physiological and psychological factors: vision, distance, lighting, time, expectations, suggestive influences, stress and anxiety. Added to these problems are the difficulties inherent in dealing with the identification of a human being. In other words, the perception process when dealing with the observation of a person varies considerably more in the eyewitness than it does with the observation of an inanimate object.

§ 2-4.1. Categorizing.

A large part of the difficulties encountered in dealing with testimony concerning identification of an individual involves the human tendency to form detailed impressions

16. Leipee, M.R., et al., 63 Journal of Applied Psychology 345 (1978).

of others very quickly and on the basis of insufficient information. This is not just a phenomenon of the witness to a crime. All of us, in our daily lives, react to people and draw conclusions about them almost instantly. Upon seeing or meeting someone new, we form first impressions, based upon a subconscious assessment of the person's physical appearance, mannerisms, clothing, from which we then infer various conclusions about his character and future behavior. This natural inclination is an attempt to simplify the world around us, to make others we deal with more understandable and predictable. At the same time, however, this categorizing process will obviously lead to general conclusions which are simply invalid. Yet the witness will be convinced that what he subconsciously concluded was what he actually observed; his perception will have been affected by categorization.

Actually, the description of another often tells us more about the perceiver than the perceived. The description will reflect how the witness "sees" people — what he thinks people are like, what qualities are considered by him to be admirable, what emotional reaction he has to different people.

It is clear that individuals will use their own list of character traits in describing others. If asked to describe five different people, an individual will invariably use perhaps a dozen or so descriptive words, repeating them in different combinations for each person described; yet another subject will probably use a completely different set of descriptive words. This tendency is so pronounced that scientists have given it the label "implicit personality theory."[17] In fact, the phenomenon is dependable enough to enable a psychologist or experienced trial lawyer to be able to predict fairly accurately how one given person will perceive another.

---

17. Bruner, J.S. & Tagiuri, R., in Lindzey, G., ed., *Handbook of Social Psychology*, Vol. 2, pp. 601-33 (Addison-Wesley 1954).

Part of implicit personality theory involves another human phenomenon: The tendency to generalize impressions as good or bad. A physically attractive person, for example, will commonly be "seen" as good, and this generalization will spill over into other observations and expectations. Experiments have confirmed this marked tendency to "see" positive traits in attractive people, while at the same time "seeing" negative traits in unattractive people.[18]

Essentially, this phenomenon of generalizing/categorizing is simply a type of stereotyping; as with so much in the field of human psychology, it reflects an attempt by the individual to simplify his world and reduce the vast amount of information around him into smaller, more manageable units. Unfortunately, there is usually a loss in accuracy which will commonly be reflected in an eyewitness' description or identification of a criminal suspect.

§ 2-4.2. Physiognomy.

Years ago some scientists were enamored of a popular theory that personality could be deduced from facial structure. In fact, this "science" is traceable as far back as Aristotle, who theorized that there were four basic facial appearances or physiognomies: melancholic (the thin face of the sensitive and withdrawn person); cholaric (the broader, more angular face which indicated openness and power); phlegmatic (the soft, round face attended by apathy and sloth); and sanguine (lacking structural definition which indicates insensitivity). Many of these scientists, including criminologists, went so far as to use this theory to explain criminal propensity in different physical types.

Whether there is any merit buried somewhere in this now-debunked theory is an open question. What is important, however, is that it reflects a characteristic common

18. Miller, A.G., 19 Psychonomic Science 214 (1970).

among eyewitnesses — a tendency to draw conclusions about an observed individual based upon physical appearance, and to subconsciously incorporate these conclusions into what is physically perceived.

Experiments have documented this tendency to attribute personality characteristics to an individual on the basis of his facial structure or appearance.[19] Men with dark complexions, for example, are commonly reported by subjects to be dishonest, unfriendly and hostile;[20] light-skinned blondes, on the other hand, are more often perceived as open and honest.

In fact this generalization process has been shown to have a probable effect on the judicial process itself. In one study clinical "jurors" were found to give noticeably longer sentences to unattractive defendants than to attractive ones; if the victim was attractive and the defendant unattractive, the prison term imposed was extremely long.[21]

Facial characteristics are not the only physical factors which will cause an eyewitness to conclude certain things about a suspect's personality and probable conduct. As with Aristotle's facial types, some scientists have theorized that basic character can be determined by body type. According to such popular theory there are three "types": the endomorph (soft-bodied, indicating an easy-going, content, sociable individual); the ectomorph (thin-bodied, showing a quiet, withdrawn, intellectual person); and the mesomorph (muscular-bodied, resulting in a confident, energetic "type"). Again, although the theory may have questionable scientific foundation, it reflects a prevalent attitude that can have a significant effect on an eyewitness' perception:

---

19. Secord, P.F., & Tagiuri, R., *Person Perception and Interpersonal Behaviour,* pp. 300-15 (Stanford Univ. Press 1958).

20. *Id.*

21. Landy, D. & Aronson, E., 5 Journal of Experimental Social Psychology 141 (1969).

The fat man *is* seen as jolly while the thin man *is* reported to be sensitive and shy.

The reverse can also be true. The character or position of an individual can affect how a witness views him physically. As an example of this, one psychological study showed that people asked to guess the heights of different persons tended to overestimate when dealing with those in positions of authority or prominence, and vice versa.[22]

§ 2-4.3. Transference of Memories.

We can all recall situations where we remembered having seen an individual at, for example, a cocktail party, only to subsequently discover he was never there and that what we had remembered was an earlier party in which the individual was present. This is an example of the commonly encountered phenomenon of "unconscious transference."

The human mind tends to integrate information, incorporating the memory of a person on one occasion into the memory of another occasion altogether, superimposing one upon the other, perhaps due to the similarity of occasions. This has been observed in situations involving eyewitnesses to criminal incidents. Commonly the witness picks out a suspect from a lineup or photograph display because he looks "familiar." The witness then subconsciously identifies the familiarity with the incident, and the two become integrated into one: the familiar face was "seen" during the perpetration of the crime. In fact, however, the witness had never seen the suspect at the time, but rather had observed him in the custody of the police some time *after* the crime had taken place. Yet the transference had taken place in the witness' mind.

An interesting illustration of this was shown in an experiment in which an assault was staged for students in

22. Dannermaier, W.D. & Thumin, F.J., 63 Journal of Social Psychology 361 (1964).

a classroom.[23] Seven weeks after the incident the students were given a display of six photographs from which to identify the assailant; one of the photos was in fact of the assailant, while one of them was of an innocent person standing nearby the assault. Forty percent of the witnesses chose the correct man. Of those who did not, however, over forty percent picked out the photograph of the innocent bystander as the guilty party!

This disturbing phenomenon was confirmed in a more recent experiment where subjects were shown a film about a crime and three days later shown a set of five photographs from which to identify the criminal.[24] The set did not contain a photograph of the actual criminal, but did include a photograph of one of the incidental characters in the film. Incredibly, *sixty percent* of the subjects picked out the incidental character as having been the person they had seen commit the crime (only twenty-four percent correctly refused to pick out anyone)!

Trial counsel will undoubtedly encounter this particular phenomenon in many eyewitness identification cases. Whether the transference comes from having seen the suspect at an earlier time (victims of store holdups sometimes pick out photos of individuals who had been customers prior or subsequent to the robbery), or from having seen him in a police-induced context (witnesses will often select a suspect from out of a lineup because they had seen him in an earlier police photo display), the result is the same. Unfortunately, it is almost impossible to determine whether the unconscious transference has taken place, since the witness himself is never aware of the process.

---

23. Buckhout, R., 23 Scientific American 231 (1974).

24. Loftus, G.R. & Loftus, E.F., *Human Memory* (Erlbaum Press 1976).

§ 3. Memory.

> "'It's a poor sort of memory that only works backwards,' the Queen remarked."
>
> Lewis Carroll

Between the time an eyewitness observes an event and the time he subsequently recollects what he observed — in reply to questioning by either police authorities or counsel — the information does not simply lie in his brain, dormant and waiting to be awakened. On the contrary, a number of things are happening which can affect the form which this "memory" will eventually take. A memory is not permanent; it can simply be lost forever. More importantly, information stored during what scientists call this "retention interval" can be actively distorted by intervening thoughts or subsequent information. To put it simply, the memory of the physical appearance of a criminal can be altered by a process of which the witness is not even aware. The witness will firmly believe he is identifying the man he saw, when in fact he is identifying the result of a continuing and unconscious process of information assimilation.

It is, of course, now accepted that memory deteriorates with the passage of time. In fact, the rate of memory loss has even been diagramed into a "forgetting curve," which indicates that memory loss is greatest right after perceiving an event, then becoming more and more gradual with the passage of time.[1] Theoretically, at least, the accuracy of an eyewitness' testimony will decrease as the perceived event

1. Loftus, E.F., *Eyewitness Testimony* (Harvard Univ. 1979).

becomes more remote in time. This has been confirmed by experiments in which subjects were shown a series of pictures and then asked to identify them after intervals of two hours, three days, one week, and four months.[2] Memory after two hours was 100 percent, but dropped steadily until there was a recognition factor of only 57 percent after four months.

But what is "memory"? Before considering some of the complex processes by which the memory of an eyewitness can be altered, counsel should attempt to understand just what memory consists of.

Essentially, psychologists agree that there are three stages to the memory process, that is, the process by which perceived information is stored in the mind. *Encoding* is the first stage, consisting of the transmission of neuronal "messages" from the sensory receptors to the brain where they are encoded as sounds, smells, or visual representations. The second stage, *storage,* varies according to the type of information the mind is dealing with. The more important types of information will be grouped or classified into smaller units of information for more efficient storage; "black," "green" and "white," for example, will be stored as "colors." Finally, *retrieval* is the process whereby stored information is recalled by the individual.

Just as there are three stages to the memory process, so there are three kinds of memory: *sensory, short-term* and *long-term. Sensory* memory is extremely short-term, representing information that is encoded immediately in terms of its physical attributes. We are constantly bombarded by stimuli that register quickly and superficially — shapes of objects, colors, distances and so on. The vast majority of this information contains little value and is rather quickly forgotten through a process of either decay or dislocation by

---

2. Shephard, R.N., 6 Journal of Verbal Learning and Verbal Behavior 156 (1967).

new information, depending on the psychological theory subscribed to. The second type of memory is the *short-term,* consisting of information that has some temporary relevance to the perceiver. Remembering the names of guests met at the cocktail party is representative of this kind of memory. The brain has limited storage capacity for such information; usually an individual can store only five or so bits of such information with any accuracy, and then only for a short period of time, perhaps for only a matter of seconds. The last — and most important to the lawyer — kind of memory is called *long-term.* This is information that is retained for an extended period of time, perhaps forever. Contrary to the other types of memory, the brain seems to have an almost infinite capacity for storing long-term memory.

Long-term memory, however, must not be viewed as a static condition. On the contrary, it is a dynamic process. The memory is constantly being reconstructed and transformed by stored experiences and by newly acquired information. When it comes time for the witness to identify or describe a criminal, he retrieves the information obtained from his earlier observations by scanning the long-term storage, zeroing in on the relevant memory, and transferring this information to the short-term storage for communication to police, lawyers or whomever. But, again, it is important to understand that what has been retrieved and communicated will *not* be what was originally perceived by the witness. Rather, it will be a subconscious product of various factors — a mixture of perception (with all of its attendant problems), of intervening thoughts, of new information, and of suggestion. It is trial counsel's job to sort through the maze of nonperceptual considerations, or, at least, to expose their influence to the trier of fact.

§ 3-1. Effect of Thought Processes on Memory.

During a witness' retention interval — *i.e.,* the time between perception of an event and later recall — there are a number of factors which can operate on the stored memory to affect its form. Among these are the intervention of independent thought processes within the witness himself.

One of these processes involves the transformation of uncertainty into certainty. It is a common experience to watch a witness at a lineup make a hesitant selection of a suspect, saying, "Well, he kind of looks like the fellow on the left, but I can't be certain." Yet this doubtful identification later is seen to harden into positive testimony at trial: "Yes, that's the man, I'm quite sure of it."

Neglecting the distinct possibilities of reenforcing conduct by the police for the moment, this phenomenon can probably be attributed to the *guessing* syndrome.[3] In essence, the witness guesses at an identification; that guess is then stored in his memory, along with the original hazy observations. Later, at trial, the witness must scan his long-term memory and recall information relevant to identifying the defendant. Meanwhile, however, the guess has hardened into identification information which has possibly merged with the original observation data. The combination is recalled as definitive information and the identification made with confidence. One of the interesting aspects of this phenomenon is the change in attitude from one of uncertainty at the lineup or photo display to one of considerable confidence at trial.

This important curiosity has been observed in a recent experiment.[4] College students were shown a series of 25 color slides portraying the mugging of a victim, and thereafter given a series of written questions concerning the incident. However, one group of students was instructed to guess at answers if they could not remember some detail, while the second group was told to reply "I don't know" in

3. Loftus, E.F., *Eyewitness Testimony* (Harvard Univ. 1979).

4. Hastie, R., et al., 19 Jurimetrics Journal 1 (1978).

such cases. After a period of time the students were again tested as to their recollection of details of the mugging. The results clearly indicated that the students who had guessed at answers in the first questionnaire were now considerably less accurate in their recall than the other group of students.

The experiment continued with subjects being shown a film about an automobile accident. Again they were asked questions concering the film, but including such questions as "What color was the station wagon that passed the accident?", when there had been no station wagon in the film. Half of the subjects were encouraged to guess at answers if they were not sure. Some time later another test was given to the students including such questions as "Did you see the station wagon that passed the accident?" This time the subjects were told to answer and also indicate the level of confidence in their answer on a five-point scale. Two days later, all students were given the same test. The results were striking. As expected, the students who had earlier been encouraged to guess at, for example, the color of the station wagon were much more likely to reply in the second test that they had actually seen the nonexistent vehicle. Interestingly, however, this group exhibited a considerably *higher* level of confidence in their memory than did the other more accurate group. Even more interestingly, this level of confidence actually continued to *rise* when the third test was administered!

Psychologists have theorized that this phenomenon is explained by the tendency of the human mind to fill in gaps in memory. The mind does not like incomplete memories, apparently, and voids are readily completed with any available relevant information. A guess, stored in memory as a guess, will be transposed into hard data and injected into the original void. Later, when questioned by police or lawyers, the witness will be completely unaware that he has constructed his own memory of the incident in question.

Furthermore, the "memory" becomes stronger and more vivid each time it is recalled as it becomes increasingly solidified. This phenomenon is reenforced by social pressure on the witness to be complete, accurate, and sure of his views.

Related to this is another psychological phenomenon called the *"freezing effect."* In this situation, a witness who had demonstrably erred in his early recollections of an event will become more and more sure in his memory as time passes. If, for example, he originally thought he saw a gun in the perpetrator's hand but realized moments later that it was a piece of pipe, his original memory will persist — "freezing" the incorrect data in his mind, and rejecting the later contradictory data.

This freezing effect has also been experimentally demonstrated.[5] Subjects were asked to read a couple of paragraphs of material, then attempt to reproduce them. They were then asked to read the material a second time and again try to duplicate it. This procedure was repeated one week later, two weeks later, and so on until six reproductions were produced by each subject. Then a final reading and reproduction was done after four months had passed. The experimenters found that errors of reproduction in one version were consistently repeated in later versions, despite the fact that the original paragraphs had repeatedly been reviewed. In fact, up to 95 percent of the errors in one reproduction would be repeated in a later reproduction. Obviously, the introduction of material to refresh the witness' recollection was broadly rejected in favor of a stubbornly maintained memory of inaccurate facts.

Finally, trial counsel should be aware of another "game" the witness will play within his memory processes: *labeling.* Simply put, the human mind will tend to label what it

5. Kay, H., 46 British Journal of Psychology 81 (1955).

perceives, and this labeling process will have a considerable impact on the memory of that perception. In another experiment,[6] subjects were shown ambiguous figures; a circular figure with outward spokes, for example, could possibly be a sketch of the sun or a ship's steering wheel, and a crescent shape could be the moon or possibly the letter "C." Half of the subjects were shown only the figures, while the other half were also given a label for the figure — *e.g.*, "ship's wheel" or "moon." Some time later, the subjects were instructed to reproduce each of the figures they had seen exactly as originally depicted. As expected, the drawings differed dramatically between the two groups of subjects. Those individuals who had been given labels along with the pictures drew objects which more closely reflected the label than the original picture. The crescent was reproduced as a moon figure, the spiked circle became a ship's wheel. Obviously, the individual's mind reshaped its memory of the perceived object to conform with the mind's image of the label.

As with any of the experiments discussed herein, trial counsel should consider the ramifications of these phenomena when dealing with an eyewitness who has been subjected to the influences of the police, lawyers or other interested individuals. In such cases, consider the possibility of labels being provided during questioning of witnesses.

§ 3-2. Effect of Intervening Information on Memory.

When an eyewitness has observed an event, such as the commission of a crime, he is often subjected thereafter to new information about the incident. He may, for example, be told by police investigators that three shotgun shells had been recovered from the scene of a robbery, contrary to the witness' recollection of only two shots being fired. Or he may read in a later newspaper account that the two robbers

6. Carmichael, L.C., et al., 15 Journal of Experimental Psychology 73 (1932).

were caught and that they were both young men, not older men as the witness had recalled. Is there any danger in a witness being exposed to such post-event information?

Psychologists have established beyond any doubt that such external data can dramatically affect a witness' memory of the original event. This is exemplified in an experiment in which subjects were shown a film of a traffic collision and then asked questions concerning it.[7] Half of the subjects were asked, for example, "How fast were the cars traveling when they *hit* each other?", while the other half would be asked, "How fast were the cars traveling when they *smashed into* each other?" Subjects exposed to the latter question generally gave considerably higher estimates of speed.

The same subjects were given another questionnaire one week later including such questions as, "Did you see any broken glass?" There was no broken glass apparent anywhere in the film. Nevertheless, over twice as many subjects who had earlier been asked the "smashed" question answered in the affirmative than did the "hit" subjects. In other words, the very form of interrogation had a marked impact on the witnesses' recollections. The information contained in the questions was absorbed by the mind, incorporated with the memory of actual observations, and later recalled as an undifferentiated whole.

The implications when applied to such activity as trial examination, witness preparation or police questioning of eyewitnesses should be apparent. We have considered the "hit vs. smashed" experiment in which subtly induced information has colored the witness' memory of related matters. But memory enhancement can be even more specific. Actual information can be directly inserted into the mind. In other words, a specific observation can be injected into

7. Loftus, E.F. & Palmer, J.C., 13 Journal of Verbal Learning and Verbal Behavior 585 (1974).

the memory, not simply a suggestive bit of information from which the witness draws inferences. A clinical experiment is perhaps the best way to both illustrate and, at the same time, document the phenomenon.

In this experiment, 200 subjects observed a series of slides showing an automobile accident.[8] Half of the subjects saw a car approaching a "stop" sign before striking a pedestrian, while the other half saw the same car approaching a "yield" sign before the accident. Each half was either asked, "Did another car pass the accident vehicle while it was stopped at the *stop* sign?", or "Did another car pass the accident vehicle while it was stopped at the *yield* sign?" For half of all subjects, the question accurately reflected what they had actually seen while the other half had been subjected to misleading information within the question itself. All subjects were then shown a pair of slides — one showing the car at a "stop" sign, one showing it at a "yield" sign — and asked to indicate which reflected what they had earlier seen.

The results should trouble any attorney. Of the subjects asked a question consistent with what they had seen, 75 percent chose the correct slide. But of those subjects asked misleading questions, only *41 percent* selected the right slide! The simple insertion of a single word in the question had significantly altered the subject's memory.

This works two ways: Information can be imparted to both *enhance* memory as well as to *alter* it. As with the previously discussed example, subjects in another experiment were shown a film about a traffic collision involving a car failing to stop at a stop sign and then turning right into traffic.[9] The subjects were then given questionnaires to answer. One of the questions concerning the speed of the car was asked as either, "How fast was it

8. Loftus, E.F., et al., 4 Journal of Experimental Psychology 19 (1978).

9. Loftus, E.F., 7 Cognitive Psychology 560 (1975).

going when it ran the stop sign?", or "How fast was it going when it turned right?" The last question was, "Did you see a stop sign?" Those subjects given the first of the two earlier questions had a much higher affirmative reply count to the last question than those asked the second question. The information contained in the earlier question had enhanced or reenforced the subject's memory of the presence of a stop sign.

A third possibility exists when introduced information mixes with the witness' memory: *compromise.* If the information is inconsistent with the information gathered from observation and stored in memory, the witness may end up recalling a compromise memory. In effect, the recalled observations, perhaps in the form of testimony, will be a blend of what was actually observed and what was subsequently learned. Yet the witness will be convinced that all of what he recalls consists of what he observed. Experiments have shown, for example, that subjects who are shown a blue color and later receive information indicating that the color was green will thereafter "recall" a bluish-green color.[10]

It should appear obvious by now that the memory of an eyewitness can be subtly changed or reenforced by the injection of information. This can easily occur during questioning by a police officer, during preparation for testimony, while reading news accounts, or even in the course of examination on the witness stand, whether unintentionally or by clever design.

But what effect does *timing* have on such questioning? Assuming one wants to alter or enhance a witness' memory, when is the best time to subject him to the desired information? Apparently, misleading or enhancing information has the greatest effect with the passage of time. When a memory is fresh, external information will have less of an

10. Loftus, E.F., 5 Memory and Cognition 696 (1977).

impact; when the memory begins to fade, induced information will have a stronger influence.[11] In other words, the longer the retention period the more susceptible the memory is to induced information.

The information recalled by the witness is not all that can be affected by injecting external data. The subjective recollections can also be changed. The feelings of the witness as he observed an event and the emotions he experienced can actually be altered by, for example, skillful questioning. In an experiment [12] subjects were shown a film of a class being disrupted by eight noisy but nonviolent demonstrators, then they were given a questionnaire to answer concerning what they remembered about the film. However, there were two versions of the questionnaire. Half of the subjects received a passive list of questions such as, "Did you notice the *demonstrators gesturing* at any of the students?" The other half were given more emotional questions, such as, "Did you notice the *militants threatening* any of the students?" One week later all of the subjects were asked further questions about the film, this time being asked to subjectively describe the incident on a scale, for example, from "quiet" to "noisy" or from "pacifistic" to "belligerent." The results demonstrated that those subjects given the earlier emotional questionnaire clearly tended to recall the incident in more violent terms, while those given the neutral questionnaire remembered those same incidents depicted in the film as more passive in nature. The simple change of a word or two in the question had a significant effect on the witness' subjective recollections of the event.

Words are not the only means of altering memory. A witness' recollections about an incident can be influenced by nonverbal methods as well. An interrogating police offi-

---

11. Loftus, E.F., *Eyewitness Testimony* (Harvard Univ. 1979).

12. Loftus, E.F., et al., 3 Journal of Police Science and Administration 162 (1975).

cer's facial expressions or tone of voice, for example, can convey information in a more subtle form to the witness and thereby affect information stored in the memory. When being shown a photographic display, a witness can easily be subconsciously influenced by an officer's gaze at a particular photo or his tone of voice as he points at each face. Once the officer's beliefs are known, there is a tendency on the part of the witness to conform his own conduct to that of the officer's expectations. This was illustrated in a study in which psychology students were told to conduct experiments on the learning ability of rats.[13] The students were advised that one group of rats had been specially bred for high intelligence, while a second group was bred for stupidity. They were then told to record how the rats performed while making their way through a maze. In fact, the rats had been selected randomly; neither group was any more or less intelligent than the other. Yet most students reported that the "intelligent" rats were much more adept at navigating the maze than the "stupid" ones.

It should be becoming increasingly apparent to trial counsel that both perception and memory are subject to numerous influences, both internal and external. A skilled police officer can, whether intentionally or not, significantly shape the substance of what any eyewitness recalls having observed. It should also be obvious that a skilled trial lawyer can also have a substantial impact on the eventual form of a witness' testimony, either through exposing the effects of police questioning, conducting his own pretrial questioning of the witness, countering suggestive questions in trial by opposing counsel, or formulating his own examination of the witness in a favorably suggestive way.

The pretrial questioning by an attorney, or lack of it, can have foreseeable consequences was demonstrated in a final

---

13. Hall, J.A., et al., 1 Human Nature 68 (1978).

experiment.[14] A group of subjects was shown a film about a fight that had taken place in a tavern in which the victim was hit over the head with a bottle. Before mock trials were to take place, each of the subjects was interviewed by a student-lawyer representing either the prosecution or the defendant. Sometime after the interview with the lawyer, the subject testified in a mock trial about what he had seen; he was subjected to examination by both sides and then a judge rendered a verdict based solely upon that testimony. In most of the "trials" the verdict was favorable to the side represented by the attorney who had earlier interviewed the witness. The results very clearly showed that a witness interviewed by the defense tended to give evidence resulting in a defense verdict, and a witness interviewed by the prosecution would give evidence tending to convict. The testimony was obviously biased in favor of the one side, often containing "evidence" directly contrary to the facts.

§ 3-3. Recall: The Psychology of Interrogation.

The effects of introducing information into the witness' memory through suggestive questioning, whether by police or counsel, and thereby altering his eventual testimony concerning an observed event have been discussed in the preceding section. Certainly the relative ease with which memory can be shaped, intentionally or unintentionally, should be appreciated by any attorney involved with trial work, and the concepts involved thoroughly understood.

However, the alteration of memory through the injection of new information is not the only means of affecting the testimony of an eyewitness. The witness' eventual recollection can be influenced by such factors as who is asking the questions, under what conditions they are being asked, and how the questions are phrased.

---

14. Vidmar, N., "Effects of Adversary Versus Non-Adversary Investigative Procedures on Testimonial Evidence" (Paper presented at the Law and Society Assoc., Minneapolis 1978).

It is perhaps helpful to understand that an interrogation is basically a conversation between two individuals — the witness and the police officer or lawyer. It is, like any conversation, an interchange of thoughts and opinions. It is important to realize that it is a *mutual* interchange — that the witness is *receiving* information and opinions from the interrogator just as he is giving them, though more subtly. At the same time, it must be understood that the individual asking the questions is, like most of us, basically egocentric in his approach to the interrogation: He is reluctant to accept new views and descriptions which do not fit with his own knowledge, experiences or theories. The lawyer or police officer will already be familiar with the facts of the case; he will presumably have formed a theory about the case and/or a bias toward one side. Therefore, whether the questioner is aware of it or not, he will be premising his questions upon that theory or bias. In other words, the questions posed to the witness will be slanted, consciously or not, to obtain a favorable reply. Nor does the bias end with the question. The examiner is also a subjective receptacle for the witness' answers. He will tend to interpret the witness' replies in a manner favorable to his own theories or biases and record them accordingly. He will again probably without realizing it have a propensity to reject data which is inconsistent with his own hypothesis and add information which supports it. Innocent, ambiguous or neutral information is modified and adapted to fit into his theories.

Subconsciously, then, the interrogator is often questioning a witness for the purpose of having him confirm the interrogator's theory of what happened or justify his bias toward one side or the other. The more convinced the interrogator is that he is correct in his view, the more likely that he will be to interpret the witness' answers as confirming his own position.

The witness' psychological stance also will tend to contribute toward the distortion of his answers. Like all of us, the witness has learned to adapt his behavior to the needs and expectations of others. During conversations all of us are constantly trying to detect the other individual's expectations and preferences; we look for slight facial movement, listen for voice inflection. Wanting to please the other person, we have learned that inappropriate comments or answers can damage the relationship. Guided by our sense of what would be appropriate to say, we choose agreeable words to relate. This universal adaptive mechanism is learned from childhood and works without our even being aware of it. It is, in fact, even accelerated in the context of interrogation. Most of us have an ingrained authoritarian respect for police officers and the courts and, as a result, an even stronger desire to please.

The interrogator, then, is perhaps subconsciously slanting his questions to get desired answers, and filtering the information he does receive. The witness, at the same time, is subconsciously trying to detect exactly what the interrogator wants to hear, and is attempting to mold his answers accordingly. The final result is very likely to be a distorted picture which is more reflective of the interrogator's preconceived views than the witness' memory.

This situation tends to perpetuate itself. Confronted with the police version of his memory, the witness' original memory becomes increasingly obscured and replaced by the police version; the images from the interrogations are superimposed on his original images. (This phenomenon has been discussed in the previous section.) By the time of his court testimony, the witness will be testifying on the basis of what the interrogator has indicated to the witness that he remembers, and he will be convinced that the interrogator's version of what he said comes from his own original observations. That this is commonplace can be shown by the frequency with which witnesses in trial ask to "refresh" their recollections with police summaries of their statements.

The degree to which this takes place can, of course, be affected by a number of factors. One of these is the type of environment in which the questioning takes place. A police station or a courtroom, for example, represents surroundings which will strongly influence the witness to modify his information to fit the apparent desires of the examining authority figure. What then is the most favorable environment for relatively unbiased examination?

Pyschologists have shown through field observations and experimentation that the grades on college students' examinations decreased markedly when they were tested in a different room from the one in which class was usually held.[15] The scores would also fall, it was found, if a person other than the professor acted as the exam proctor; the students produced the worst scores when both the room and the proctor were changed.

Apparently, the atmosphere of a new environment will inhibit recognition. This would seem to apply with added strength to a particularly strange environment such as a police station or courtroom. As one noted psychologist has observed, "The proper way to obtain successful recognition is not to bring the witness into the police court, but to bring the supposed lawbreaker to the scene of the crime and have the witnesses look at him precisely in the same surroundings and from the same angle at which he saw him originally." [16] Obviously, this procedure will not usually be possible, but counsel should attempt to minimize the strangeness of the environment and maximize its familiarity and informality if he wants to obtain a fair

---

15. Abernathy, E.M., 10 Journal of Psychology 293 (1940).

16. Feingold, G.A., 5 Journal of Criminal Law and Criminology 39, 43 (1914).

eyewitness identification. If he wants to lessen the impact of police authority on identification procedures, he should try to convince the police or prosecutor that the lineup or photographic display should take place at the scene of the criminal conduct, at the witness' home, or at least at a neutral site for the most accurate results. If, on the other hand, counsel feels he must counter suggestive police tactics, he might consider conducting a defense lineup or deposing the witness with as much authoritarian formality as possible — in a vacant courtroom or at least in a law office with stenographic reporters and fellow counsel present.

Just who is conducting the interrogation can also have a significant effect. In one experiment,[17] psychologists had their subjects view a film about an incident; they were then interrogated by trained drama students in either a challenging or a supportive way. The supportive examiner, for example, would permit the subject to freely tell what he had observed — *i.e.*, in narrative form — while all the time indicating approval through smiles, nods and words of praise. The challenging interrogator, on the other hand, would stare in silence, disagree periodically, and make occasional negative comments. The completeness and accuracy of the subjects' observations about the film was then compared. Surprisingly, there was no significant difference in accuracy of recall between the subjects interviewed by the two "types" of interrogators.

In another experiment,[18] however, law students and police trainees observed a film of an incident, and were given questionnaires concerning what they could remember about it. Half of them were instructed by figures of authority — a police captain or a law professor — after the film and

17. Marquis, K.H., et al., 2 Journal of Applied Social Psychology 167 (1972).

18. Marshall, J., *Law and Psychology in Conflict* (Bobbs-Merrill 1966).

before questioning that it was important that they be accurate and complete. These authority figures remained during the completion of the questionnaires. The results indicated that the group answering questions under the influence of an authority figure gave significantly longer answers than did the group without such influence. Interestingly, the "authority" group of law students was much more likely to draw inferences about such things as motives than were the "authority" group of police trainees or either neutral group; the "authority" trainees, on the other hand, were considerably more accurate than the "authority" students or either neutral group.

Judging from these two experiments, it would appear that whether an interrogator plays "Mr. Nice Guy" or not has no effect on accuracy and completeness of recall. His status or credibility, however, can apparently have a decided effect — though perhaps varying according to the type of personality reflected in the witness.

Yet another factor in interrogation is the phraseology employed by the examiner. As has been observed in the previous section, the use of suggestive words can result in the incorporation of the interrogator's views into the witness' memory. But the suggestiveness can be far more subtle, resulting from a mere shift in pronoun or adjective beyond the awareness of either questioner or witness. Consider, for example, an experiment in which one hundred students viewed a short film about an automobile accident. Of the six key questions in the subsequent questionnaire, three asked about things that had not been present in the film. These questions were asked in two ways of two groups of subjects, differing only in a single seemingly insignificant word. Thus, the subject was asked either, "Did you see *a* broken headlight?" or "Did you see *the* broken headlight?" Obviously, use of the article "the" carries with it an assumption on the part of the examiner that there was, in fact, a broken headlight in the film. The results clearly indicated that witnesses asked a "the" question were much more likely to have "seen" something that was not really present. On the other hand, an "a" question was two to three times more likely to result in an "I don't know" answer.

An even more striking result was obtained by Professor Loftus when she was retained by a marketing research firm to investigate product preference for headache remedies in a supermarket.[19] Professor Loftus decided to ask two of the survey questions in two different ways. In the first question, she asked half of the shoppers she interviewed: "How many other headache products have you tried? 1? 2? 3?"; the other half were asked: "How many other headache products have you tried? 1? *5? 10?*" In the second question she asked half the shoppers: "Do you get headaches *frequently* and, if so, how often?"; the remaining half were asked: "Do you get headaches *occasionally* and, if so, how often?" Amazingly, the shoppers asked the 1-2-3 question replied with an average of 3.3, while the 1-5-10 respondents gave an average answer of 5.2! The "frequently" shoppers experienced 2.2 headaches per week, while the "occasionally" subjects had an average of only 0.7 headaches — one-third as many!

Even the unintentional changing of a single word in a question can have a significant impact on a witness' answer. Consider, for example, the effect of a police interviewer asking a critical eyewitness, "Did you see *the* pistol?", rather than, "Did you see *a* pistol?"

The form of an answer called for can have as much of an impact on the answer as the wording. In experiments conducted many years ago, psychologists established that asking questions requiring a narrative answer generally resulted in fewer errors than questions requiring short, specific replies.[20] At the same time, however, the answers tended to be less complete. When, for example, a subject was

19. Loftus, E.F., *Eyewitness Testimony* (Harvard Univ. 1979).

20. Cady, H.M., 35 American Journal of Psychology 110 (1924).

asked, "What can you remember about the incident?", the answer was less complete but more accurate than if he was asked a series of questions such as, "What was the assailant wearing?", "How tall was he?", etc.

Confirming the results of this experiment, a more recent study involved the viewing of a film by a number of subjects about a robbery.[21] The film contained approximately 150 details for the subjects to later recall. Half of the subjects were questioned in the narrative form, while the other half were questioned with the more limiting interrogative form. The results were dramatic: subjects replying in the narrative form recalled only 21 percent of the details but were 91 percent accurate, while those questioned in the interrogative form were able to recall 75 percent of the details but with only 56 percent accuracy.

The lessons are again obvious. If completeness is important, then the interrogative form traditionally employed by police and lawyers should be employed. But if accuracy is the critical factor, then the witness should be questioned in the narrative form. The best procedure would of course be a combination of the two: Allow the witness to ramble on about what he observed in his own words and when he is finished with his narrative, then ask him a series of specific questions. The result will be initial accuracy, with the range of recall expanded by subsequent interrogative inquiries.

§ 3-4. Remembering Faces.

Just as individuals have unique difficulties when it comes to accurately perceiving other individuals (see § 2-4), so the human mind encounters special problems in remembering and later recalling the human face. Psychologists are unable to explain why the face presents such difficulties to

21. Lipton, J.P., 62 Journal of Applied Psychology 90 (1977).

the memory; they can only confirm that such difficulties do, in fact, exist.

A rather dramatic example of the failure of short-term memory was offered when a psychologist arranged an experiment in cooperation with a New York television station.[22] The station's audience was shown a film depicting a purse-snatching incident; the thief's face was clearly seen for a few seconds. Later, a lineup of six men was presented, and the television audience was invited to call in and identify which, if any, of the men in the lineup was the culprit. The station received over two thousand calls in reply. Incredibly, only *14.1 percent* of the viewers correctly identified the man in the lineup who had taken the purse! This figure, incidentally, approximates the percentage expected from sheer chance — *i.e.,* if the viewer-witnesses were merely guessing (14.2%).

§ 3-4.1. Facial Features.

Certain features of the face seem more critical to memory and subsequent recognition than others. Yet exactly which features are most important has been the subject of some disagreement among psychologists. One experiment will indicate that the mouth is most important, followed by the eyes and forehead and then the nose,[23] while another will tend to show that the eyebrows and the mouth are the most critical.[24] Yet another study seems to indicate that the hair and forehead are the central factors in identification, with the nose and chin being least relevant.[25] In studies of sections of the face, one early experimenter found greater difficulty in memory and later recognition where the lower parts of the face were covered (as with the classic

22. Buckhout, R., 2 Social Action and the Law 7 (1975).

23. Friedman, M.P., et al., 10 Perception and Psychophysics 47 (1971).

24. McKelvie, S.J., 14 Perception and Psychophysics 343 (1973).

25. Ellis, H.D., et al., 89 International Journal of Psychology 357 (1971).

bandana),[26] while a more recent study offers evidence that covering the upper half of the face (as with the "Lone Ranger" mask) will inhibit recognition to a greater degree.[27] In fact, one experiment apparently establishes that the right half of the face is more important than the left half of the face for witness identification.[28]

The general consensus of modern psychological studies seems to be that witnesses concentrate to a greater degree on the upper half of the face — the eyes, forehead and hairline. Yet an analysis of individual features does not necessarily produce an understanding of the memory-recall process as applied to the human face. Some faces are simply more difficult to remember and/or recognize than others, causing a greater number of false identifications. In a series of clinical experiments, it was shown that certain faces were often mistaken for the face of another, while other faces were hardly ever incorrectly identified.[29] The disturbing implication of this, of course, is that certain types of suspects will tend to be incorrectly identified by multiple witnesses.

The physical attractiveness of a face will not only result in certain conclusions about the owner's character (see § 2-4.2), but will also apparently make identification easier. In one study, two groups of facial photographs were presented of a number of male subjects — one consisting of attractive men, the other of unattractive men.[30] The subjects — both male and female, young and old, white and black — were able to recognize only 36% of all faces

---

26. Howells, T.H., 33 Journal of Abnormal and Social Psychology 124 (1938).

27. Daires, G., et al., 63 Journal of Applied Psychology 180 (1978).

28. Liggett, J., *The Human Face* (Constable 1974).

29. Goldstein, A.G., et al., "Face Recognition and Verbal Descriptions of Faces From Memory" (Paper presented at the annual meeting of the Psychonomic Society, Washington, D.C. 1977).

30. Cross, J.F., et al., 10 Perception and Psychophysics 393 (1971).

presented to them. Of these, however, the attractive faces were recognized 57% of the time.

The intangible "likability" of a face is also apparently a helpful factor to the human mind in remembering and identifying faces. In a study of faces categorized by attractiveness,[31] likability and distinctiveness of features, it was found that later recognition was greatest where the face appeared likable; attractiveness was the second most important factor.

Why do such considerations as attractiveness or likability significantly affect the ability of a witness to remember and later identify a face? One theory is that such factors facilitate the encoding process of the mind — *i.e.,* the process whereby the mind organizes what the eye has seen into more easily stored units. A series of features making up a face may be difficult to store, where a total impression of a face is a more easily managed unit.

The expression on a face can also have an effect on a witness' later recognition. Studies have shown, for example, that witnesses seeing faces with friendly expressions later recall them as being larger or closer than faces with unfriendly expressions.[32] In another experiment, subjects were shown photographs of a number of individuals whose faces were changed from friendly to unfriendly, or vice versa.[33] In most cases a particular individual's face became more difficult to identify when his expression was changed.

Apparently, an expression is itself stored in the memory and becomes an additional "feature" to identify. However, the mind may tend to reject unpleasant faces as being, perhaps, threatening, and embrace faces which seem to offer acceptance or openness. When an expression is changed, the memory reacts much like it would if the eyes

31. Yarmey, A.D., *The Psychology of Eyewitness Testimony* (Free Press/Macmillan 1979).

32. Smith, G.H., 49 Journal of General Psychology 46 (1953).

33. Galper, R.E., 19 Psychonomic Science 207 (1970).

or nose were changed, and identification becomes more difficult.

What is the effect on a witness when he is called upon to identify a suspect whose appearance has changed from when he was originally observed? Can the mind compensate for the changes and recognize the underlying face?

One investigation of this problem involved the addition or removal of eyeglasses, moustaches, beards, or changes in hair style.[34] The study indicates that growing or shaving beards and moustaches seems to have the greatest impact on identification efforts, while the addition or subtraction of eyeglasses had the least. These results were basically confirmed in yet another experiment where such changes in appearance dropped accuracy of recognition from 98% to 45%.[35] These studies seem to indicate that facial disguises can be quite effective but need not be elaborate to throw off identification attempts.

§ 3-4.2. Descriptions and Identification.

In most crime situations, eyewitnesses are called upon to give the police as detailed a description of the individual observed as possible. This description is then used in attempts to find the suspect, and later used to compare the suspect in attempts to confirm him as the perpetrator. In some cases, the witness will give a continuing description to a police artist for drawing a sketch or arranging a mechanical composite of the face. What is the effect, if any, of the eyewitness' verbal descriptions on his later attempts to identify a suspect in person?

Apparently, the human mind recognizes objects more readily when they are easily encoded in the memory.

---

34. Laughery, K.R. & Fowler, R.H., Factors Affecting Facial Recognition (Univ. of Houston, Mug File Project, Report No. UHMUG-3, 1977).

35. Patterson, K.E. & Baddeley, A.D., 3 Journal of Experimental Psychology 406 (1977).

Encoding may be facilitated when the object is more readily verbalized or has in fact been verbalized. One theory (the "verbal loop" hypothesis) holds that the encoding process consists of a mental verbalization of the perceived image; [36] later recall then is a reverse of the process — transforming the word description back into an image. Language, so the theory goes, has a direct correlation with — and effect on — memory.

Whatever the theoretical reasons, repeated experiments have clearly established that memory of objects is improved when those objects are labeled.[37] This ability to remember and later recognize is even more enhanced when the object contains a number of identifying characteristics, and when the labels directly relate to those characteristics.[38] Yet this improved memory with verbalization seems to have relatively little effect when it comes to the identification of faces. In one experiment, subjects viewed facial photographs and then wrote down some things about each face which would help them remember it.[39] A second group merely viewed the faces, with no attempts to verbalize or describe them. The results indicated that describing the faces improved recognition one week later to only a slight degree. This would seem to contradict the general phenomenon of increased recall through verbalization, and perhaps indicates once again that perceiving, remembering, and identifying the human face is a unique process for the human mind.

---

36. Glanzer, M. & Clark, W.H., 77 American Journal of Psychology 621 (1964).

37. Ellis, H.C. & Daniel, T.C., 90 Journal of Experimental Psychology 18 (1971).

38. Ellis, H.C., 78 Journal of Experimental Psychology 401 (1968).

39. Chance, J. & Goldstein, A.G., 7 Bulletin of the Psychonomic Society 384 (1976).

§ 3-4.3. Prosopagnosia.

Prosopagnosia is a fairly rare mental defect involving damage to the brain's right hemisphere (the part of the brain which processes visual information). A primary symptom of this condition is the inability to recognize faces, even faces very familiar to the person such as a wife, parent or best friend. In fact, prosopagnosiacs will be unlikely to be able to even recognize a photograph of themselves or a photograph of a person holding his own photograph.

Individuals suffering from this problem are aware of their disability. They realize that what they are looking at is a face and can describe some of the features of the face, but the totality of the face appears distorted. As a result, identification is usually attempted through isolated features such as hairstyle, a unique scar, voice or clothing. The individual having this condition, though, will often also suffer from other defects, such as spatial agnosia (disorientation of surroundings), color agnosia (inability to differentiate colors) or object agnosia (inability to identify objects together when they can be identified separately).

Prosopagnosia usually occurs, as has already been noted, when there has been damage to the brain's right hemisphere. There does not appear to be a localized area of the brain, however, where damage results in the condition; prosopagnosia has been found to occur when the injury is to various parts of the right hemisphere. In fact, the condition has even resulted, in relatively rare cases, from damage to the left frontal lobe. For further information concerning prosopagnosia, see Hecaen, H., and Angelergues, R., "Agnosia for Faces" in 7 Archives of Neurology 92 (1962).

§ 4. Scientific Determination of Truth.

> "Whoever undertakes to set himself up as a judge in the field of Truth and Knowledge is shipwrecked by the laughter of the gods."
>
> Albert Einstein

One of trial counsel's primary functions is to attempt to draw out the truth from an adverse witness. Traditionally, this attempt takes the form of cross-examination — "the greatest touchstone of truth ever devised."[1] Yet as every lawyer well knows, cross-examination is far from being the foolproof path to justice that a public fed on Perry Mason reruns believes it to be. A skilled attorney can accomplish much in the course of his questioning, but rarely will a jury ever be treated to the cliche of a broken, sobbing witness recanting his testimony. Despite the potentials of cross-examination, a simple fact remains: Most witnesses will never change the essence of their testimony. Trial counsel, then, is usually limited to demonstrating through cross-examination such things as inconsistencies of testimony, prior inconsistent statements, and bias.

However, relatively recent and much-publicized developments in the scientific and quasi-scientific fields have opened other possibilities for determining the truth. Hypnosis, for example, was once reserved for the exclusive use of entertainers, mystics and quacks; today, it is a medi-

1. Thomas, E.I., 15 Defense Law Journal 247 (1965).

cally accepted procedure. The polygraph, or "lie detector" as it is commonly known, has graduated from the "magic box" stage to widespread employment by private corporations and governmental agencies, and an occasional court. The effects on truthfulness of various chemical compounds when injected into an individual are still being explored; some of these "truth sera" are already being utilized in different fields. Instruments which analyze minute variations in a person's voice patterns to detect the presence of stress are the most recently hailed in the continuing attempt to scientifically detect or induce truth. Psychological testing of an individual to determine his ability to perceive and remember or his propensity to fabricate is yet another development — not to mention the availability of such expert witnesses as psychiatrists and psychologists to testify concerning the credibility of a given witness or the shortcomings of eyewitness identification generally. There will, of course, continue to be scientific developments in this area in the coming years.

We may live to see a machine permanently mounted next to the witness stand which will accurately detect "auras" radiating from the witness, indicating falsehood or lack of sincerity. For now, however, trial counsel is faced with only a few scientific or quasi-scientific methods for detecting or inducing truth in a witness or accused. The problem becomes not one so much of their availability as one of their reliability and admissibility. Historically, the courts are reluctant to receive new forms of evidence, scientific or otherwise, and this resistance has certainly been applied to the various "truth detectors" — often with good reason. But cracks are appearing in the wall and some courts are now beginning to accept various types of truth detection in evidence. In time, such forms of evidence will undoubtedly be commonplace, but for now counsel must deal with the realities of a generally cynical judicial attitude.

There is reason for this cynicism. As with any new development, there are flaws and limitations inherent in each of these relatively new methods for detecting or inducing truth. When contemplating the use of one of these methods, therefore, or when his client or a defense witness is confronted with one of them, it is incumbent upon trial counsel to understand as thoroughly as possible the strengths and shortcomings of the particular instrument or procedure to be used. Counsel should, for example, be aware of the risks involved if he is considering subjecting his client to questioning with a polygraph — particularly if he has chosen to stipulate with the prosecutor that the results can be received in evidence. At the same time, he should understand the possibilities and limitations of such procedures as hypnosis if a hostile witness has agreed to be subjected to this procedure. In other words, counsel should familiarize himself with the particular method used or being contemplated, whether he plans to use the results to discredit a witness or to attack the results when used by the opposing party.

Counsel should also keep in mind one serious drawback to some of these methods: They may work only when the witness is consciously lying. In the great majority of cases, a witness will differ in his version of what he saw from the truth only because he is honestly mistaken. The average witness, in other words, is merely in error — not lying; what he testifies to is what he believes he really saw, regardless of how wrong he is shown to be. Faulty perception, inaccurate memory, the subtle influence of suggestion and other factors can cause a change in what a witness saw and what was later recalled. If the witness is only mistaken, none of the truth detection devices will work. Polygraphy, voice-stress analysis, truth serum and hypnosis will all indicate that the witness is telling the truth — and he is as *he* knows it. Hypnosis, and possibly truth serum, may, however, be used to reach into the subconscious and detect thoughts and memories not readily accessible to the witness himself.

The following material will serve to generally familiarize counsel with the most common of the current processes for determining truth, while at the same time dealing with the limitations of each as well as the legal problems of admissibility.

§ 4-1. Physiological Detection.

In many ways, the most recent methods of physiologically detecting falsehoods are not basically different from those used in the more distant past. All operate on the assumption that an individual telling a lie will respond differently in his physiological reactions than when telling the truth. Such functions as perspiration, blood pressure, muscular tension, pulse and breathing will be affected by his attempt to knowingly mislead the questioner.

There is considerable evidence that such bodily reactions are in fact indicative of lying, and that methods of detection can be fairly reliable in assessing the truthfulness of a witness or a suspect. There is also evidence, however, that some individuals are capable of "fooling" the examiner. Pathological liars, for example, may have little or no physiological reaction when telling a lie. At the same time, it must be recognized that the accuracy of the method employed and, more importantly, the abilities of the operator/examiner, are critical to the accuracy of any conclusions.

Partly because of the potential for error, and mainly because of the courts' reluctance to recognize relatively recent developments, the results of physiological detection techniques have generally been considered inadmissible — at least, absent any stipulation between opposing counsel. This situation may change as more and more courts recognize the *potentially* probative value of such techniques.

§ 4-1.1. The Polygraph.

The polygraph, or "lie detector" as it has commonly been referred to, is basically a machine that is hooked up to the subject in such a way that his respiration rate, perspiration (through detection of skin conductivity), blood pressure and/or pulse is recorded as he answers questions posed by the examiner. The theory is that a suspect's or witness' awareness that he is lying, combined with concern over being caught in a lie, create emotional disturbances which are transformed into physiological changes which can be detected by the machine. When there is an increase in perspiration or more rapid breathing in response to a critical question, for example, the conclusion may be that the subject is lying.

As with most methods of lie detection, the polygraph technique depends heavily upon the abilities of the examiner for accuracy. The machine itself records only physiological functions; the examiner must determine what questions to ask to obtain these bodily reactions, how to ask them, and then how to interpret the results. His decisions are usually based upon his personal assessment of the subject's behavior—before, during and after the examination. In fact, one of the primary assets of a good polygraph examiner is his ability to convince a guilty party to confess to his crime. Obviously, the polygraph method is to a large degree subjective, relying upon the skills and judgments of the examiner.

There are basically two different techniques followed by polygraph examiners. The *deception* test consists of asking a number of questions of the subject, some relating to irrelevant matters and some relating to the crime. The subject may be asked, for example, "Did you eat breakfast this morning?", "Do you now have on a blue shirt?", and "Did you kill Mrs. Johnson?" Theoretically, the first two questions establish a pattern of physiological responses for the subject, and a significant departure from this pattern in the answer to the third question would indicate deception. Unfortunately, it is entirely possible for a subject telling the truth to react stressfully to the third type of question; innocent as well as guilty people can be sensitive to critical questions.

A variation on the deception technique involves use of the *control* question.[2] Using this method, the subject is asked a question designed to produce anxiety or guilt feelings irrelevant to the crime, such as, "Have you ever struck your child?" or "Have you ever cheated on your income taxes?" The truthful subject will have greater autonomic reactions to these questions — again theoretically — than he will to a relevant question such as, "Did you kill Mrs. Johnson?" The guilty subject, however, should have equal or greater reactions to the relevant question.

The second technique commonly employed is the *information* test.[3] This method operates on the assumption that only a guilty party has knowledge of certain facts about a crime. Confronted with a question concerning such facts, the innocent subject will respond no differently than he would to any other question, while a guilty party will have autonomic reactions because of his knowlege of the facts contained in the question. For example, assume that a murder case involves the use of an ice pick and the incidental theft of a purse containing twenty dollars — facts unreported by the newspapers. The examiner would tell the subject: "We are looking for the man who killed Mrs. Johnson. If you are the killer, you will know what she was killed with. Now, I'm going to name some weapons, and as

2. Barland, G.H., and Raskin, D.C., 12 Psychophysiology 321 (1975).
3. Lykken, D.T., 44 Journal of Applied Psychology 258 (1960).

I do, I want you to repeat it after me. Was it a gun? An axe? An ice pick? A knife? A hammer?" The guilty subject will have an autonomic response to hearing "ice pick," particularly when he must repeat it for the examiner. But there is always the possibility that an innocent subject may react by chance to the key question, or that he may be aware of the answer through other sources. To reduce this chance to mathematically impossible odds, a number of such key questions will be asked, each containing information known only to the police and the guilty party. Again, for example, the subject will be told: "If you are the murderer, you will know what you stole from her. Repeat after me each item. Was it a bracelet? A purse? A watch? A necklace?" And so on.

How accurate is the polygraph? As has been repeatedly stated, accuracy with this method depends heavily upon the subjective skills of the operator. An innocent subject may react to questions in a guilty way because of his fear or his suspicion of the machine. On the other hand, some subjects are apparently capable of controlling their autonomic responses to a considerable degree, either through conscious suppression or because of a natural lack of emotional response (such as may be found in a psychopath). In fact, clinical studies have shown that individuals can "fool" the polygraph. In one such study, individuals were able to distort test results by inducing autonomous reactions through simply flexing their toes.[4] In another, subjects were able to control test results by learning how to inhibit their own perspiration (much as is done with "biofeedback").[5]

Generally speaking, however, it seems clear that the polygraph method *can* be accurate. Clinical studies have established the relevance of autonomic responses to control

---

4. Smith, B.M., 216 Scientific American 1 (1976).

5. Dean, S.J., et al., 3 Journal of Experimental Research in Personality 71 (1968).

questions in detecting deception.[6] Assuming administration by a competent examiner, laboratory studies have indicated that the polygraph is accurate anywhere from 70 to 85% [7] to fully 90% [8] of the time. In fact, one of the most noted experts on polygraphy in America has estimated that an expert examiner should be in error on an average of only once in every twenty tests.[9] Of the two basic operator techniques, studies indicate that the information test appears to be definitely the superior.[10]

It must again be repeated that the accuracy of the polygraph depends upon the skills and subjective judgment of the operator. In the hands of a relatively unskilled examiner, the results are considerably less than worthless — they can tend to incriminate an innocent person. Even with the most competent of operators the machine has been shown in some studies to be, at best, inaccurate five or ten percent of the time.

Despite the relative reliability of the polygraph when properly administered, American courts have generally refused to admit evidence of the results of such tests.[11] The usual reason given for this refusal is that polygraphy is simply not sufficiently advanced, not scientifically accepted, and not demonstrably reliable. However, it seems clear that it will be only a matter of time before the traditionally conservative judicial system accepts this relatively new form of evidence. As McCormick has written in his celebrated work on evidence:

> [The] technique has much to contribute to the difficult

---

6. Barland, G.H. & Raskin, D.C., 12 Psychophysiology 321 (1975).

7. Yarmey, A.D., *The Psychology of Eyewitness Testimony* (Free Press 1979).

8. Lykken, D.T., 29 American Psychologist 725 (1974).

9. Inbau, *Lie Detection and Criminal Investigation* (2d ed. 1948).

10. Ben Shakhar, G., et al., 54 Journal of Applied Psychology 409 (1970), & Davidson, P.O., 52 Journal of Applied Psychology 62 (1968).

11. 29 Am. Jur. 2d, § 831.

> process of judicial factfinding. It has been widely and successfully employed in criminal investigation and in business. We cannot in our hearts be so confident of the reliability of the present system of resolving conflicts in testimony by impeachment, cross examination and inferences from demeanor, that we can afford to reject scientific aid in the task. . . . Obviously, the lie detector tests have substantial probative worth. . . . [The] courts' wholesale exclusion of lie detector test results, for want of scientific acceptance and proved reliability, is not supported by the facts. Many courts can easily recede from this position, in a case where the foregoing facts as to acceptance and reliability are adequately proven by the expert himself as a foundation for his testimony giving the test results. In most of the cases where the results were held inadmissible no such foundation was laid.[12]

McCormick is joined in his rather strong opinion by another expert in the field of identification, Patrick Wall, who stated:

> . . . an increasing use of the polygraph should be made in difficult identification cases. There is little question but that the result of a polygraph examination administered by an expert is far more reliable than most types of identification evidence. It is hardly fair to subject a defendant to possible imprisonment on the basis of an identification obtained by means of a suggestive procedure, for example, without giving him an opportunity to support his claim of innocence by the only means which may be available to him. . . . The polygraph, it is submitted, will eventually find at least a limited place in the criminal trial; perhaps the place for it to start is in identification cases, where it is most needed.[13]

The courts nevertheless continue to almost uniformly refuse to accept polygraph evidence for either the defense or prosecution, at least absent a stipulation. Some of the

---

12. McCormick, C.T., *Evidence,* p. 369 (West Publ. 1954).

13. Wall, P.M., "Eyewitness Identification in Criminal Cases," p. 204 (Charles C. Thomas 1975).

appellate decisions hold that the results are simply inadmissible, while others indicate that their admission is within the discretion of the trial judge. In some cases, the courts have gone so far as to hold that polygraph evidence is inadmissible even when both parties stipulate to their introduction into evidence.[14]

There are, however, indications of a change in this attitude. By far the earliest of these is *People v. Kenny,*[15] a 1938 New York case accepting polygraphy results in evidence where the foundation for the accuracy of the polygraph was laid by testimony from a Fordham University professor. More recently the appellate courts of New Mexico have twice ruled the results of polygraph examinations admissible upon the laying of a proper foundation.[16] In Illinois, polygraph evidence has been held admissible in a civil case.[17] In Michigan, evidence of the results of a criminal defendant's polygraph test was held properly received by a trial court when offered by the defendant in his motion for a new trial.[18]

The foundational requirement for admission into evidence of polygraph evidence is usually recognized to be the so-called *Frye* test: "While the courts will go a long way in admitting expert testimony deduced from a well-recognized scientific principle or discovery, the thing from which the deduction is made must be sufficiently established to have gained general acceptance in the particular field in which it belongs."[19] Most jurisdictions today still apply the *Frye*

---

14. *See, e.g.,* State v. Hill, 40 Ohio App. 16, 317 N.E.2d 233 (1963); People v. Hargrove, 80 Misc. 2d 317, 363 N.Y.S.2d 241 (1975).

15. 167 Misc. 51, 3 N.Y.S. 2d 348 (1938).

16. State v. Dorsey, 88 N.M. 184, 539 P.2d 204 (1975); State v. Shaw, 90 N.M. 540, 565 P.2d 1057 (1977).

17. Moskos v. National Ben Franklin Ins. Co., 60 Ill. 3d 130, 376 N.E.2d 388 (1978).

18. People v. Barbara, 400 Mich. 352, 255 N.W.2d 171 (1977).

19. Frye v. United States, 54 App. D.C. at 47, 293 F. at 1014 (1923).

standard, requiring the proponent of polygraph results to produce evidence of the method's reliability and scientific acceptance. However, a recent comment on *Frye* is of note. In *United States v. De Betham,*[20] the trial court noted that *Frye* did not intend "to require a specially rigorous standard of admissibility for [polygraph] evidence,"[21] and then critically observed that courts have applied *Frye* in such a way as "to require more of the polygraph than of other types of scientific evidence."[22] Although bound to apply the jurisdiction's law of inadmissibility of polygraph results, the *DeBetham* court found that the polygraph had probative value and that there was no valid policy considerations to prevent its introduction into evidence.

In a similar vein, the court in *United States v. Zeiger* concluded that "polygraphy" has emerged from ... [the] twilight zone into an established field of science and technology.... [The] polygraph has been accepted by authorities in the field as being capable of producing highly probative evidence in the court of law when properly used by competent, experienced examiners."[23]

At the present time, therefore, it may be said that polygraph evidence is generally held to be inadmissible, although this position appears to be in the initial stages of change. Most jurisdictions will admit polygraph evidence where there is a stipulation, whether arrived at before or after the administration of the test. In some jurisdictions, polygraph evidence is simply inadmissible, while in others it is admissible within the sound discretion of the trial judge after the laying of a sufficient foundation.

Perhaps the current status of the admissibility of polygraph evidence is best summarized by the court in

20. 348 F. Supp. 1377 (S.D. Cal. 1972).

21. *Id.* at 1382.

22. *Id.* at 1383.

23. 350 F. Supp. at 690 (D.D.C. 1971), *rev'd,* 155 U.S. App. D.C. 11, 475 F.2d 1280 (D.C. Cir. 1972).

United States v. Ridling, rejecting the *Frye* test and holding that "the scientific psychological basis for the polygraph examination is well established":

> When opinions interpreting the results [of a new form of evidence] are first offered in Court, the underlying premises require a great deal of proof, as well as does the proper use of these premises, the necessary controls used in the specific cases and the appropriate qualifications of the expert. On proper proof, the evidence becomes admissible. The attention of the Courts at this point seems to be directed at the proper qualification of an expert witness, including testimony, establishing the underlying theory.
>
> Finally, the underlying principle and premises become so well established and known that the only real issues for determination in connection with the reception of evidence is the proper use of the principles, premises and theories and the use of adequate controls in the specific case to assure good results. In other words, at this stage the Courts judicially notice the basic theories and premises. They need no longer be proved.[24]

The Court observed that while polygraphy is still in the first stage, "the scientific psychological basis for the polygraph examination is well established." [25] It then rejected the *Frye* standard and held that "[the] theory of the polygraph is sound and that it is directly relevant to this case [a perjury case], and that therefore the cases denying admissibility on these grounds are not controlling." [26]

The polygraph remains a potential tool for the defense attorney as well as for the prosecutor. It can be used both to establish the truth of a defendant's protestations of innocence, and to either verify or refute the honesty of an eyewitness' account. It cannot, however, do anything to detect inaccuracies in a witness' recollections or errors in

---

24. 350 F. Supp. at 94-95 (E.D. Mich. 1972).

25. *Id.* at 93.

26. *Id.* at 95.

identification. It is a tool that depends very much upon the operator's abilities, and one which is only beginning to achieve reluctant acceptance by the courts.

§ 4-1.2. Voice-Stress Analysis.

A fairly recent development in lie detection technology is the voice-stress analyzer. This device is similar in many respects to the polygraph but requires less of the operator's subjective skills. Consequently, the results are less dependent upon the operator and can be objectively analyzed. At the same time, detractors of the analyzer claim that it is less reliable than the polygraph.

Voice-stress analysis originated with voiceprint identification. Each person has his own unique patterns and sounds of speech, and these can be graphically recorded on a sound spectrogram. As with fingerprints, no two individuals will have the same graphic voice "prints," and so it becomes possible to match the prints of two different recordings and determine if they came from the same person. Later the technique was applied to lie detection when it was noticed that an individual's voiceprint changed in appearance when he was under stress.

The following excerpt from an advertisement by a manufacturer of a voice-stress analyzing unit, the Psychological Stress Evaluator (PSE), describes in greater detail the general theory behind the machines:

> Superimposed on the audible voice are inaudible frequency modulations. The FM quality of the voice is susceptible to the amount of stress that one may be under when speaking. To the human ear, a person may sound perfectly normal, free of tremors or "guilt-revealing" sound variations. The PSE senses the difference and records the changes in the inaudible FM qualities of the voice on a chart. When the chart is interpreted by an experienced examiner it reveals the key stress areas of the person being questioned.
>
> The human body has two nervous systems — central

> nervous system and autonomic nervous system (and their various subdivisions). In each of these there are voluntary and involuntary reactions: those reactions controlled by the brain (voluntary) or those not controlled by the brain (involuntary, or reflex actions). The [PSE] is designed to detect the inaudible effect on the human voice of the involuntary reactions.
>
> When one speaks the voice has two modulations — audible and inaudible. The audible portion is what we hear. The inaudible modulation comes from the involuntary areas (those not totally controlled by the brain or thought processes). Internal stress is reflected in the inaudible variations of the voice. These differences cannot be heard, but they can be detected and recorded by the PSE.
>
> The key to successful use of the PSE is the preparation of simple selected questions keyed to the individual and structured to reveal normal or truthful answers and answers that are false. Once the personal pattern has been established any evasive or false answers reveal stress; if a person is not telling the truth then analysis of his voice pattern will show it.

The theory of voice-stress analysis, then, is that attempts to lie result in emotional reactions of stress which are manifested in vocal vibrations or microtremors that are picked up by a tape recorder and then fed through an electronic processing unit which detects the changes in electrical energy caused by the vibrations. These graphic changes, it is claimed, can be easily observed by the examiner and interpreted as deception or truth.

Obviously, many of the same considerations relevant to the polygraph apply to the voice-stress analyzer (see § 4-1.1). It is probable, for example, that certain individuals will remain capable of "fooling" the instrument because of their ability to control — or not have — emotional reactions. It is equally probable that truthful individuals will react emotionally because of the nature of the question or because of fear or distrust, resulting in false readings. Despite claims of less dependence upon operator skill, it is clear that the form and manner in which questions are posed will have a significant effect on the technique's success; information tests will probably continue to be more effective than deception tests (see § 4-1.1).

As to the accuracy of this new method, the few clinical studies conducted to date have produced widely varying results. Generally, however, the results have been disappointing. In one clinical study comparing voice-stress analysis with polygraphy,[27] the polygraph was the clear winner. In a field study involving actual criminal suspects,[28] the voice-stress analyzer was successful in only 50-60 percent of the cases — a figure representing little more than pure chance.

One interesting study of the reliability of voice-stress analyzers was commissioned by the United States Army in 1973. In that study conducted by Professor Joseph Kerbis of Fordham University's Department of Psychology, researchers used two different analyzing instruments (the Psychological Stress Evaluator and the Voice Stress Analyzer), and after extensive experimentation finally concluded that the use of voice-stress analysis instruments was not valid as a method for detecting deception.[29] This finding was confirmed in separate studies conducted by the National Security Agency and the United States Air Force. In an article reflecting the results of those tests, the following comments were made:

> [H]ard evidence that the voice analysis lie detection technique is effective has not been introduced. It further seems that, at a minimum, much further testing and refinement will be required before voice analysis can be considered useful for military lie detection. Resolution of these problems does not seem to be enhanced

27. Horvath, F., 63 Journal of Applied Psychology 338 (1978).

28. Rice, B., Psychology Today 61 (June 1978).

29. Technical Report No. LWL-CR-03B70, August 1973, U.S. Army Warfare Laboratory, Aberdeen Proving Grounds, Maryland.

> by inconsistent statements made by the experts in voice analysis. Until a scientifically acceptable validity rate for voice analysis (that approaches the validity rate of the polygraph technique) is established and, until the boundaries are clearly established for what voice analysis can and cannot do, it does not seem reasonable that voice analysis for lie detection ought to be adopted by any of the military services.[30]

The voice-stress analysis process, then, should be viewed as still in the developmental stage. Although it may in the near future be perfected to the point of general acceptance by the experts, it remains today a technique of dubious reliability.

As a new process, the admissibility of voice-stress analysis has yet to be ruled upon by the higher courts. However, it would clearly appear that an application of the *Frye* test (see § 4-1.1) or any variation of its reliability/scientific acceptance standard would preclude acceptance of voice-stress results into evidence. In time, of course, the technique may be perfected and the courts eventually take notice of its value. At present, it is doubtful that a trial court would accept the results of voice-stress analysis even with a stipulation between opposing counsel.

Currently, the following represent voice-analyzing instruments offered for sale by manufacturers:

The Psychological Stress Evaluator (Dektor Counterintelligence and Security Co., Inc.)

The Voice Stress Analyzer (Decision Control, Inc.)

The Hagoth (Hagoth Corp.)

The Mark II Voice Analyzer (Law Enforcement Associates, Inc.)

The Mark IX-P Voice Stress Analyzer (Communications Control System, Inc.)

---

30. Link, "Lie Detection Through Voice Analysis," 3 Military Police Law Enforcement Journal 38 (1976).

§ 4-2. Inducing Truth and Recall.

In addition to methods for detecting deception, there exist certain techniques that have been employed with varying degrees of success to induce a witness or defendant to tell the truth. These involve placing the individual in a state of mind in which his desire to fabricate is, theoretically, "short-circuited" for a period of time.

These same techniques may be used not only to prevent fabrication, but to delve into an individual's memory. As has been seen in earlier chapters, the memory is imperfect to say the least; an eyewitness is rarely able to recall all that he has seen or heard on an earlier occasion. With "truth serum" or hypnosis, he *may* be able to go beyond his normal memory and actually recall other — more critical — aspects of the event he witnessed.

§ 4-2.1. "Truth Serum."

One highly-publicized method of inducing an individual to tell the truth is through injecting him with a drug, such as sodium pentothal, or "truth serum" as it has been popularly termed. This drug, as well as such other commonly employed compounds as scopolamine, sodium amytal and thiopental sodium, acts essentially as a combination tranquilizer and anesthetic, relaxing the subject and lowering his "will power" and resistance. In this state of inhibited control over his nervous system, the subject is questioned by a qualified expert such as a psychiatrist, using free-association techniques much as is employed during psychoanalysis. In such a condition and under such skilled interrogation, the individual supposedly loses the capacity to fabricate, while at the same time experiencing an improved memory.

The method has been used successfully on patients in psychotherapy, and there are claims of success when applied to forgetful or lying witnesses or defendants. Certainly, sodium pentothal will produce vivid memories, but it has not been proven whether these memories are necessarily accurate or not. Many experts in the field view the technique with considerable skepticism.[31]

Professor A. Daniel Yarmey, for example, has flatly stated that "any attempt to discover truth through the use of so-called truth drugs such as sodium pentothal should be discouraged, since it does not produce the desired results."[32] While the drug will relax an individual and lower his resistance, it will not guarantee that the individual will tell the truth or that his seemingly improved recall is accurate. In fact, one study has shown that people under the effects of the drug are still fully capable of lying.[33] In another study, psychologists concluded that individuals who have confessed to crimes after being injected with sodium pentothal would have confessed without it; apparently, subjects will confess under the drug's influence only if they want to anyway.[34]

Insofar as the question of admissibility of the results of "truth serum" examination into evidence, the courts have generally taken the same position as they have with polygraph tests (see § 4-1.1). In fact, there has apparently yet to be an appellate decision recognizing the admissibility of "truth serum" evidence to prove the truth of the matter asserted.[35] However, the courts have recognized the results of such examinations when offered on the question of insanity at the time of committing an offense[36] or to show

---

31. *E.g.,* Loftus, E.F., *Eyewitness Testimony* (Harvard Univ. 1979).

32. Yarmey, A.D., *The Psychology of Eyewitness Testimony,* p. 175 (Free Press/Macmillan 1979).

33. Frank, G., *The Boston Strangler* (New American Library 1966).

34. McMahon, F.B., *Psychology: The Hybrid Science* (3d ed. Prentice-Hall 1977).

35. *E.g.,* People v. Johnson, 32 Cal. App. 3d 988, 109 Cal. Rptr. 118 (1973); Knight v. State, 97 So. 2d 115 (Fla. 1957); State v. Levitt, 36 N.J. 266, 176 A.2d 465 (1961); State v. Arizona, 79 Ariz. 158, 285 P.2d 612, *cert. denied,* 350 U.S. 950, 76 S. Ct. 326, 100 L. Ed. 828 (1955).

36. People v. Cartier, 51 Cal. 2d 59, 335 P.2d 114 (1959).

sex deviation.[37] Whether "truth serum" evidence offered to prove a defendant's or witness' state of mind at a given time would be admissible is an interesting issue. For the present time, at least, the use of such "truth drugs" as sodium pentothal is largely limited to investigative procedures.

§ 4-2.2. Hypnosis.

Hypnosis has, of course, graduated from the carnival stage to become an accepted medical practice. In recent years, it has also become an increasingly accepted technique within the criminal justice field. The Los Angeles Police Department, for example, has used departmental hypnotists extensively since 1970, primarily as an aid to witnesses in helping them recall details of observed crimes. The Israeli National Police Force maintains a staff of hypnotists for investigative work, and claims to have solved twenty-five cases through their efforts in one recent four-year period.

Acceptance of hypnosis as at least a potentially valuable tool in criminal matters has been accelerated by its highly-publicized employment in the investigations of such cases as Sam Shepherd; the Boston Strangler; and the Chowchilla kidnapping. The latter case, involving the hijacking of a schoolbus filled with children in 1976, presented the F.B.I. with a difficult situation: Neither the children nor the bus driver could identify their three abductors, nor could they supply any information that might lead to their identification. The F.B.I. finally called in a hypnotist, Dr. William Kroger, to hypnotize the bus driver. While under hypnosis, the bus driver was able to recall all but one digit of the kidnappers' license plate number. Armed with this information, the three men were soon found, arrested and convicted.

It seems clear that hypnosis, if used correctly, *can* be a

37. People v. Jones, 42 Cal. 2d 219, 266 P.2d 38 (1954).

valuable tool to the investigator — and to the trial lawyer. But just what *is* hypnosis? Quite simply, medical and psychological experts do not agree on what hypnosis consists of. It is not, contrary to popular belief, a state of deep sleep; the brain activity, respiration and heart rate of an individual in a hypnotic "trance" does not resemble that of one who is asleep.[38] It more closely resembles the normal waking state and can perhaps best be described in terms of its effects: "Hypnosis is said to exist when suggestions from one individual seemingly alter the perceptions and memories of another."[39] Hypnosis, then, is characterized primarily by increased suggestibility; a secondary characteristic is post-hypnotic amnesia, whereby the subject forgets what happened during hypnosis when told to do so by the hypnotist.

The medical world cannot explain exactly what hypnosis is, nor can they agree on how effective or dependable the technique is. One expert in fact has come to the conclusion after twenty years of careful study that hypnosis is little more than a myth — that the same effects can be achieved through simple relaxation and concentration.[40] This seems borne out by an experiment in which hypnotized subjects and subjects who were only simulating hypnosis were compared for memory performance:[41] Interestingly, the *simulators* showed dramatic improvement in their abilities to recollect.

Most experts, however, will agree that hypnosis can be helpful in assisting a witness to recall events that his normal memory processes have failed to bring back. Whether

---

38. Yarmey, A.D., *The Psychology of Eyewitness Testimony,* p. 176 (Free Press/Macmillan 1979).

39. Orne, M.T., 19 International Journal of Clinical and Experimental Hypnosis 183 (1971).

40. My, C., 7 Human Behavior 43 (1978).

41. O'Connell, D.N., et al., 76 Journal of Abnormal Psychology Monograph No. 3, Part 2 (1970).

this occurs because of some unexplainable altered state of consciousness, or simply because of the benefits of concentration and a rested mind, the phenomenon appears to exist. Psychological studies seem to indicate that individuals under a hypnotic "trance" experience improved memory, particularly when the memory concerns a traumatic event.[42]

Critics of hypnotic technique, on the other hand, claim that an individual under hypnosis is subject to the same errors of perception and memory as any other person. In fact, because of the increased suggestibility of the hypnotized subject, he is much more likely to be influenced by external factors in his recollections than would be the non-hypnotized witness. A very recent and interesting study [43] showed this when a film about a traffic accident was shown to a group of subjects who were afterwards given questionnaires about the film which contained some misleading information. Some time after completing the questionnaire the subjects were questioned individually in a suggestive and leading way, some of them while under hypnosis. The results indicated that the hypnotized subjects were clearly less accurate than their non-hypnotized counterparts, especially when the answers were in reply to leading questions. Apparently, witnesses placed under hypnosis will be more susceptible to suggestive or manipulative influences, whether the suggestion or manipulation by the examiner is intended or not. Suggestion though is not the only cause of error with hypnosis. According to one study, hypnotized subjects are sometimes likely to "recall" incidents which simply never took place.[44]

Perhaps the most disturbing fact brought forth by the

---

42. Goldstein, M.S., and Sipprelle, C.N., 18 International Journal of Clinical and Experimental Hypnosis 211 (1970).

43. Loftus, E.F., *Eyewitness Testimony,* p. 107 (Harvard Univ. 1979).

44. Orne, M.T., in Lindzey, G., et al. (eds.) *Psychology,* p. 150 (Worth 1975).

critics is the apparent ability of hypnotized subjects to lie. Despite their state of hypnosis, subjects have been shown in clinical studies to be fully capable of hiding information and deceiving even the most experienced hypnotist.[45]

Summarizing the pitfalls of hypnosis, consider the following quotation by two leading experts in the field taken from an *American Bar Association Journal* article: "People can flat-out lie under hypnosis, and the examiner is no better equipped to detect the hypnotic lie than any other kind. Even more serious, a willing hypnotic subject is more pliable than he normally would be, more anxious to please his questioner. Knowing even a few details of an event, often supplied in early contacts with police, may provide the subject with enough basis to create a highly detailed 'memory' of what transpired, whether he was there or not."[46]

On the issue of admissibility, the courts have very generally taken a position somewhat similar to that taken for polygraphy, voice-stress analysis and "truth serum" examinations — *i.e.*, the results are usually held inadmissible when offered to prove the truth of the matter asserted, at least when results come from hypnosis of an accused[47] and in the absence of a stipulation between opposing counsel. However, there appears to be an increasing willingness of some courts to recognize that hypnosis has reached the state of scientific acceptance which will support introduction into evidence.

In discussing the admissibility of hypnosis-related evidence, it must be realized that there are basically three kinds of such evidence: evidence of statements made by a hypnotized witness (or defendant); testimony of a witness

---

45. Field, P.B., and Dworkin, S.F., 67 Journal of Psychology 47 (1967).

46. American Bar Association Journal, p. 187, Feb. 1978.

47. *E.g.*, People v. Busch, 56 Cal. 2d 868, 366 P.2d 314 (1961); State v. Pusch, 77 N.D. 860, 46 N.W.2d 508 (1951).

(or defendant) while hypnotized; and opinion testimony of experts as to truthfulness of a hypnotized witness or defendant. Usually, such evidence is offered either by the defense, in the form of explanatory statements obtained from hypnosis of the defendant, or by the prosecution, in the form of facilitated recollection of a witness with a faulty memory. Very generally speaking, the courts have been unreceptive to introduction of the former, and considerably more willing to accept the latter.[48]

Evidence of statements made by a hypnotized witness or defendant has generally been held to be inadmissible.[49] As one court has put it, the "vast majority of authorities" have concluded that hypnotic evidence is not admissible because of its unreliability.[50] However, there appears to be a considerably more receptive attitude toward allowing witnesses to testify at trial concerning matters as to which memory was restored through hypnosis, with an increasing number of courts permitting this procedure.[51]

Reflecting a possibly changing attitude, some courts have suggested that certain guidelines be followed when attempting to assist an eyewitness recalling past events through hypnosis.[52] Thus the hypnotist should be a qualified psychiatrist or psychologist; all information given to the hypnotist should be recorded; the hypnosis session should be filmed or videotaped; and the witness and the

---

48. *See generally* 92 A.L.R.3d 442.

49. *E.g.*, People v. Shirley, 641 P.2d 775 (Cal. 1982); Rodriguez v. State, 327 So. 2d 903 (Fla. 1976); Creamer v. State, 232 Ga. 136, 205 S.E.2d 240 (1974); State v. Pusch, 77 N.D. 860, 46 N.W.2d 508 (1951).

50. Greenfield v. Commonwealth, 210 Va. 710, 204 S.E.2d 414 (1974).

51. *E.g.*, Creamer v. State, 232 Ga. 136, 205 S.E.2d 240 (1974); Harding v. State, 5 Md. App. 230, 246 A.2d 302, *cert. denied*, 395 U.S. 949, 89 S. Ct. 2030, 23 L. Ed. 2d 468 (1968); State v. McQueen, 295 N.C. 96, 244 S.E.2d 414 (1978); State v. Jorgensen, 8 Or. App. 1, 492 P.2d 312 (1971).

52. People v. Hughes, 99 Misc. 2d 863, 417 N.Y.S.2d 643 (1979); State v. Hurd, 173 N.J. Super. 333, 414 A.2d 291 (1980).

hypnotist should be alone during the session. If the session was conducted at the prosecution's request, the defense should be made aware that the eyewitness has undergone hypnosis. Finally, a pretrial hearing should be held to determine the effect of the hypnosis and the reliability of the witness' expected testimony.

Permitting a witness to testify at trial while under a hypnotic state is a fairly recent development, usually involving the testimony of the defendant himself. Whether or not it is a valid technique, the few courts addressing this issue have rejected the procedure.[53] However, testimony under hypnosis may be permissible if stipulated to by both sides.[54]

Finally, the courts have generally excluded the testimony of experts as to opinions formed during hypnosis of a defendant concerning his guilt or state of mind at the time of the crime.[55] Similarly, expert opinion testimony as to the truthfulness or reliability of statements made by a defendant under hypnosis have been rejected.[56] Oddly enough, however, a hypnotist's opinion concerning the reliability of memories induced in a *prosecution* witness by hypnosis has been held admissible.[57] This reflects a general suspicion among the courts of evidence by hypnosis when offered as to the defendant, but a greater willingness to consider such evidence when it relates to a prosecution witness.

In attempting to offer or oppose any evidence of hypnosis, counsel must always bear in mind the foundational require-

---

53. *E.g.,* Greenfield v. Commonwealth, 212 Va. 710, 204 S.E.2d 414 (1974).

54. *See* Diloff, G., 4 Ohio North Law Review 1 (1977); Spector, G., et al., 38 Ohio St. L.J. 567 (1977).

55. *E.g.,* People v. Busch, 56 Cal. 2d 868, 366 P.2d 314 (1961); Jones v. State, 542 P.2d 316 (Okla. 1975).

56. *E.g.,* State v. Pusch, 77 N.D. 860, 46 N.W.2d 508 (1951); Jones v. State, 542 P.2d 1316 (Okla. 1975).

57. Harding v. State, 5 Md. App. 230, 246 A.2d 302, *cert. denied,* 395 U.S. 949, 89 S. Ct. 2030, 23 L. Ed. 2d 468 (1968).

ments of establishing through proper testimony (presumably of expert hypnotists) the reliability and scientific acceptance of hypnosis as an analytical tool. Evidence concerning the uses, techniques, effects, and general reliability of hypnosis has generally been held properly received in criminal trials. In addition, the expertise of the hypnotist who conducted or is conducting the hypnosis must be shown through his education, training and experience. If the hypnotist is testifying as to earlier statements of a witness or defendant, the hearsay rule must be kept in mind.

§ 4-3. Psychological Detection.

The law relevant to eyewitness identification has concerned itself primarily with pretrial confrontations — with the fairness of police identification procedures and with the right to counsel at this stage. The actual issue of the reliability or unreliability of eyewitness testimony itself has not really been dealt with by the courts, other than to perhaps require corroboration of a witness' testimony, or a judicial warning to the jury in the form of an instruction. An instruction supplies no guidelines to the juror on how to assess the testimony of an eyewitness. Simply excluding eyewitness evidence when the trial judge feels it to be unreliable would be a dangerous imposition on the jury's province. Yet it is a proven fact that the average person has an unrealistic confidence in eyewitness testimony. How, then, to deal with this misplaced faith without abrogating the role of the juror?

One possible answer is to permit the jury to hear evidence concerning the psychology of the eyewitness. In other words, expose the trier of fact to the testimony of an expert witness concerning factors that affect perception, memory and the reliability of eyewitness accounts. The expert could testify generally to considerations in eyewitness identification, describing clinical experiments that have been conducted, or he could go farther and consider the psychological aspects of the particular eyewitness involved in the case. Either way, the jury is supplied with sufficient knowledge about the psychology of eyewitnesses to evaluate the eyewitness' testimony accordingly.

§ 4-3.1. The Psychologist as Expert Witness.

It is clear that the average juror views eyewitness testimony with a considerable amount of trust. It is equally clear that such testimony is inherently unreliable. Yet the courts have generally been reluctant to permit expert testimony as to the psychology of eyewitness identification. Permitting such testimony will inevitably result in a war of experts, it is reasoned, with each side calling more of its own psychologists to refute the other side's psychologists. Of course the trial judge can always exercise his discretion in limiting the number of such witnesses to be called; the same problem has been dealt with in murder cases involving the insanity issue.

The more commonly asserted objection to permitting testimony on eyewitness identification is that it invades the province of the jury. The trial courts have broad discretionary powers when it comes to admitting or excluding such evidence, and many of them have opted for the latter on the theory that "it would not be appropriate to take from the jury their own determination as to what weight or effect to give to the evidence of the eyewitness and identifying witnesses and to have that determination put before them on the basis of the expert witness testimony as proffered." [58]

A number of relatively recent decisions have confirmed the discretionary right of trial courts to exclude psychological evidence should they deem it appropriate. One of the more significant of these decisions is *United States v. Amaral,*[59] wherein the testimony of a psychologist

---

58. United States v. Amaral, 488 F.2d at 1153 (9th Cir. 1973).

59. 488 F.2d 1148 (9th Cir. 1973).

concerning the effects of stress on perception in a robbery trial was excluded. The appellate court backed the trial court's exercise of discretion, reasoning that the jury's own common sense and the availability of cross-examination of the eyewitness constituted a sufficient check on unreliable identification evidence. Yet the decision provided no guidelines to assist the trial court in exercising its discretion. The general foundational requirements for the admissibility of expert testimony were reiterated in the *Amaral* decision: The witness must be qualified; his testimony must concern a proper subject matter; it must comply with a generally accepted scientific method or theory; and its probative value must outweigh its potentially prejudicial effect. But the decision offered no standards for the trial court to apply in deciding each foundational requirement. How does the trial court decide whether testimony conforms to a generally accepted method or theory? What is a "proper subject matter"? How is probative value to be weighed against potential prejudice?

In an interesting review of the *Amaral* case,[60] one commentator analyzed each of the four foundational requirements restated by the court as they apply to psychologists. Certainly, determining the expertise of such a witness causes no problems. Whether his testimony is a "proper subject matter" for expert testimony is a more difficult question. Jurors lack sufficient knowledge about the reliability of eyewitness accounts, the commentator argued, and their "intuition" about such matters is unsupported by scientific research. Since jurors do not have sufficient knowledge of the field, therefore, expert testimony is "proper." It does not invade the province of the jury because the expert does not testify whether a particular witness is accurate or truthful; he testifies only to general psychological factors affecting an eyewitness identification. He is, in

60. Woocher, F.D., 29 Stan. L. Rev. 969 (1977).

other words, testifying only about witnesses in general, and the jury is free to give whatever weight it wishes to both his testimony and that of the eyewitness.

The third foundational requirement, conformation to a scientifically accepted method or theory, presents somewhat of a problem. Although applied by the *Amaral* court, this requirement has generally been applied to such relatively new devices as the polygraph, voice-stress analyzer and the like; the concern of the courts is that the devices have found scientific acceptance. The testimony of psychologists, however, does not fall into this category. Rather, it should be grouped with the testimony of physicians and psychiatrists — neither of which have ever had the "scientific acceptance" standard applied to them.

Finally, the commentator addresses the issue of probative value versus prejudicial effect. Obviously, the testimony of an expert on eyewitness psychology is probative; it is relevant to the reliability of critical evidence. It has value; it tends to supply jurors with information to eyewitness identification which they do not have. As to prejudicial effect, the trial judge can minimize this possibility through cautionary instructions and limitation of the scope of the expert's testimony.

Applying the standards restated by the *Amaral* court, the commentator concludes that they have been satisfactorily met when dealing with expert testimony on eyewitness identification. Yet federal and state courts continue to uphold the trial courts' discretionary refusal to permit such testimony. It must be kept in mind that cases where it is received in evidence are not usually appealed on that issue, since it is usually the defense that offers the evidence to refute a prosecution eyewitness, and as a result there is a scarcity of appellate decisions upholding the admissibility of such testimony. Some courts have established a rule that the proponent of eyewitness expert evidence must prove to the court that the issues are beyond the ability of the jury to determine through application of their common experience, and as a result, expert testimony has been ruled inadmissible.[61] Other courts have simply held that such expert testimony, whether offered as to eyewitness identification generally or as to the particular identification involved in the case, invades the province of the jury and takes up too much time relative to its probative value.[62] Cross-examination of the eyewitness provides sufficient opportunity for checking the reliability of an eyewitness' identification, according to yet other courts, precluding the necessity for expert witnesses.[63] Some courts have rejected expert evidence on the grounds that it was simply not sufficiently accepted by the scientific community as a valid method or theory.[64]

On the other hand, a small but growing number of appellate decisions are recognizing the value of expert testimony on the question of the reliability of eyewitness testimony, and are approving its use in criminal trials.[65] As in so many other areas of the law, eventual change is being preceded by scholarly criticism [66] — in this case by the failure of trial judges to recognize the value of psychological

---

61. United States v. Burke, 506 F.2d 1165 (9th Cir. 1974), *cert. denied,* 421 U.S. 915 (1975).

62. United States v. Brown, 501 F.2d 146 (9th Cir. 1974); United States v. Brown, 540 F.2d 1048 (10th Cir. 1976); People v. Johnson, 38 Cal. App. 3d 1, 112 Cal. Rptr. 834 (1974); State v. Reed, 226 Kan. 519, 601 P.2d 1125 (1979).

63. United States v. Amaral, 488 F.2d 1148 (9th Cir. 1973); Caldwell v. State, 594 S.W.2d 24 (Ark. 1980).

64. United States v. Watson, 587 F.2d 365 (7th Cir. 1979).

65. United States v. Green, 525 F.2d 386 (8th Cir. 1975); United States v. Harris, 528 F.2d 914 (4th Cir. 1975), *cert. denied,* 423 U.S. 1075 (1976); United States v. Snow, 552 F.2d 165, *cert. denied,* 434 U.S. 970 (6th Cir. 1977).

66. Tyrrell, C., 37 Alabama Law Review 563 (1976); Woocher, F.D., 29 Stan. L. Rev. 969 (1977); Partman, D., 3 Criminal Defense Magazine (1976); Sobel, N.R., *Eyewitness Identification* (Boardman 1972).

evidence to jurors unfamiliar with the vagaries of eyewitness identification.

§ 4-3.2. Psychological Testing of Witnesses.

In 1895 a noted psychologist predicted that the reliability of any given eyewitness could be scientifically measured and his testimony be given a corresponding weight by the jury.[67] He felt that "a numerical correction could be introduced for lapse of time, average lack of truthfulness, average effect of personal interest, etc. The testimony could be collected independently and given to experts who could affirm, for example, that the chances are 19 to 1 that the homicide was committed by the defendant, and 4 to 1 that it was premeditated."[68]

The psychologist went a bit too far in his confidence that science could solve the eyewitness problem with mathematical precision. But the concept that the accuracy of any given identification or account can be at least roughly approximated by psychologically testing the eyewitness is potentially a valid one. Psychologists today have the means for testing individuals as to each of the traits critical to perception, memory and identification. Although the courts have yet to be called upon to rule on the admissibility of such test reults, it would seem to be only a matter of time before they are. After a traditional period of resistance, the results of these tests may find their way into evidence. The day will come, in other words, when a witness can be psychologically tested and rated as to the reliability of his testimony, and his evidence weighed accordingly.

Dr. Robert Buckhout, Professor of Psychology and Director of the Center for Responsive Psychology at the Brooklyn College for the City University of New York, describes a recently developed test using "signal detection theory" as "a means of coping with the fact that an

---

67. Cattell, J.M., 2 Science 761 (1895).

68. *Id.* at 765-66.

observer's attitude interferes with his detection, processing and reporting of sensory stimuli." [69] The subject is given a stimulus (sight, sound or whatever) and asked to reply "yes" or "no" to a question concerning it; some stimuli are purposely false. For example, an auditory signal is sent in the midst of confusing noise; sometimes only the noise is sent. Is a signal heard? The examiner then counts the correct "yes" answers ("hits") and the incorrect "yes" answers ("false alarms"). A cautious person will have very few "false alarms" and a high proportion of "hits"; a less cautious person will have more "hits", but at the cost of a large number of "false alarms". From the test data is drafted a "witness sensitivity curve" — a theoretical indication of the propensity for that person to give a "false alarm" — that is, to mistakenly identify a suspect.

---

69. Buckhout, R., 23 Scientific American 231 (1974).

PART TWO

PRETRIAL IDENTIFICATION

§ 5. Police Procedures.

> "The influence of improper suggestions upon identifying witnesses probably accounts for more miscarriages of justice than any other single factor — perhaps it is responsible for more such errors than all other factors combined."
>
> *United States v. Wade*[1]

In any criminal trial involving the issue of the identity of the perpetrator, the eyewitness will be asked by the prosecutor to point to the man whom he saw commit the crime. Invariably, of course, the witness will indicate the defendant seated at counsel's table. The identification has been dramatically made before the jury's own eyes, and the impact on their thinking will be considerable.

Such in-court identifications have very little intrinsic value, and are done primarily for effect and to supply the technical requirements of the prosecution's case. Both counsel realize that the witness has already identified the defendant during the police investigation. Furthermore, every person who watches television knows that the defendant is the nervous-looking fellow seated next to the attorney at

1. 388 U.S. at 229, 87 S. Ct. 1926, 18 L. Ed. 2d 1149 (1967) (quoting from Wall, P.M., *Eyewitness Identification in Criminal Cases* (Charles C. Thomas 1965)).

the defense table; he may as well have a neon sign hanging from his neck.

The cold fact of criminal justice is that identifications are made long before this supposed "confrontation" at trial. The charade of in-court identification is, in most cases, the *pro forma* acting out of an earlier identification or identifications. It is these *pretrial* identifications, then, which are critical to the whole issue and which must be thoroughly understood by counsel. It is at these pretrial identifications that the witness is originally confronted with the suspect and makes his decision — a decision which will later be reenforced by police or the prosecutor, and a decision which will become increasingly committed.

These pretrial identifications almost invariably take place in police stations or in the field. Because of this, they immediately take on two very ominous characteristics: They are removed from the protective rules of procedure and evidence of the courtroom, and they offer tremendous opportunity for suggestive influences. Thus the eyewitness is usually being asked to identify a suspect under circumstances which — intentionally or not — act upon him in such a way as to produce a result desired by the police.

There are two primary causes for misidentification by an eyewitness. The first involves the human frailties of perception and memory discussed in the previous sections. It is now time to consider the second cause: suggestive police identification procedures.

§ 5-1. Identification Methods.

It is a common practice for law enforcement authorities to offer an eyewitness to a crime the opportunity to identify the perpetrator by confronting him or his likeness. The purpose of such a confrontation is to (1) identify the suspect, (2) confirm suspicions about a suspect temporarily being detained, or (3) strengthen evidence on a suspect against whom charges have already been or are being filed.

There are several commonly used methods of pretrial identification, each with its own strengths and weaknesses. Probably the most common, and certainly the most suggestive, of the procedures is the *showup.* Although the term is often used interchangeably with "lineup," here it will be treated as referring to a one-to-one confrontation — *i.e.,* the eyewitness viewing the isolated suspect. Commonly, it is conducted at the scene of the crime, shortly after the crime has taken place and a suspect detained, and while the incident is still fresh in the witness' mind. Another often-used showup procedure is to take the witness to the jail cell where the suspect is being held. There are few precautions taken; the police point out the often-handcuffed suspect and ask, "Is that him?" Although the showup procedure is simple, short, and inexpensive, it involves tremedous risk of prejudicial influence from the police and from the circumstances.

A more controlled version of the showup is the *lineup.* A lineup may be conducted before charges have been filed, in an attempt to determine whether a detained or arrested suspect is the guilty party, or after the filing of a complaint or indictment, to strengthen the prosecution's case against the defendant by crystallizing his identity in the eyewitness' mind. The lineup is often held on a stage and usually at a police station or jail facility. In some situations, the witness will be making his observations of individuals on a lighted stage from a darkened audience or from behind a one-way mirror, thus preventing the suspect from seeing him. The lineup will consist of the suspect and perhaps five or six others roughly similar in basic physical characteristics. These others are often inmates from the jail, but will sometimes be police officers. The people in the lineup stand shoulder-to-shoulder, facing the witness; they may be made to turn sideways for a profile, walk, or speak a given phrase. The witness may be alone, with a police officer and/or in the company of other witnesses.

Another method of identification commonly used in the early stages of an investigation is the *photographic display,* or "mug shot lineup" as it is sometimes called. A series of photos of individuals roughly similar to the suspect are shown to the witness. This may be done one at a time or in sets of perhaps five or six photos mounted on a strip. Preferably, there will be no names or booking numbers on the photos, and all will be of the same quality. But many of the same problems found in lineups are present, resulting in a subtle suggestion that the photo of the suspect is the one the witness is looking for.

Occasionally, police will use other means of identification when appropriate. If the voice of the perpetrator was heard, the witness may be asked to listen to the suspect talk; if the voice was recorded, voice analysis may be employed. If a witness was able to work with a police artist, a sketch or mechanical composite may be used in initially identifying the perpetrator and in later corroborating the identification.

In most cases involving pretrial identification, counsel will encounter a combination of these procedures. Typically, the police will show a photograph display to the witness, then have him view the suspect in a lineup, and finally refresh his recollection with the photograph before testifying. But the inherent dangers of these individual practices are geometrically increased by their cumulative effect, as will be seen in the following sections.

§ 5-2. The Showup.

The experts in the field of law and police methods have been uniform in their condemnations of the showup procedure. Patrick Wall has written that it "constitutes the most grossly suggestive identification procedure now or ever used by the police."[2] Wigmore states that "there is no

---

2. Wall, P.M., *Eyewitness Identification in Criminal Cases,* p. 28 (Charles C. Thomas 1965).

excuse for jeopardizing the fate of innocent men by such clumsy, antiquated methods; a recognition under such circumstances is next to worthless." [3] Felix Frankfurter has argued that the use of showups is a "violation of approved police methods" and will "fatally impair" the value of any identification that results.[4]

The Supreme Court of the United States has recognized the inherent dangers of the traditional showup procedures. In *Stovall v. Denno* [5] the Court noted that "the practice of showing suspects singly to persons for the purpose of identification and not as part of a lineup, has been widely condemned." However, the Court went on to determine that use of showups *per se* would not constitute a denial of due process, but rather that the "totality of the circumstances" surrounding the particular showup must be considered in determining the fairness of the procedure. (see § 8 *infra*).

Police agencies throughout the United States have been surprisingly oblivious to the almost uniform criticism of showups. The method continues to be routinely used in the field and in the station house. Many police investigators, however, are not content with the already considerable suggestiveness inherent in a normal one-on-one showup identification, and often see fit to add extra embellishments designed to further guarantee a positive identification. It is not enough that the witness is strongly influenced by the presentation by the police of only one suspect — an individual he presumably believes the police feel is the guilty party. To ensure an identification, some police officers will take the witness to the jail cell where the suspect is being detained, possibly in jail clothing. If there was any doubt in the witness' mind, viewing the suspect in such a setting

3. Wigmore, 4 *Evidence* § 1130, n. 20 (3d ed. 1940).

4. Frankfurter, F., *The Case of Sacco and Vanzetti,* pp. 12, 31-32 (1927).

5. 388 U.S. at 302, 87 S. Ct. 1967, 18 L. Ed. 2d at 1206.

would certainly tend to dispel it. Why, he reasons, would the individual be held in custody unless the police were already convinced of his guilt?

A variation on this involves an at-the-scene presentation of the suspect to the witness while in handcuffs and in an obvious custody situation. As Wigmore has said concerning the witness' predictable reaction to such a confrontation, "the suggestion of guilty identity could not have been more violent."[6]

There are other ways for further increasing the likelihood that a witness will identify the police investigator's favorite suspect. Simply pointing him out as the chief suspect before the showup, for example, can do much to ensure a favorable result. Telling the witness that there is a lot of evidence against the individual, or that he has confessed, or that he is, in fact, guilty — all of these can be quite effective, even though unethical and grossly unfair. Often, suggestiveness can be accomplished in subtle ways, such as telling the witness that "it's okay to make an identification, because where he's going he'll never be able to hurt you again."

Another method police have for further corrupting an already prejudicial identification procedure is to require the suspect to repeat emotion-laden words uttered by the perpetrator at the scene of the crime, such as, "Keep your hands up or I'll blow your head off!" It does not take a psychologist to realize the effect on a witness of hearing such a phrase again.

Related to this is the common practice of requiring the suspect to wear clothing similar or identical to those described by the witness. In many cases, the witness will recall the clothing worn by a culprit more effectively than he will the culprit's face or other physical characteristics. He may, in effect, identify the clothing rather than the suspect himself.

---

6. Wigmore, 25 Ill. Law Review at 551 (1931).

Faced with such inherently suggestive procedures, what has been the attitude of the courts toward showup identifications? A specific discussion of the factors relevant to the due process considerations of suggestiveness at a showup will be left for later in this text — including the question of admissibility of a showup identification in trial (§ 11-2.2) as well as the effect of a suggestive showup on the admissibility of an in-court identification (§ 10-3). For now, however, it is useful to distinguish the use of showups in two quite different situations: in the field and at the station house.

Generally speaking, the courts have been fairly permissive when dealing with in-the-field showups, at least, as to those that occur very soon after the commission of a crime.[7] This is due to a recognition of the practical realities of police work. When a suspect has been caught immediately after a crime has taken place, it would be unreasonable to deny the police the opportunity to confront the witness with him in the field right away. Most courts have recognized the value of a prompt confrontation, reasoning that a negative identification would permit the police to continue their search for the perpetrator and that, in any event, such a procedure is in the suspect's best interest since a failure to identify would prevent possible arrest and overnight detention pending the organization of a lineup.

This sanctioning of showup procedures in the face of *exigent circumstances* has been extended to the "hospital confrontation." In this situation, the eyewitness is usually the victim of bodily injury inflicted by the perpetrator, and is either in danger of dying or is simply physically incapable of being transported to a lineup. There seems to have been relatively little discussion in court decisions of this type of

---

7. *E.g.*, Bates v. United States, 132 U.S. App. D.C. 36, 405 F.2d 1104 (D.C. Cir. 1968); Jackson v. State, 269 N.E.2d 23 (Minn. 1978); State v. Strickland, 63 Or. App. 119, 584 P.2d 310 (1978).

procedure as to the merits of bringing a lineup to the hospital.

The courts have generally been somewhat less receptive to showups of the second type — that is, to showups that take place in the station house. There is usually little reason for showing a suspect to a witness in his jail cell, or in an interrogation room from behind a one-way mirror. In such situations, the police have ample opportunity to put together a lineup of prisoners or police officers, usually with no pressing reasons for not doing this. The time differential in such a situation is usually no more than a half-hour or so. Accordingly, the courts tend to find undue suggestiveness where an identification resulted from a showup conducted at a police station — particularly where the suspect was in a jail cell,[8] or was wearing handcuffs.[9]

Other considerations will, of course, render a showup identification inadmissibly unfair. Holding it at an unusually late hour, for example, may lead the witness to conclude that he would not have been asked to view the suspect unless the police were quite sure of his guilt.[10] Having the witness view the suspect in two or more showups has been held unduly suggestive.[11]

Nevertheless, trial counsel must be aware that despite the occasional finding of a violation of due process amounting to the necessity for a reversal, courts in the United States are generally reluctant to deal with the issue. Where the English and Commonwealth courts have soundly

---

8. *E.g.*, In re Hill, 71 Cal. 2d 997, 458 P.2d 449, *cert. denied*, 397 U.S. 1017, 90 S. Ct. 1254, 25 L. Ed. 432 (1969).

9. *E.g.*, State v. Kennedy, 249 S.E.2d 188 (W. Va. 1978); State v. Williams, 545 P.2d 938 (Ariz. 1976).

10. United States v. O'Connor, 282 F. Supp. 963 (D.D.C. 1968), *aff'd*, 137 U.S. App. D.C. 76, 420 F.2d 644 (D.C. Cir. 1969).

11. People v. Blumenshine, 42 Ill. 2d 508, 250 N.E. 152 (1969); Harris v. State, 350 A.2d 768 (Del. 1975).

condemned the use of showups — and will reverse a conviction where the showup identification constitutes the primary evidence of guilt — the American courts have apparently taken the position that while showups should be disapproved, the jury should determine the credibility of such identification (absent complete unfairness after viewing the "totality of circumstances"). In other words, counsel is faced with overcoming a judicial inertia when attacking identification procedures which have been judicially condemned.

§ 5-3. The Lineup.

Generally speaking, a lineup involves considerably less suggestiveness to an eyewitness than does a showup. However, this assumes that the lineup is conducted in a fair and imparital manner by the police authorities — an asumption that all too often cannot be made. As with any identification procedure, the authorities can administer the lineup in such a way as to almost direct the witness to select a suspect if that is their desire. Unlike the showup, a suggestive lineup has an added danger with which defense counsel must contend: The jury will tend to accept the identification as reliable since the lineup procedure appears on its face to be completely fair to the accused.

Why are lineups presented in a suggestive manner by the police? There is always the very real possibility that the police are consciously trying to get a witness or witnesses to identify the man they are trying to arrest or convict. The more difficult situation to detect, however, involves the subconscious motivation of police officers with a strong sense of duty. His expectations or theories of the case will be communicated to the witnesses in subtle ways which he may not even be aware of, thus influencing their identifications. This phenomenon is so prevalent that psychologists refer to it as the "Rosenthal effect."[12] It can become even more pronounced as the relative status of the officer with regard to position, age, sex, or race is elevated over that of the witness.[13] A white male lieutenant in his middle years, for an extreme example, would have a considerable suggestive influence over an older black woman who works as a domestic.

The psychology of the witness must also be understood. The witness is aware that the lineup has been organized for his benefit at considerable expense, and that the police hope — and perhaps expect — him to succeed in his identification. In essence, he is being asked to take a multiple-question recognition test, and he is quite well aware that all this effort is not being wasted on a meaningless procedure: The guilty party *is* somewhere in the lineup. Thus, the eyewitness makes the assumption that one of the individuals in the lineup is the culprit, and it becomes a question not of whether any of them is the person he saw at the scene of the crime, but of which one *most closely resembles* that person. This predisposition to make an identification is further strengthened by the natural tendency of witnesses to want to please the police officers — whom many view as authority figures dispensing approval or even praise.[14]

A lineup identification, then, must be viewed with a healthy degree of skepticism, and the procedures employed carefully examined for suggestive influences. These influences are usually of four types: pre-lineup police conduct; the composition of the lineup; police administration of the lineup; and post-lineup police conduct. Pre-lineup conduct involves such activities as "preparing" the witness for an

12. Rosenthal, R., *Experimenter Effects in Behavioral Research,* (Appleton Century Crafts 1966).

13. Kintz, B.L., et al., 63 Psychological Bulletin 223 (1965).

14. Orne, M.T., 17 American Psychologist 776 (1962).

identification at the lineup by having him pick out the suspect from a biased photo display; "accidentally" letting him see the suspect in a custodial setting before the lineup; or telling him that the guilty party will definitely be in the lineup. The composition of the lineup can have a tremendous influcence on a witness' identification. If the suspect is the only individual in the lineup who resembles the description given the police, then his selection becomes more likely. The administration of the lineup itself can have a similarly suggestive influence, such as where the witnesses are permitted to make their identifications in a group, or where only the defendant is made to utter an emotional statement heard at the scene. Finally, police conduct during the post-lineup stage can also have a pronounced effect: Urging an equivocal witness to commit himself, for example, or reenforcing a witness' tentative identification with photographs of the suspect or information about his criminal record.

Assuming that counsel has been retained or appointed to represent a suspect being exhibited in a lineup (see § 7, *infra*), he should make every effort to ensure the fairness of the proceedings. He should, however, be aware of one basic fact: The police authorities will probably consider him as a necessary nuisance or a source of obstruction, and may give only token recognition to his role in the lineup procedures. Although some police agencies will offer counsel an active role in the composition and conduct of the lineup, many others will ignore his presence or even attempt to subvert his role in the proceedings. Such conduct may later subject the prosecution's case to suppression of identification evidence.

A sympathetic consultation with the supervising police officer can prove helpful, particularly if he is encouraged to understand that a suggestive lineup may result in the suppression of all the identification evidence. Where a one-person showup is being considered, the merits of a seven-person lineup should be argued and eventually demanded; where a normal lineup is being arranged, the use of a "blank lineup" (one in which the client is not present) preceding it should be suggested. The composition of the lineup should be made as uniform as possible; the client/suspect should not stand out in any respect from the others in the lineup. Care should be taken to explain to the witnesses that the person observed at the crime scene may *not* be in the lineup. Any instructions or statements by the police that tend to suggest the client to a witness should be recorded. Any showing of photos to a witness should be noted, and the photos examined for suggestiveness.

Where there is more than one witness at the lineup, counsel should attempt to have them isolated from one another, and their comments written down silently rather than made orally to the police. Any uncertainties shown by a witness ("I think," "maybe") should be noted, as well as any selections of individuals in the lineup other than the client. In fact, counsel should attempt to interview the witnesses himself both before and after the lineup, with notes of the conversations carefully taken. Descriptions of the person seen committing the crime should be obtained in as great a detail as possible *before* they have viewed the lineup. The names and addresses of the witnesses should also be taken.

Counsel must keep careful notes of the lineup procedures for possible later use in a motion to suppress identification evidence. If possible, photographs should be taken of the lineup itself. The simple fact of counsel taking notes and photos can have a decided effect on the police authorities in their conduct of the lineup, swaying them toward less suggestive procedures.

In most cases, however, counsel will not have had the opportunity to be present at his client's lineup. He will then be limited to reviewing the facts surrounding the identification procedures, with an eye to arguing that the "totality of circumstances" indicate a lineup so suggestive as to constitute a denial of due process. If he is successful, he will be able to have evidence of the pretrial identification suppressed and, possibly, even any in-court identification of his client. These matters will be discussed in later sections of this book.

§ 5-3.1. Composition.

The composition of a lineup is critical. If the suspect is the only black in the lineup, for example, or the only one wearing clothing fitting the descriptions of the eyewitnesses, then the entire procedure becomes a farce. The eyewitnesses, already strongly motivated to make a selection regardless of their degree of confidence, will tend to select anyone that stands out in any significant respect.

The first consideration in assessing the fairness of a lineup is the number of individuals placed in it. Wigmore has suggested that a lineup should contain twelve persons,[15] thus reflecting the practice in England; Wall has indicated that "at least five or six, and more if possible" should be used.[16] The effectiveness of a lineup decreases as the number of individuals contained in it decreases; as the number shrinks to four or less, the entire procedure will begin to reflect many of the problems of a showup.

The next concern is that of a physical similarity of the persons arranged together in the lineup. Obviously, the suspect should not differ significantly in appearance from those accompanying him in the lineup. Placing an Oriental suspect in a lineup of Caucasians would, by itself, be prejudicially suggestive. Similarly, displaying a young, tall suspect with five or six older and shorter people would

15. Wigmore, 3 *Evidence* 164 (3d ed. 1940).

16. Wall, P.M., *Eyewitness Identification in Criminal Cases*, p. 53 (Charles C. Thomas 1965).

hardly constitute a fair presentation. The participants in the lineup should be of the same race and sex, and roughly similar in age, height, weight and physical build. Unusual characteristics, such as a beard, outstanding scar or shrivelled arm, would tend to immediately disqualify a person as a participant. Descriptions given by the witnesses should be considered. If an eyewitness has described the person he saw as having blue eyes, the lineup should not contain a blue-eyed suspect and eight brown-eyed individuals next to him. In other words, consistent with witnesses' descriptions and the suspect's own physical features, the lineup should contain individuals of like characteristics. As Justice Frankfurter has observed, the process becomes "identification through accentuation"[17] where a lineup is presented to an eyewitness in which the suspect stands out in some respect.

Clothing and eyeglasses present yet another potential problem. There is an understandable tendency to identify an individual on the basis of what he is wearing, rather than on the basis of his physical features. If the perpetrator was wearing blue jeans, for example, and the suspect is the only one in the lineup wearing blue jeans, the eyewitness may be likely to identify him because of that fact alone. Lineups have been held unnecessarily suggestive by the courts where a suspect is dressed in clothing resembling that described by witnesses earlier.[18] Similarly, the presence of eyeglasses may trigger a false identification, and lineups have been found constitutionally defective where only the suspect was wearing glasses after witnesses had earlier reported that an outstanding feature of the perpetrator of the crime was his glasses.[19] Indicating a

---

17. Frankfurter, F., *The Case of Sacco and Vanzetti* 32 (1927).

18. People v. Franklin, 22 Ill. App. 3d 775, 317 N.E.2d 611 (1974); State v. Boyd, 294 A.2d 459 (Me. 1972); United States ex rel Cannon v. Smith, (W.D.N.Y.) 388 F. Supp. 1201, *aff'd,* 527 F.2d 702 (2d Cir. 1975).

19. Israel v. Odom, 521 F.2d 1370 (7th Cir. 1975).

continuing confusion in definite guidelines, however, it must be recognized that there are as many cases holding that such practices are *not* unduly suggestive, and that they relate only to the weight of the evidence, or that any suggestiveness was overcome by independent sources of identification.

Whatever the judicial ruling as to clothing, the solution to any prejudicial practices should be apparent: The suspect's clothing should not differ significantly from those of his companions in the lineup. If he is wearing clothing similar to those described earlier by witnesses, then he should be presented in different clothes. The fact of similar clothing can always be used as evidence of guilt in trial by the prosecutor. If he is wearing glasses, either have them taken off or have everyone in the lineup wear glasses.

Finally, the type of individuals used in the lineup can have a greater effect on the outcome than would at first be realized. The ideal source for lineup participants is the public at large — ordinary citizens who resemble the suspect. This, however, involves obvious difficulties and leads us to the second-best choice: prisoners being held in or near the station house where the lineup is being conducted. Yet despite the availability of such prisoners (and it must be recognized that there are occasions when sufficient prisoners similar in characteristics to the suspect are simply not available), the police authorities continue to employ the third — and worst — source of lineup participants: police officers.

It is, of course, much easier for the officer conducting the lineup to simply summon four or five of his fellow officers from around the station house for brief "lineup duty" rather than deal with the problems inherent in searching the cells for appropriate prisoners and supervising them during the lineup. But there are inherent dangers in using police officers in a lineup. For one thing, officers have a distinctly different bearing and attitude than has the suspect. Most of them will reflect confidence, companionship and even humor; contrast this with the nervous, isolated and depressed mannerisms of the suspect. For another, there is all too often a tendency on the part of the officers in the lineup to glance at the suspect, to shy away from him, and in other ways to perhaps unintentionally communicate the suspect's status to the witness.

A related problem involves the appearance of other suspects in the same lineup. Although this would seem to emphasize the suspect through a guilt-by-grouping effect, at least two courts have held that this factor does not, by itself, constitute an unfair lineup.[20] Nevertheless, the less suggestive approach would clearly be to place only one suspect in a lineup at a time.

Eventually, counsel will probably be arguing that the composition of the lineup was unfair — either to the court, in an attempt to suppress identification evidence, or to the jury, as part of an attempt to discredit the identification. In either case, the benefits of a photograph of the actual lineup should be obvious. If counsel has any prior knowledge that a lineup will take place, he should make every effort to have it photographed by himself or, if possible, by the police at his specific request.

In considering the issue of fairness of composition, counsel may wish to consider the use of expert psychological testimony. Professor Loftus describes a simple procedure [21] for testing the validity of a lineup whereby a random sampling of citizens are given brief descriptions of the suspect, and then a photograph of the lineup is shown to them (if such a photo does not exist, one might be created by reassembling the participants or by placing their individual photos in a strip display). The subjects are asked to pick out the

---

20. People v. Tuttle, 3 Ill. App. 3d 326, 278 N.E.2d 458 (1972); Burton v. State, 84 Nev. 191, 437 P.2d 861 (1968).

21. Loftus, E.F., *Eyewitness Testimony,* p. 146 (Harvard College 1979).

culprit from the description. If the suspect is chosen more often than chance would indicate (assuming ten photos, ten percent of the time), then the lineup was unfair: The participants in the lineup simply did not resemble the description closely enough to provide a valid test of the witness' identification.

In a slightly more complex procedure, another psychologist developed a method for determining the functional size of any lineup.[22] Again, individuals are shown a photograph of the lineup and are given a rough description of the suspect. The total number of individuals tested is then divided by the number of individuals who selected the suspect, and the functional size computed. If, for example, one hundred people were given the description and shown the photo and twenty-five of them picked out the suspect, then the functional size of the lineup was four. Never mind that there were eight individuals actually in the lineup, the realistic effect was such that it consisted functionally of only four people.

§ 5-3.2. Police Conduct of Lineup.

Although the physical composition of the lineup may be satisfactory, the circumstances surrounding its presentation to the eyewitnesses may be defective. Where, for example, a witness is shown two successive lineups and the suspect is the only participant present in both, the procedure is unduly suggestive — and courts have so held.[23] Similarly, a lineup preceded by a showup of the suspect has been held to be defective,[24] although not necessarily so suggestive as to require exclusion of the eyewitness' later testimony in court.[25]

---

22. *Id.* at 148-49.

23. Foster v. California, 394 U.S. 440, 89 S. Ct. 1127, 22 L. Ed. 2d 402 (1969); Commonwealth v. Lee, 215 Pa. Super. 240, 257 A.2d 326 (1969).

24. Foster v. California, note 23 *supra*.

25. State v. Summers, 445 S.W.2d 369 (Mo. 1969); Beaupre v. State, 526 S.W.2d 811 (Tex. Crim. 1975).

This problem of emphasizing a suspect through repetition is most often encountered in the practice of "photo-biased lineups." A common police procedure is to show the witness a series of facial photographs, among which is one or two of the suspect, and then to have him view a lineup; the suspect is the only individual in the lineup who appeared in any of the photographs. The obvious effect of this is to trigger a vague, perhaps subconscious, recognition in the witness: He identifies the suspect as the person he thinks he saw at the crime scene, but in fact he is recognizing him from the police photo display.

Psychologists refer to this dangerous but predictable phenomenon as "unconscious transference." In a recent study,[26] "witnesses" were shown photographs of ten "criminals" and told to study them carefully since they might have to identify them later in a lineup. An hour and a half later they were shown fifteen photos, including some of the "criminals" and some of random citizens. One week later a series of lineups were conducted, containing some of the "criminals," some of the innocent citizens in the photographs, and some persons not seen before. The results were disturbing: While eight percent of those in the lineups who had not been seen before were mistakenly identified as "criminals," this figure rose to fully *twenty* percent where an innocent citizen's photograph had been included in the second set of photographs! In other words, the mere viewing of an individual's photo more than doubled the chances of his being mistakenly identified in a subsequent lineup. Counsel should keep these findings in mind when arguing the admissibility or weight of identification evidence resulting from a photo-biased lineup.

One of the primary questions concerning a lineup is just who should conduct it. In almost all cases, lineups are con-

---

26. Browne, E.K., et al. 62 Journal of Applied Psychology 311 (1977).

ducted by the investigating officer on the case. But this is the very official who is most involved in the matter — the person who has probably already formulated theories of the case and strong suspicions as to who is the guilty party, the person who probably arrested the suspect, and the person who may have a personal and/or professional stake in the outcome. This officer may have spent many long hours working the case up to the point of an arrest and a lineup, and he may well be tempted to take steps to ensure that the eyewitness makes a positive identification of the man whom the officer "knows" to be guilty.

What is the alternative? Consider the practice in England: All lineups are conducted by members of the uniformed police staff— officers who are not involved in the case in any way. The investigating officers are simply not permitted to take a direct part in the identification procedures. Thus the lineup is still conducted by the police, but by relatively disinterested parties with no reason to encourage any particular result.

Another problem is the physical facilities in which the lineup is to be held. A common practice is to insulate the witness from fear of retribution by having him view the lineup from behind a two-way mirror or through a peephole. However, there are certain drawbacks to this procedure. For one, the suspect is usually unaware of exactly when he is being observed by the witness and he is likely to exhibit nervousness, anxiety or fear because of the circumstances — emotions which tend to isolate him as the suspect to the witness. For another, the conduct of the police and witness during the identification cannot be observed by the suspect. Quite simply, there will be no defense witness to whether the officer made suggestive comments, or whether the witness initially failed to make a positive identification or was reluctant in his identification. If such secrecy is deemed necessary (as, for example, when the witness is a child or emotionally distraught), the police should at least advise the suspect of exactly when he is being observed.

The question of multiple witnesses presents further problems. Where there are two or more witnesses, they are often permitted to view the lineup together. But the dangers here should be apparent: Each will be influenced by the conduct of the others. Where a given witness may initially be unsure or even unable to make an identification, he becomes quite confident in his selection of the suspect once his fellow witnesses have picked him out. No one likes to appear stupid, incapable, or not a member of the group. Elementary psychology tells us that the actions of one witness will have an effect on the actions of another, and the conduct of a group of identifying witnesses can have a considerable impact on a lone non-identifying witness.

For the same reason that we exclude witnesses from the courtroom during the testimony of other witnesses, so should the police isolate witnesses during lineup procedures. Each witness should observe the lineup by himself and make his identification and/or comments beyond the sight and hearing of other witnesses. If the police insist on having all witnesses view the lineup at the same time due to cost and man-hour considerations, they should at the very least require the witnesses to make their identifications silently by writing comments on paper.

As a corollary of this, proper procedure would dictate that the witnesses be kept apart before and after the lineup as well. If they are permitted to discuss matters before the lineup they may influence one another by describing what they had seen. One witness who has been shown a photograph of the suspect may, for example, describe his facial features to the others, thus influencing the others to identify the man whom they realize the police believe committed the crime. Discussions after the lineup can also be harmful; witnesses who identified the suspect may influence witnesses who did not, to the degree that these non-identifying witnesses will later identify the suspect at trial. Of course, little can be done if the witnesses are friends or fellow workers.

Counsel should always be aware of the possible existence of another prejudicial police practice: The "Oklahoma Showup." The "Oklahoma Showup" is an insidious procedure whereby police arrange to have the witness "accidentally" see the suspect in an incriminating context, such as during booking procedures or while the suspect is being taken from the jail cell to the lineup room in handcuffs and/or jail clothing. Having been seen in this manner just before the lineup, the suspect's subsequent identification is almost assured. A variation on the "Oklahoma Showup" involves permitting the witness to see the other participants in the lineup before it takes place, as where police officers to be used in the lineup wander freely through the squad room where the witness is waiting.

The most prevalent — and damaging — problem existing in present-day lineup procedures, however, involves suggestive statements made by the police. These statements can have considerable inpact on the witness, as members of the public tend to trust police officers and even subconsciously view them as father or authoritarian figures. There is a marked tendency on the part of witnesses to accept what officers say as truth, and at the same time to want to please them by performing to their satisfaction — *i.e.,* to choose the man whom police have indicated they believe is the culprit. Whether as a sole instance of suggestive conduct in a lineup or as an instance in a larger "totality of circumstances," then, statements made by police to witnesses in the context of a lineup should be studied carefully for any suggestive statement or innuendo.

The statements can take place before the lineup, during the actual conduct of the lineup, or afterwards when the witness is making or has made his decision. In each stage, suggestive comments can have a critical effect on the witness. Thus, for example, where a witness identified a car as having been used by the perpetrators and the officer informed him that the suspect had been picked up in the car and was in the lineup, the court ruled that the lineup was improperly conducted.[27] As another illustration, a court reversed a conviction where a witness picked a suspect from a lineup, then changed her mind because the suspect's hair color was wrong, and changed it back after police told her that they were sure they had the right man and that the suspect's brother was a hair stylist who could have changed the hair color.[28] On the other hand, courts have disapproved the practice of telling a witness that he had "done well" in picking out a suspect, but have refused to reverse on those grounds; the suggestive conduct was not considered as materially affecting the witness' certainty as to identification.[29]

The types of statements are endless and seem limited only by the police officer's imagination. Whether telling a witness to "try harder," to "take a closer look at that man on the far right," or "take your time — we have all day," the effect of the statements is the same: In subtle and not-so-subtle ways, the witness is clearly subjected to the suggestive influence of the police. Either the suspect is emphasized in some way as the guilty party, or the witness is gently pressured into making or changing an identification.

The problem is one of proof. How does counsel prove what was said by the police officers? The witness will often not remember what seemed to be innocuous conversation, the suspect was probably not present, and the officer is unlikely to admit his conduct (or perhaps is even unaware of it). For

---

27. Commonwealth v. Lee, 215 Pa. Super. 240, 257 A.2d 326 (1969).

28. State v. Torres, 81 N.M. 521, 459 P.2d 166 (1970).

29. United States v. Person, 155 U.S. App. D.C. 455, 478 F.2d 659 (D.C. Cir. 1973).

this reason if for no other, the presence of counsel (or a delegate) at lineup procedures as an observer is invaluable.

§ 5-4. Photographic Displays.

The effect on a lineup identification of exhibiting a photographic display to a witness prior to his viewing the lineup has been covered in the discussion on "photo-biased lineups" (§ 5-3.2). However, the presentation of the photographs can be done in such a suggestive manner as to almost assure a desired choice of the photos themselves.

It must be recognized at the outset that identification through the use of photographs or "mug shots" has been permitted by the United States Supreme Court.[30] At the same time, however, the Court expressly recognized the risks inherent in such procedures and affirmed the possibility that suppression was in order if, after a review of the "totality of circumstances," the identification was the result of prejudicial influences. In the absence of any unfairness in the presentation of photos then, most courts have permitted the admissibility into evidence of a witness' prior identification of a suspect's photograph. But where the manner of presenting the photo is improper, such as where it is *per se* suggestive, the courts have often granted motions to exclude or suppress the photographs and the prior identification of them. Most importantly, it may be possible to exclude an in-court identification if it can be shown that it is based largely on the unfair photographic identification.[31] (See § 10-3, *infra*).

There are basically two kinds of photographic presentations to a witness, analogous to the showup and the

---

30. Simmons v. United States, 390 U.S. 377, 88 S. Ct. 967, 19 L. Ed. 2d 1247 (1968).

31. *See, e.g.,* United States v. Marson, 408 F.2d 644 (4th Cir. 1968); Commonwealth v. Nassar, 354 Mass. 249, 237 N.E.2d 39 (1968); State v. Standley, 1 Wash. App. 148, 459 P.2d 808 (1969).

lineup: the single photo and the photo display. Having a witness view a single photo has all the dangers inherent in having him view only one suspect — *i.e.,* a showup. The obvious conclusion is made by the witness that the photo is of the man whom the police believe committed the crime; anxious to please and assuming that the police have the right man, the witness is very likely to make an identification which he would not otherwise make. Once he has made the initial suggestive identification, the witness will tend to solidify his identification until he points to the defendant at trial — identifying not the man he saw commit the offense, but the man he saw in a photograph. Clearly, the use of single photos is suggestive and prejudicial in the extreme and the practice has been roundly condemned.

The police continue to utilize the procedure. The courts, though not condoning the practice, have failed to find it so suggestive per se as to require a suppression of in-court identification testimony — absent any suggestive conduct or statements by the police.

By far the preferable way of presenting photos to a witness, then, is through the use of multiple photo displays. Such displays consist of a series of photographs presented either one-at-a-time or as a fixed display. The fixed display may be simply a mug shot catalog or, preferably, a grouping of photographs such as in a fixed strip of eight or ten, resembling a lineup. As with lineups, there are different ways of presenting such displays, and infinite ways of influencing a witness' decision.

To begin with, the display should have at least six or eight photographs. As with a lineup, any fewer in number and the procedure begins to resemble a one-photo showup. In England, as an example, some police regulations require a minimum of eight photographs be used.

The next consideration is that the display be presented in such a way that it does not suggest any one photo as the suspect. If the photos are shown to the witness one-at-a-time, for example, it would be obviously suggestive if the suspect's photo were displayed for a longer period of time than the others; the police officer's facial expressions, or question such as "Is this the one?" while showing the suspect's photo would be equally suggestive.

The fixed display is much the better procedure, but again, there is plenty of room for prejudicial influence. The photos must be of individuals that roughly approximate the suspect's description: sex, age, race, height, weight, gross physical characteristics. Nothing about the photos themselves should suggest anything to the witness; showing him six candid snapshots taken at random along with one police mug shot of the suspect would be unduly suggestive. Similarly, presenting a photo of the suspect with a police booking number on it would clearly indicate to the witness that the man was a known criminal and possibly that he had been booked for the crime witnessed. Showing a photo of the suspect with his name on it after the name had become known to the witness would also be clearly unfair.

Comments on conduct by the police during the presentation of a photo display can have the same effect they do when made during a lineup. Suggesting that the photo of one individual represents a prime suspect would be grossly prejudicial, as would pointing at a photo and asking if that was not the person the witness saw. Asking a witness to "try harder," continually staring at the suspect's photo, or telling the witness that the guilty party is in one of the photos are only a few examples of the innumerable instances of police misconduct that have occurred in the past and will occur in the future.

Counsel should make every effort to have the photographs used in the identification procedure preserved for use later in a suppression hearing or in trial. At present, there is no constitutional right to a lawyer at a photographic display,[32] but counsel should make a demand upon the police agency as well as the prosecuting agency for preservation and/or production of the photographs in the form presented to the witnesses as soon as possible.

Even if the trial court rules that the pretrail photographic identification was not unduly prejudicial or that the in-court identification of the suspect by the eyewitness is independent of any suggestive prior identification, counsel should still strongly emphasize to the jury the suggestive effect of such photographic identifications. This can be done not only in argument, but by an effective cross-examination of both the eyewitness and the officer who showed the photographs. The possibility of suggestion is always present, and the witness has a tendency to subsequently identify a suspect based on an earlier identification of his photograph. Yet the photographic identification may have been based on an insufficient observation at the scene, a vague memory, or suggestive police conduct. Unsure of himself, embarrassed by his inability and perhaps intimidated by police authority, the witness picks one of the photos rather than none. This witness will thereafter adopt the photograph as the person he saw; his own faulty observations at the scene will fade from his memory. This very common phenomenon should be clearly brought out in cross-examination and argument.

§ 5-5. Composites and Artists' Sketches.

A common technique employed by police agencies in their attempts to identify unknown perpetrators of criminal conduct is to employ an artist to recreate the individual's facial features from descriptions given to him by one or more eyewitnesses. Usually, the eyewitness works directly with

32. *See* United States v. Wade, 388 U.S. 218, 87 S. Ct. 1926, 18 L. Ed. 2d 1149 (1967); Gilbert v. California, 388 U.S. 263, 87 S. Ct. 1951, 18 L. Ed. 2d 1178 (1967).

the artist, in a fluid arrangement, directing him to change various features as the face takes shape. If there are two or more witnesses, the final drawing will reflect a more or less agreed-upon blend of their recollections.

While artists' sketches are the most common means of recreating a suspect's features, other means have also been employed. An officer or other person loosely fitting the suspect's description may be used, with a makeup artist changing his appearance at the witness' direction. Sculptured busts have been employed. The most prevalent and rapid-growing technique, however, has been the development of composite kits. These commercially prepared kits have the advantage of not requiring the services of an expensive and perhaps unavailable artist. An added advantage is that some of them are designed so that the code numbers of facial parts can be relayed by telephone to distant police stations where the face can be reconstructed from a similar kit, thus permitting almost instant communication of the composite face to anywhere desired.

Composite kits are designed upon the theory that all faces consist of a limited number of parts — *e.g.*, eyes, nose, mouth, etc. — and that each of these can be reduced to a relatively few types. Thus, under "eyes" there will be green, blue, hazel, etc. — each in various configurations, such as oval, narrow, baggy and so on. Theoretically, any individual's face can be at least roughly reconstructed using the parts in the kit.

The most common of the commercially available composite kits are the Identi-Kit, the MIMIC (Multiple Image Maker and Identification Compositor) and the Photo-Fit. The Identi-Kit is composed of 544 transparent celluloid sheets, each containing a facial feature such as a set of eyebrows, a hairline, wrinkles, or a pair of eyeglasses. These features, which were drawn from over 50,000 photographs of individuals of different races, are then laid one upon another at the witness' direction until a likeness appears.

The MIMIC system employes a film projector. As the witness describes a feature of the suspect's face, the police officer or technician selects a corresponding film according to a coding system. Finally, six separate films are imposed upon one another, representing eyes, nose, mouth, hair, chin and "accessories." As with the Identi-Kit, any appropriate changes can be made by the witness until he is satisfied with the final image. As with the Identi-Kit, the likeness can be relayed to any other police agency by simply telephoning the six film code numbers.

Photo-Fit is basically similar. This system distinguishes five different facial "zones": eyes, nose, mouth, chin, and forehead-and-hairline. The witness chooses photographs of the various types of each zone, and these are then mounted together on a board. Again, the witness simply has the police technician rearrange different photos until a satisfactory image is formed.

At the outset, it should be observed that a sketch or composite done by police to identify a suspect comprises hearsay evidence in that it rests on the veracity and competence of someone other than the artist.[33] Courts have even excluded such sketches or composites when only offered to bolster a witness' identifying testimony.[34] However, they have sometimes been held admissible as a prior consistent statement exception to the hearsay rule where the eyewitness' testimony was impeached.[35]

---

33. *E.g.,* People v. Turner, 91 Ill. App. 2d 436, 235 N.E.2d 317 (1968); Commonwealth v. McKenna, 355 Mass. 313, 244 N.E.2d 560 (1969).

34. *E.g.,* People v. Jennings, 23 A.D.2d 621, 257 N.Y.S.2d 456 (1965); Commonwealth v. Rothlisberger, 197 Pa. Super. 451, 178 A.2d 853 (1962).

35. *E.g.,* People v. Coffey, 11 N.Y.2d 142, 227 N.Y.S.2d 412, 182 N.E.2d 92 (1962); People v. Peterson, 25 A.D.2d 437, 266 N.Y.S.2d 884 (1966).

Whatever the admissibility of such evidence, any identification of a defendant based in any part upon a police employee's sketch or composite should be suspect and closely examined. As with a photo display or lineup, these techniques always present the danger of suggestion. The eyewitness may refer to the sketch or composite, fixing that in his mind rather than the face of the person he observed at the scene. On viewing the suspect in person, the witness then has a tendency to identify him upon the basis of his resembling the sketch or composite. If the police had the suspect in mind when drawing the sketch or presenting the composite, it may very well reflect the police version of their suspect. The witness, then, perhaps unsure of himself, vague in his memory, and/or influenced by police authority, adopts the sketch or composite suggested to him as being of the person he saw. A subsequent identification at a lineup or in court may simply be a matching of the suspect to the sketch rather than to the witness' recollection.

The ability of a witness to supply accurate descriptions to the police technician is also subject to question. Obviously, the sketch or composite can be no better than the data provided by the witness. Examinations concerning the descriptions provided may indicate superficial or inaccurate observations, hence an unreliable likeness.

Psychologists have conducted various experiments concerning both the ability of witnesses to direct a reconstruction of an observed face and the effect of that reconstruction on later in-person identification. One of the most interesting of these involved subjects who were shown a photograph of a man's face and later asked to identify him in a lineup.[36] Before the lineup, however, an artist worked with some of the subjects in putting together composite drawings of the man's face. The results: The subjects who

36. Loftus, E.F., *Eyewitness Testimony* 151 (Harvard College 1979).

had engaged in the drafting of a composite averaged 40 percent errors in their identifications at the lineup, while those who had not engaged in the drafting averaged only 31 percent.

In an interesting review of the research accomplished in the area by various scientists, Professor Yarmey has made the following general conclusions about the efficacy of sketches and composites: [37]

1. Artist sketches are better representations of real faces than Identi-Kit composites.
2. The limiting factor in the use of Identi-Kits is not the skill of the technician, but the inherent weakness of the composite technique itself. Witnesses may have accurate memories and good communication skills, but these assets may be lost because of the deficiencies of the Identi-Kit technique.
3. The quality of images generated by witnesses is best for faces of the same race than for faces of another race.
4. Image generation of faces, either through helping a sketch artist or helping a technician generate an Identi-Kit composite, acts to "stamp in" the long-term memory of the created face. Witnesses are able to make almost perfect identifications of a created face from a set of photographs, six to twelve months after creating the image.

§ 5-6. Voice Identification.

It is a common practice of police authorities to require a suspect to demonstrate his voice to a witness. Often, the crime was committed in the dark, or in another room; perhaps the witness is blind. A recurrent criminal situation involves contact by way of telephone; this is often the situation in cases involving such conduct as extortion,

37. Yarmey, A.D., *The Psychology of Eyewitness Testimony* 151 (Free Press/Macmillan 1979).

kidnapping, solicitation, conspiracy, and obscene conduct. In such situations, the perpetrator's voice may be the primary — or only — evidence linking him to the crime.

A witness is permitted to testify as to the identity of a suspect on the basis of his having heard the voice and having compared it to the defendant's. The prevalent opinion is that such evidence is direct and positive proof, a "conclusion reached directly and primarily from an operation of the sense of hearing." [38] However, such evidence can as well be viewed as mere lay opinion evidence, subject to the infirmities of lay opinion testimony.[39] Although the general rule is that voice recognition testimony is direct evidence, it has also been considered to constitute circumstantial evidence.[40]

Whatever its legal status, voice comparison testimony by a lay witness should be examined closely. The circumstances under which the voice was heard should be thoroughly investigated. Often, because of the nature of the crime, the acoustics were poor, the distances extensive, and/or there was a series of different voices. The emotional condition of the witness at the time may have been one of fear, excitement, anger, surprise, or terror — conditions which would tend to preclude an accurate and objective witnessing of the voice. Certainly the sound of the voice itself is usually the last thing on the witness' mind under such circumstances. The physical conditions and the witness' emotional state at the scene of the offense should be contrasted with the calm and controlled environment offered by police authorities when the suspect's voice was presented.

---

38. People v. Sica, 112 Cal. App. 2d 574, 247 P.2d 72 (1952).

39. *E.g.*, Henderson v. State, 209 Ga. 238, 71 S.E.2d 628 (1952); State v. Kilpatrick, 110 Utah 355, 173 P.2d 284 (1946).

40. United States v. Zweig, 467 F.2d 1217 (7th Cir. 1972), *cert. denied*, 409 U.S. 1111, 93 S. Ct. 921, 34 L. Ed. 2d 692 (1973).

The physical ability of the witness to perceive and compare sound should not be overlooked. It is not uncommon for a witness, particularly an older witness, to suffer from hearing disabilities. Such impairments can, to varying degrees, affect hearing considerably more at the scene of a crime than inside a police station or acoustical laboratory.

The discovery process may be used to elicit a witness' medical treatment for hearing problems. The possibility of testing the witness' ability to hear and compare one voice with another should not be overlooked; the results of such tests conducted out of court have been held admissible, assuming foundational showings of similar conditions, etc.[41] As to experiments or demonstrations conducted in court, however, the prevailing attitude appears to be that such procedures are inadmissible; [42] this may be discretionary with the court, of course.

The types of phrases the suspect is made to utter should be considered. A truly objective and effective comparison would dictate the use of neutral phrases — words having no emotional meaning and no relation to the words used by the perpetrator at the scene. Often, however, police will have the suspect repeat phrases heard by the witness at the scene. The danger here is that the witness will tend to identify the words spoken, rather than the voice itself. The emotional impact of again hearing words from a probably traumatic experience may trigger a false recognition in the witness' mind. Even the use of phrases or words not heard at the scene can have an emotional effect on the witness; hearing "gun," "kill" or "cops" can cause a tendency to relate the suspect to a crime.

The effect of voice identification during pretrial proce-

41. *E.g.*, Starr v. People, 28 Colo. 184, 63 P. 299 (1936).

42. *E.g.*, Bland v. State, 129 Tex. Crim. 553, 89 S.W.2d 996 (1936).

dures on testimony in trial cannot be overstated. The jury is deeply impressed when the court orders the defendant to repeat a phrase in front of the witness, and the witness then identifies him as the culprit. Yet all too often such testimony is merely a recitation of pretrial comparison. The witness, having seen the defendant in a police station and having identified his voice, now simply confirms it; subconsciously or otherwise, he has already decided the voice is the same because of the police procedures. It is the task of cross-examination to point out that identification in trial is based on identification in the police station, and that the comparison at the station was made under suggestive influences.

A recent development in criminology has been the appearance of the "voiceprint" method of identification. If the witness or police are able to tape record the voice, they can later compare it with the voice of a suspect on the spectrographic voice analyzer. Using this instrument, police technicians claim that they can identify a speaker by comparing his voiceprint to that made from an earlier recording of his voice. The theory is that every person has a unique system of tremors and speech patterns in his voice, and that spectroscopic graphs of these can be visually compared much like is done with fingerprints or handwriting analysis.

The man who developed this technique, Lawrence Kersta, claims that, based upon his own laboratory studies, the procedure is accurate 99 percent of the time.[43] However, the experts in the areas of linguistics, acoustics and phonetics have simply not accepted Kersta's claims. They point to the fact that his studies failed to simulate actual conditions; the examiners knew in advance, for example, that a voice would match one of the available voiceprints, and they were asked only to determine which spectrogram was the best available

43. Kersta, L., 1253 Nature 1256 (1962).

match. In fact, the Technical Committee of the Speech Communicaitons Section of the Acoustical Society of America has expressly stated that "reliable machine methods for voice identification have not yet been established." [44]

On the other hand, Dr. Oscar Tosi, a professor of physics and audiology at Michigan State University, has conducted extensive studies from which he has concluded that spectroscopic voice analysis is relatively reliable.[45]

Faced with such voiceprint evidence, counsel should consider both the constitutional and foundational aspects first. The courts have generally held that a defendant's Fifth Amendment privilege against self-incrimination is not violated by requiring him to demonstrate his voice for identification purposes, whether in a face-to-face confrontation with a witness or for a voiceprint recording for technical analysis.[46] This seems to be true even where the defendant is asked to speak words identical to those used by the perpetrator at the time of the offense.

The foundational issue of admissibility involves the question of which test the court will apply. If the *Frye* test is employed,[47] then the question is whether the voice analysis technique has become sufficiently established to have gained general acceptance in the scientific community. In other words, before voiceprint evidence is deemed admissible, it must not only meet the usual test of reliability, but it must also be shown by competent expert testimony to be a procedure generally accepted by experts in acoustics, audiology and physics. When dealing with voice analysis,

---

44. Jones, W.R., 11 American Criminal Law Review 549 (1973).

45. Tosi, O., et al., 51 Journal of Acoustical Society of America 2030 (1972).

46. United States v. Wade, 388 U.S. 218, 87 S. Ct. 1296, 18 L. Ed. 2d 1149 (1967).

47. Frye v. United States, 54 App. D.C. 46, 293 F. 1013 (D.C. Cir. 1923).

this is a difficult test to satisfy as there is no shortage of experts who do not accept the method's validity. Thus, there is a general consensus among courts applying the *Frye* test that voiceprint evidence is not admissible in either a criminal [48] or civil [49] trial.

The *Frye* test has been criticized by some courts, however, and an approach advocated by Professor McCormick has been adopted: Any relevant evidence supported by a qualified expert should be admissible. Applying this standard, the general lack of acceptance within the scientific community of voice analysis is irrelevant; if an expert can be found to testify to the relevance and reliability of the procedure, then the results are admissible. As a result, courts applying this test have generally permitted the introduction into evidence of spectroscopic voice analysis.[50]

---

48. *E.g.*, United States v. Addison, 162 U.S. App. D.C. 199, 498 F.2d 741 (D.C. Cir. 1974); Brown v. United States, 384 A.2d 647 (1978); People v. Kelly, 17 Cal. 3d 24, 549 P.2d 1240 (1976); Reed v. State, 283 Md. 374, 391 A.2d 364 (1978); People v. Tobey, 401 Mich. 141, 257 N.W.2d 537 (1977).

49. D'Arc v. D'Arc, 157 N.J. Super. 553, 385 A.2d 278 (1978).

50. *E.g.*, United States v. Baller, 591 F.2d 463 (4th Cir. 1975); United States v. Jenkins, 525 F.2d 819 (6th Cir. 1975); State v. Williams, 388 A.2d 500 (Me. 1978); State v. Andretta, 61 N.J. 544, 296 A.2d 644 (1972).

§ 6. The Right Against Self-Incrimination in Identification Proceedings.

> "The dictum that truth always triumphs over persecution is one of those pleasant falsehoods which men repeat after one another 'till they pass into commonplace, but which all experience refutes."
>
> John Stuart Mill

Until relatively recently there was considerable authority available for the proposition that requiring a suspect to cooperate in his own identification to the extent of demonstrating his voice, wearing suspected clothing, repeating certain acts, or even appearing in a lineup against his will constituted compulsory self-incrimination. The United States Supreme Court, however, in *United States v. Wade* [1] and related decisions, severely limited the application of the Fifth Amendment to pretrial identification procedures. The Court drew a distinction between "an accused's communications in whatever form, vocal or physical, and compulsion which makes a suspect or accused the source of real or physical evidence." [2] The protection extends only to compulsion used to obtain communications, not to the use of the suspect's physical characteristics against him.

§ 6-1. The Nature of the Right.

Prior to 1966, there appeared to be some authority for the proposition that compelling a suspect to appear in a lineup violated his Fifth Amendment rights. Then, in *Schmerber*

1. 388 U.S. 218, 87 S. Ct. 1926, 18 L. Ed. 2d 1149 (1967).
2. *Id.* at 223.

v. California,[3] the Supreme Court dealt with a situation where blood was extracted from a drunk driving suspect without his consent. In affirming the right of the police to obtain physical evidence from a suspect without violating his right against self-incrimination, the Court held that

> the privilege protects an accused only from being compelled to testify against himself, or otherwise provide the State with evidence of a testimonial or communicative nature .... Since the blood test evidence, although an incriminating product of compulsion, was neither petitioner's testimony nor evidence relating to some communicative act or writing by the petitioner, it was not inadmissible on privilege grounds.[4]

Chief Justice Warren dissented, joined by Justices Black and Douglas who felt that withdrawal of blood did constitute a violation of the privilege against self-incrimination. Yet, the decision seemed to indicate that requiring a suspect to appear in a lineup was not a Fifth Amendment violation, as there would be no communicative conduct. However, the issue had to be clarified. One year later, the Court did just that in very clear language in *Wade*:

> We have no doubt that compelling the accused merely to exhibit his person for observation by a prosecution witness prior to trial involves no compulsion of the accused to give evidence having testimonial significance. It is compulsion of the accused to exhibit his physical characteristics, not compulsion to disclose any knowledge he might have. It is no different from compelling Schmerber to provide a blood sample . . ."[5]

Again, separate opinions filed by Justices Douglas and Black indicated their feelings that compulsory appearance in a lineup constituted a Fifth Amendment violation, but the issue was finally resolved.

---

3. 384 U.S. 757, 86 S. Ct. 1826, 16 L. Ed. 2d 908 (1966).

4. *Id.* at 761, 765.

5. 388 U.S. at 222.

There remained, however, certain nagging questions concerning just how far the police could constitutionally go in their lineup procedures. Could they, for example, use force to make a suspect appear in a lineup? Could an individual be exhibited if his presence had been obtained by the police without probable cause? Are the police permitted to require the suspect to wear certain clothes, utter specific phrases, or alter his physical appearance in any way?

It appears that physical force may be used to make a suspect appear in a lineup, at least where the police obtain a court order requiring him to appear.[6] However, the comments of the *Schmerber* court must be kept in mind when the required force becomes excessive. Just as extraction of a blood sample may not be tolerable where "an unjustified element of personal risk of . . . pain"[7] to the suspect is present, so may appearance in a lineup become intolerable if such force is necessary that the suspect may be harmed.

Where a suspect is in custody, most courts have held that he can be required to appear in a lineup — even if there is no probable cause to arrest him for the offense relating to that lineup.[8] The reasoning here is that since he is already in custody on another matter, exhibiting him to witnesses involves no increased infringement of his freedom. However, there are jurisdictions which have held that an individual in custody on another charge cannot be required to appear in a lineup unless there is probable cause to arrest him for the offense relating to that lineup.[9]

---

6. *See* United States v. Cunningham, 509 F.2d 961 (D.C. Cir. 1975).

7. 384 U.S. at 772.

8. *E.g.*, United States v. Anderson, 490 F.2d 785 (D.C. Cir. 1974); People v. McClain, 88 Misc. 2d 293, 389 N.Y.S.2d 976 (1976); People v. Hall, 24 Mich. App. 509, 180 N.W.2d 363 (1970).

9. *E.g.*, New Jersey v. Foy, 146 N.J. Super. 378, 369 A.2d 995 (1976).

As to suspects not in custody being required to appear in a lineup, there is a split of authority. Some jurisdictions permit their courts to issue orders compelling a suspect to appear in a lineup despite the fact that there existed no probable cause to arrest him.[10] In fact, a number of states now have statutes which authorize court orders to compel appearance in identification procedures on less than probable cause.[11] Others, however, have specifically held that probable cause to arrest must exist before an individual could be required to take part in a lineup.[12]

The Fifth Amendment is not violated by requiring the suspect in a lineup to wear certain clothing (presumably clothing similar to that described by witnesses). Although such procedures have at times been held to constitute compulsory self-incrimination, the Supreme Court in *Holt v. United States* ruled that this would be "an extravagant extension of the Fifth Amendment."[13] In *Holt,* the Court dealt with a case where a key question had been whether a shirt belonged to the defendant, and it affirmed a conviction based in part upon evidence that he had been forced to put it on in court and that it had fit him:

> [T]he prohibition of compelling a man in a criminal court to be witness against himself is a prohibition of the use of physical or moral compulsion to extort communications from him, not an exclusion of his body as evidence when it may be material.[14]

Although the *Holt* court did not direct itself to the question of whether a suspect could be required to parade before

---

10. *E.g.,* Wise v. Murphy, 275 A.2d 205 (D.C. 1971).

11. *E.g.,* Ariz. Rev. Stat. Ann. § 13-1424 (Supp. 1973); Neb. Rev. Stat. § 29-3301-07 (Supp. 1974); N. C. Gen. Stat. § 15A-271-82 (1973).

12. *E.g.,* Alphonso C. v. Morgenthau, 50 A.D.2d 97, 376 N.Y.S.2d 126 (1975).

13. 218 U.S. 245, 31 S. Ct. 2, 54 L. Ed. 1021 (1910).

14. *Id.* at 252-53.

witnesses in clothing supplied by the police and described by those witnesses, *Wade* seems to infer that such a procedure would be acceptable. Most jurisdictions today permit the police to engage in such conduct. There are, however, some older state decisions extending the privilege against self-incrimination to requiring a defendant to wear suspected apparel at his trial, in the presence of witnesses and the jury.[15] These decisions seem to make the distinction that evidence from pretrial procedures comes from the witnesses, while evidence produced by wearing the clothing during trial comes from the defendant. Nevertheless, *Wade* seems to draw no distinction between pretrial and trial procedures.

Just how far can the police go in changing the appearance of a suspect in a lineup? Requiring him to remove or wear eyeglasses is probably permissible,[16] as may be making him wear a wig or a beard.[17] One court has even condoned the alteration of a suspect's appearance by a makeup artist to make him look like an earlier photograph of himself.[18] However, the courts begin to split when the question of requiring the suspect to permanently change his appearance presents itself. This problem is usually encountered where an individual is suspected of having grown a beard and/or moustache since his observation by witnesses. Faced with the police practice of making a suspect shave off his facial hair for his lineup appearance, some courts have held that it is impermissible [19] while

---

15. *E.g.*, Ward v. State, 27 Okla. Crim. 362, 228 P. 498 (1924); Allen v. State, 183 Md. 603, 39 A.2d 820 (1944); People v. Mead, 50 Mich. 228, 15 N.W. 95 (1883).

16. *E.g.*, People v. Sanders, 58 A.D.2d 525, 395 N.Y.S.2d 190 (1977).

17. *E.g.*, People v. Cwikla, 46 N.Y.2d 434, 386 N.E.2d 1070 (1979).

18. State v. McBain, 30 Or. App. 1055, 569 P.2d 630 (1977).

19. *E.g.*, People v. Vega, 51 A.D.2d 33, 379 N.Y.S.2d 419 (1976).

others have condoned it[20] — at least where there is evidence that the hair was grown for disguise purposes.[21]

Prior to *Wade* there appeared to be some authority for the proposition that compelling a suspect to demonstrate his voice to a witness was a violation of his Fifth Amendment right against self-incrimination. This was especially so where the suspect was required to repeat the very phrases the witness heard at the scene of the offense. Some courts reasoned that this went further than merely requiring the suspect to show a physical characteristic, and in effect forced him to reenact the crime. The *Wade* court, however, held that requiring a detained suspect to exhibit his voice to a witness did not constitute impermissible self-incrimination:

> [C]ompelling Wade to speak within hearing distance of the witnesses, even to utter words purportedly uttered by the robber, was not compulsion to utter statements of a "testimonial" nature; he was required to use his voice as an identifying physical characteristic, not to speak his guilt.[22]

It is interesting, however, to note that Chief Justice Warren and Justice Fortas joined Justices Black and Douglas' position when it came to this issue in *Wade*. Thus, where the justices were split 7 to 2 on the issue of whether appearance in a lineup constituted compulsory self-incrimination, the vote was only 5 to 4 on the question of requiring a suspect in a lineup to utter words or phrases.

As to the constitutionality of requiring a suspect to engage in certain acts or make specific gestures, such as pointing a gun or running, the *Wade* court again seems to

---

20. *E.g.*, United States v. Crouch, 478 F. Supp. 867 (E.D. Cal. 1979).

21. United States v. Lamb, 575 F.2d 1310 (10th Cir.), *cert. denied*, 439 U.S. 854 (1978).

22. 388 U.S. at 222-23.

have decided such procedures do not violate the provisions of the Fifth Amendment:

> [The privilege] offers no protection against compulsion to . . . appear in court, to stand, to assume a stance, to walk, or to make a particular gesture.[23]

§ 6-2. Comment Upon Refusal to Appear in Lineup.

Assuming that a suspect refuses to take part in a lineup procedure and is not physically forced to do so, is it a violation of his Fifth Amendment protections for the prosecutor to advise the jury of that refusal and further, to comment upon the probable reasons for the refusal? The Supreme Court did not address this issue in their *Wade* decision. However, those few jurisdictions which have appear to permit such comment. In the District of Columbia Court of Appeals, for example, the flight of a suspect after being served with a subpoena to appear in a lineup was considered proper subject matter for comment by the prosecutor.[24] In a Ninth Circuit case, the court sanctioned a cross-examination of the defendant on the issue of why he had refused to participate in a lineup, specifically stating that argument on the refusal was permissible comment as to evidence of consciousness of guilt.[25]

At least one recent decision, however, has held that it was reversible error to permit the jury to hear evidence of the defendant's refusal to take part in a lineup.[26] Unfortunately, the decision may be distinguishable on the facts: The jury was not advised that the lineup the defendant had adamantly refused to participate in was for another crime altogether, and therefore they may well have

23. *Id.* at 223.
24. Christian v. United States, 394 A.2d 1 (D.C. 1978).
25. United States v. Pahrms, 424 F.2d 152 (9th Cir. 1970).
26. Commonwealth v. Nichols, 400 A.2d 1281 (Pa. 1979).

concluded that he was exhibiting consciousness of guilt for the crime charged. The California Supreme Court has held that evidence that the defendant refused to speak for voice identification could not be used against him where the refusal might have been the result of a police warning that he had a right to remain silent.[27]

---

27. People v. Ellis, 65 Cal. 2d 529, 421 P.2d 393 (1966).

§ 7. The Right to Counsel at Identification Proceedings.

> "The trial which might determine the accused's fate may well not be that in the courtroom but that at the pretrial confrontation, with the State aligned against the accused, the witness the sole jury."
>
> *United States v. Wade*[1]

Prior to 1967, the question of the right to legal representation at pretrial identification procedures was largely ignored by the courts. Despite the critical nature of these procedures, there was simply no right of a suspect to have a lawyer present to represent his interests. The Supreme Court then handed down its now famous trilogy of decisions in *Wade — Gilbert — Stovall (United States v. Wade,*[2] *Gilbert v. California,*[3] and *Stovall v. Denno).*[4] These decisions dramatically altered a defendant's constitutional rights at such police proceedings as lineups. Unfortunately, however, the decisions left many issues unanswered, and in the following years both inconsistent and apparently contradictory decisions would serve to limit their effect.

---

1. 388 U.S. at 235, 87 S. Ct. 1926, 18 L. Ed. 2d 1149 (1967).

2. *Id.* at 218.

3. 388 U.S. 263, 87 S. Ct. 1951, 18 L. Ed. 2d 1178 (1967).

4. 388 U.S. 293, 87 S. Ct. 1967, 18 L. Ed. 2d 199 (1967).

§ 7-1. The Nature of the Right: Wade — Kirby.

The Supreme Court, in its *Wade* decision, recognized the pitfalls of pretrial police identification procedures and enumerated the inherent risks.

> A major factor contributing to the high incidence of miscarriage of justice from mistaken identification has been the degree of suggestion inherent in the manner in which the prosecution presents the suspect to witnesses for pretrial identification. . . .
>
> Suggestion can be created intentionally or unintentionally in many subtle ways. And the dangers for the suspect are particularly grave when the witness' opportunity for observation was insubstantial, and thus his susceptibility to suggestion the greatest.
>
> Moreover, "[i]t is a matter of common experience that, once a witness has picked out the accused at the lineup, he is not likely to go back on his word later on, so that in practice the issue of identity may (in the absence of other relevant evidence) for all practical purposes be determined there and then, before the trial". . . .[5]
>
> [A]s is the case with secret interrogations, there is serious difficulty in depicting what transpires at lineups and other forms of identification confrontations. "Privacy results in secrecy and this in turn results in a gap in our knowledge as to what in fact goes on . . ." *Miranda v. Arizona* (cite). For the same reasons, the defense can seldom reconstruct the manner and mode of lineup identification for judge or jury at trial . . . . . [N]either witnesses nor lineup participants are apt to be alert for conditions prejudicial to the suspect. . . . Improper influences may go undetected by a suspect, guilty or not, who experiences the emotional tension which we might expect in one being confronted with potential accusers. Even when he does observe abuse, if he has a criminal record he may be reluctant to take the stand and open up the admission

5. Quoting from Wall, P.M., *Eyewitness Identification in Criminal Cases* (Thomas 1975).

of prior convictions. Moreover, any protestations by the suspect of the fairness of the lineup made at trial are likely to be in vain; the jury's choice is between the accused's unsupported version and that of the police officers present. In short, the accused's inability effectively to reconstruct at trial any unfairness that occurred at the lineup may deprive him of his only opportunity meaningfully to attack the credibility of the witness' courtroom identification.[6]

Having specifically isolated the dangers involved in lineups and showups, the Court then went on to clearly establish the right of a suspect to legal counsel at a pretrial lineup:

> Insofar as the accused's conviction may rest on a courtroom identification in fact the fruit of a suspect pretrial identification which the accused is helpless to subject to effective scrutiny at trial, the accused is deprived of that right of cross-examination which is an essential safeguard to his right to confront the witness against him . . . .
>
> Since it appears that there is grave potential for prejudice, intentional or not, in the pretrial lineup, which may not be capable of reconstruction at trial, and since presence of counsel itself can often avert prejudice and assure a meaningful confrontation at trial, there can be little doubt that for Wade the post-indictment lineup was a critical stage of the prosecution at which he was "as much entitled to aid [of counsel] . . . as at the trial itself" (cite). Thus, both Wade and his counsel should have been notified of the impending lineup, and counsel's presence should have been a prerequisite to conduct of the lineup, absent an "intelligent waiver" (cite).[7]

The Court's holding, then, was clear: A suspect in a pretrial lineup had a constitutional right to have counsel

6. 388 U.S. 229-32.

7. *Id.* at 235-37.

present. His presence would, the Court reasoned, lessen the chances of a suggestive presentation; with a lawyer observing, the police are less likely to engage in unfair practices. At the same time, counsel's presence would permit the suspect to effectively challenge the basis for the identification either at trial or at a motion to suppress.

The remedy for denying a suspect his right to have counsel present was also made clear, if somewhat difficult to determine:

> Where, as here, the admissibility of evidence of the lineup identification itself is not involved, a *per se* rule of exclusion of courtroom identification would be unjustified . . . .
>
> We think it follows that the proper test to be applied in these situations is that quoted in *Wong Sun v. United States,* 371 U.S. 471, 488, "[W]hether, granting establishment of the primary illegality, the evidence to which instant objection is made has been come at by exploitation of that illegality or instead by means sufficiently distinguishable to be purged of the primary taint." Application of this test in the present context requires consideration of various factors; for example, the prior opportunity to observe the alleged criminal act, the existence of any discrepancy between any pre-lineup description and the defendant's actual description, any identification prior to lineup of another person, the identification by picture of the defendant prior to the lineup, failure to identify the defendant on a prior occasion, and the lapse of time between the alleged act and the lineup identification.[8]

Thus, the Court held that where counsel is denied to a suspect, evidence of the pretrial identification is inadmissible in trial. Further, any in-court identification resulting from a pretrial identification in which counsel was not made available to a suspect will be suppressed. This latter sanction, however, was qualified: The in-court iden-

8. *Id.* at 240-41.

tification should not be suppressed "without first giving the Government the opportunity to establish by clear and convincing evidence that the in-court identifications were based upon observations of the suspect other than the lineup identification." [9] In other words, an in-court identification would be permitted if its independent source could be proven by "clear and convincing" evidence.

Nothing in the *Wade* decision appeared to limit the right to counsel to any particular time framework. Although the facts in *Wade* involved a lineup held after the defendant's indictment, the Court nowhere in its decision indicated that the right to counsel was to be limited to post-indictment (or post-arraignment) identification proceedings. In fact, the reasoning of the Court in setting forth the reasons for requiring counsel — preventing an unfair confrontation and permitting effective challenge in court — are applicable whether dealing with a pre-indictment or post-indictment lineup. It seems clear from a reading of *Wade* that the Court intended no distinction between the two; the occasional use of the term "post-indictment" simply referred to the fact situation before the court. In fact, the subsequent decisions of the United States Courts of Appeal uniformly applied the right to counsel to both pre- and post-indictment situations.[10]

Yet the Supreme Court severely limited the application of *Wade* when five years later it expressly held that the right to counsel was only to be applied to post-indictment situations. In *Kirby v. Illinois,*[11] the Court held that "a person's Sixth and Fourteenth Amendment right to counsel attaches only at or after the time that adversary proceedings have been initiated against him . . . . [W]hether by way of formal charge, preliminary hearing, indictment, information or

---

9. *Id.* at 240.

10. *See, e.g.,* Wilson v. Gaffney, 454 F.2d 142 (10th Cir. 1972).

11. 406 U.S. 682, 92 S. Ct. 1877, 32 L. Ed. 2d 411 (1972).

arraignment."[12] Interestingly, the *Kirby* Court was split 5-4, with Justice Brennan (Justices Douglas and Marshall joining) pointing out in his dissent that nothing in *Wade* or *Gilbert* reflected an intention of the Court to limit the holding to the facts, and that: "In view of *Wade,* it is plain, and the plurality today does not attempt to dispute it, that there inhere in a confrontation for identification conducted after arrest the identical hazards to a fair trial that inhere in such a confrontation conducted 'after the onset of formal prosecution proceedings'."[13]

The law of *Wade — Kirby* remains: A suspect must be afforded counsel if he is required to take part in a post-indictment lineup or showup. In practice, the right established by *Wade* has been effectively emasculated by the *Kirby* decision. By limiting the right to counsel to post-indictment proceedings, the *Kirby* Court has eliminated the presence of counsel at almost all identification proceedings in which identification is a critical issue.

Post-indictment lineups are usually held either to refresh a witness' memory or to otherwise strengthen the case. Since the suspect has already been formally charged, there already exists a sufficiently strong case to prosecute him: Either there is sufficient independent evidence (fingerprints, confession, etc.) or the eyewitnesses have already identified the defendant in photographs or in a pre-indictment lineup or showup. In other words, *Kirby* grants the defendant the right to counsel when he *least* needs it.

Consider, on the other hand, the pre-indictment lineup. Generally, the police have insufficient evidence to ask the prosecutor to file formal charges against the suspect: Almost by definition, the very fact that the lineup is being conducted before the bringing of formal charges infers that

12. 406 U.S. 688-89.

13. *Id.* at 697-98.

there is insufficient evidence to indicate the suspect is guilty. In such situations, the identification by one or more eyewitnesses becomes critical. It is largely upon the basis of such identification that charges will be brought. If the lineup identification was not critical to the case, then the suspect would already have been charged. In such situations, it is readily apparent that the conduct of the pretrial identification procedure is critical to the eventual resolution of the case. Yet it is at this critical stage that *Kirby* denies the right to counsel.

The reaction of police authorities has been predictable. Freed from the cumbersome and awkward requirement of having defense counsel present, the number of pre-indictment lineups has increased. In fact, police will now often delay the bringing of formal charges so that a lawyer-free lineup can be conducted. Post-indictment lineups, on the other hand, have almost disappeared, only to be replaced by the increased use of lawyer-free photographic displays.

There has been no shortage of criticisms of the *Kirby* decision by commentators and legal scholars.[14] While most lower courts have applied the decision without comment, many have been openly critical.[15] In fact, a number of state courts have flatly refused to impose the *Kirby* ruling, electing instead to extend the right to counsel to pretrial identification situations occurring prior to indictment/arraignment.[16] Thus, the Michigan Supreme Court has held that since *Kirby* was not binding upon the states, it was free to require that counsel be available to a suspect

14. *See, e.g.,* 72 Mich. L. Rev. 717 (1974); 7 Suffolk L. Rev. 587 (1973); 22 DePaul L. Rev. 660 (1973).

15. *See, e.g.,* People v. Chojnacky, 8 Cal. 3d 759, 505 P.2d 530 (1973) (Justice Mosk concurring); State v. Gray, 503 S.W.2d 457 (Mo. 1973).

16. *See, e.g.,* Blue v. State, 558 P.2d 636 (Alaska 1977); Commonwealth v. Richman, 458 Pa. 167, 320 A.2d 351 (1974); State v. Kiraly, 56 Ohio App. 2d 37, 381 N.E.2d 649 (1977).

at any lineup or showup conducted after his arrest.[17] In Tennessee, the right to counsel at pretrial identification procedures attaches when an arrest warrant has been issued.[18] In New York, Louisiana and Alabama, a suspect must be permitted to have previously retained counsel present at the pre-indictment lineup or showup.[19]

Perhaps reacting to criticisms of the *Kirby* decision, the Supreme Court in 1977 made certain rather obvious concessions. In *Moore v. Illinois,*[20] the Court clarified the question as to when the right to counsel accrued by conceding that a defendant in a preliminary hearing or other pretrial judicial proceeding where an identification is made has a right to counsel even though no formal indictment has been filed. Further, the Court confirmed that the post-indictment right to counsel applied to showups as well as to lineups.

§ 7-2. The Role of Counsel at Lineups.

The Supreme Court in its *Wade* decision was vague — perhaps purposely vague — when it came to describing the role counsel was to play at a police lineup. Because of this, many courts have felt that the role should be a passive one: The purpose of counsel is to be an objective observer, with no right to interfere in the proceeding or even to make suggestions.[21]

---

17. People v. Anderson, 389 Mich. 155, 205 N.W.2d 461 (1973); People v. Jackson, 391 Mich. 323, 217 N.W.2d 22 (1974).

18. State v. Mitchell, 593 S.W.2d 280 (Tenn. 1980).

19. People v. Blake, 35 N.Y.2d 331, 320 N.E.2d 625 (1974); State v. Vaughn, 378 So. 2d 905 (La. 1979); Sparks v. State, 376 So. 2d 834 (Ala. 1979).

20. 434 U.S. 220, 98 S. Ct. 458, 54 L. Ed. 2d 424 (1977).

21. *See, e.g.,* Bruce v. State, 375 N.E.2d 1042 (Ind. 1977), *cert. denied,* 439 U.S. 988 (1978).

The language in *Wade,* however, seems to contemplate a more active role:

> In our view counsel can hardly impede legitimate law enforcement; on the contrary . . . law enforcement may be assisted by *preventing* the infiltration of taint in the prosecution's identification evidence. (Emphasis added.)[22]

The Court could hardly have envisioned defense counsel in a passive role as mere observer when it expressed its belief that counsel's role would help *prevent* an unfair lineup. Further, the Court reasoned in general language that the presence of counsel would help eliminate suggestive police practices and ensure a meaningful confrontation; it is unlikely the Court felt this would all occur simply through counsel's silent presence.

The courts have been in considerable disagreement since *Wade* in their attempts to define the role of counsel at a lineup. Certainly, counsel should be supplied with any information relevant to the proceedings, a view expressed by the District of Columbia Circuit Court:

> It would seem that appellant's counsel might be best able to serve his client's interest and the interest of justice if he is given in advance of the lineup the names of witnesses who would attend; the time, place and nature of the crimes involved; and the descriptions of the suspect, if any, which the witnesses had given to the police. Counsel also might be allowed to have a role in setting up the lineup and proposing changes to avoid suggestive features.[23]

This last suggestion, however, has proven to be the cause of major conflict among decisions in the area. On the one hand, a majority of courts have flatly held that a defendant does not have a right to have his attorney take an active

22. 388 U.S. at 238.

23. United States v. Allen, 408 F.2d at 1289 (D.C. Cir. 1969).

part in the selection and conduct of the lineup; such a situation, it is argued, would unduly interfere with the right of the prosecution to gather evidence.[24] On the other hand are a few courts which reason, as did the District of Columbia Court, that *Wade* envisioned defense counsel in an active role at the lineup.

The dispute as to counsel's role has focused on the subject of post-lineup identifications: Does defense counsel have a right to be present *after* the lineup when the witnesses make and discuss their identifications with the police? The California Supreme Court has decided that refusal to permit counsel to be present at such a critical stage of the procedure constitutes a denial of the right to counsel:

> It is not the moment of viewing alone, but rather the whole "procedure by which [a suspect] is identified" that counsel must be able to effectively reconstruct at trial. (Cites.) If defense counsel is to be able to intelligently cross-examine the witness, he cannot be excluded from the moment of identification any more than he can be excluded from the lineup itself.[25]

It would seem obvious that counsel's presence is meaningless if he is not permitted to observe how and in what manner the witness makes his identification. A bold conclusion that the witness identified the client is almost meaningless without knowing whether, for example, the identification was tentative, whether the client was the second or third person identified, or whether the identification was made at the suggestive urging of the police.

Many jurisdictions have expressed accord with the position of the California Supreme Court.[26] However, at least as

---

24. *See, e.g.,* United States v. Crouch, 478 F. Supp. 867 (E.D. Cal. 1979).

25. People v. Williams, 3 Cal. 3d at 856, 478 P.2d at 944 (1971).

26. *E.g.,* State v. McGhee, 350 So. 2d 370 (La. 1977); People v. Sweeney, 57 Ill. App. 3d 879, 373 N.E.2d 663 (1978); Richardson v. State, 600 P.2d 361 (Okla. Crim. 1979).

many have taken a contrary position.[27] The Fourth Circuit, for example, has forcefully stated that: "It is not claimed that to date the Supreme Court has required the presence of counsel during the interrogation of all witnesses, and we will not so require with regard to the interrogation of identification witnesses once the actual confrontation has been completed." [28]

The exact role of counsel at pretrial identification proceedings constitutes an area of conflicting and changing law. Accordingly, defense counsel should attempt to take as active a role in the lineup as the police will permit and make known his objections to any limitations. Besides establishing a record for a later suppression hearing or appeal, an adamant effort to take part in the proceedings may well work with police officials who are as unsure of the law as are some courts.

If possible, then, counsel should attempt to accomplish certain minimal tasks at a police lineup. First, he should obtain information from the police and/or the witness concerning previous descriptions of the suspect given by the witness; any previous identifications of the defendant or other individuals, such as in a photographic showup or earlier lineup. The witnesses themselves should be interviewed before the lineup. This is an area where counsel is especially likely to encounter police resistance.

The composition of the lineup should be reviewed by counsel before it is presented to the eyewitness. If the client stands out in any significant manner, counsel should insist that changes be made to make the presentation fairer. Resistance to "interference" with the conduct of the lineup is again likely, but a reminder to the police that the removal

27. United States v. Rich, 580 F.2d 929 (9th Cir.), *cert. denied,* 439 U.S. 935 (1978); United States v. Bierey, 588 F.2d 620 (8th Cir.), *cert. denied,* 440 U.S. 927 (1979).

28. United States v. Cunningham, 423 F.2d at 1274 (4th Cir. 1970).

of unfair aspects is in their interests since subsequent identifications are less likely to be suppressed can sometimes be effective. In any event, counsel should take careful notes of all proceedings, including a detailed physical description of the participants in the lineup; if possible, names and addresses of the participants should be obtained so that the lineup or photos of the participants can later be recreated. If counsel has a camera, photographs of the lineup itself should be taken. In many cases the mere presence of counsel taking notes and photographs can have a sobering effect on the officer conducting the lineup.

Counsel should definitely suggest the use of a *"blank" lineup.* A "blank" lineup is simply a lineup in which the suspect does not actually appear; instead, he will appear in a second lineup. Alternatively, the witness is advised beforehand that there will be two lineups, and the suspect can appear in either the first or second. Either way the procedure tends to avoid the ever present problem of the witness who believes that the culprit is, in fact, one of the men in the lineup, and so is motivated to choose not the person he saw at the crime scene but the person who most closely *resembles* him in the lineup. Once again, resistance from the police may be expected, particularly since the use of a "blank" lineup involves obtaining more suitable individuals for two separate lineups. To overcome this understandable objection, counsel might suggest that rather than have one lineup of eight individuals, two lineups of five each would be more effective and involve little extra work.

Counsel should attempt to ensure that his client is made aware of exactly when he is being observed by a witness. Thus he will not be engaged in conduct on the stage which will tend to throw him in a negative light for the witness hidden behind the one-way mirror, seated in the darkened auditorium, or looking through a peep-hole.

The conduct of the police before, during, and after the lineup should be carefully observed and noted if at all possible. Any suggestive statements or gestures by police should be taken down. Similarly, any statements or unusual conduct on the part of the witness or witnesses must be recorded. If a witness is hesitant while observing the lineup, asks questions, or expresses doubt, these must also be observed and written down. Counsel should attempt to ensure that the witnesses are kept separate before, during, and after the lineup to avoid any possible influence. If this is not possible, observations of or communications between the witnesses should be carefully noted.

The post-lineup identification is critical and counsel must make every effort to be present. It is at this point that the witness makes a choice, if any, and expresses reluctance or reservations. If he selects another individual in the lineup, counsel should be there to know of it; the exculpatory fact may not appear in subsequent police reports. Similarly, if the choice is affected by suggestive comments or urging on the part of the supervising officer, this fact will go unknown unless observed by counsel.

Finally, counsel should attempt to interview the witness or witnesses after the lineup proceeding is over. He should ask them whom they chose, why, and what their degree of certainty is. Any statements by the police or conduct of the lineup that affected them in any way should be determined. The witnesses might also be approached concerning participation in a later defense lineup or photograph display.

Having observed the lineup, counsel now becomes a potential witness. The ethical problem of conflict then arises. Counsel is in the awkard position of attempting to be both a witness and an advocate, of trying to argue his own credibility. Consequently, it may be advisable to employ substitute counsel at the lineup.

§ 7-3. Substitute Counsel.

One of the problems left unresolved by the *Wade* Court was whether a suspect has a right to demand the presence of a specific lawyer, or whether the police were free to ask any available attorney — such as a Public Defender — to handle the job.

> [W]e leave open the questions whether the presence of substitute counsel might not suffice where notification and presence of the suspect's own counsel would result in a prejudicial delay.[29]

In a footnote to this quotation the Court went on to say:

> Although the right to counsel usually means a right to the suspect's own counsel, provision for substitute counsel may be justified on the ground that the substitute counsel's presence may eliminate the hazards which render the lineup a critical stage for the presence of the suspect's *own* counsel.[30]

It would appear, then, that the Court has left the door open for police to provide their own version of counsel, despite a suspect's demand that his own attorney be present. In fact, a number of jurisdictions have accepted the coincidental presence of defense counsel not representing the suspect as satisfying *Wade*'s requirements.[31]

A separate issue altogether presents itself where defense counsel appears at a pretrial police lineup for the purpose of observing any suggestive procedures. Counsel has now become a potential witness. Thus a problem in professional ethics presents itself, since counsel has placed himself in the difficult position of being both advocate and witness — a

---

29. 388 U.S. at 237.

30. 388 U.S. at 237, fn. 27.

31. *See, e.g.* Commonwealth v. Shoatz, 469 Pa. 545, 366 A.2d 1216 (1976); Washington v. United States, 377 A.2d 1348 (Pa. 1977).

conflict situation in which he will be trying to argue his own credibility. Faced with the potential for such a situation, it is probably advisable to arrange for substitute counsel to represent the client's interests at the lineup. The alternative may well be that counsel will have to remove himself from the case at a later stage.

The issue may not even be one the resolution of which is left to the ethical discretion of counsel. The Arizona Supreme Court has specifically held that a defense attorney cannot testify concerning what he saw or heard at a lineup unless he first withdraws permanently from the case.[32] This fairly recent decision may well be followed by other jurisdictions in future years. The result could be the birth of a new specialist within the legal community, familiar with both eyewitness identification techniques and the law: the "lineup lawyer."

§ 7-4. Waiver of Counsel.

The *Wade* Court specifically recognized that a suspect in a pretrial identification proceeding could waive his right to have counsel present — assuming that the waiver is intelligently made.[33] As with *Miranda* advisements, this leaves a number of questions to be answered. Does silence on the part of a suspect constitute a waiver? Must he be specifically advised of his *Wade* rights? What if chosen counsel fails to appear?

The United States Supreme Court decision in *Carnley v. Cochran,*[34] cited by the *Wade* Court in its brief reference to waiver of counsel, has held that the failure to demand counsel does not amount to a waiver of counsel. *Wade,* therefore, appears to have applied *Carnley's* interpretation of the

---

32. State v. Caldwell, 117 Ariz. 464, 573 P.2d 864 (1978).

33. 388 U.S. at 237.

34. 369 U.S. 506, 82 S. Ct. 884, 8 L. Ed. 70 (1962).

right to counsel under *Miranda* to a pretrial identification situation: Silence does not constitute a waiver.

One rather interesting Fourth Circuit decision, however, stands for the proposition that if a suspect at a pretrial lineup can afford to hire his own attorney and delays doing so for an unreasonable period of time, he is deemed to have waived his right.[35] Representing the other extreme, a New York court has held that an indicted defendant could not waive his right to counsel at a lineup unless he does so in the presence of an attorney.[36]

As to advisement of *Wade* rights, the issue was first addressed by the Fifth Circuit in 1968: The suspect "must be warned of his right to counsel prior to the confrontation." [37] Some states have followed this interpretation, requiring the police to tell a suspect of his right to have an attorney present at a lineup.[38] The California Supreme Court has gone even further, requiring that "[w]hen the right to counsel at a lineup has attached, the suspect is entitled to be so notified and to be notified that counsel will be appointed if necessary." [39]

What is the result if counsel fails to appear at the pretrial identification proceeding? In the very few cases addressing the issue, courts have held that failure to appear within a reasonable period of time will result in a waiver of the defendant's right to have counsel present.[40]

---

35. United States v. Clark, 499 F.2d 802 (4th Cir. 1974).

36. People v. Settles, 46 N.Y.2d 154, 385 N.E.2d 612 (1978).

37. Rivers v. United States, 400 F.2d at 940 (5th Cir. 1968).

38. *See* State v. Connally, 36 N.C. App. 43, 243 S.E.2d 788 (1978); People v. Evans, 60 A.D.2d 892, 401 N.Y.S.2d 292 (1978).

39. People v. Fowler, 1 Cal. 3d at 345, 461 P.2d at 651 (1969).

40. *See, e.g.,* People v. Styles, 90 Misc. 2d 861, 395 N.Y.S.2d 1007 (1977); State v. Smith, 357 So. 2d 798 (La. 1978).

§ 7-5. The "Lawrence Lineup."

Many police agencies have found an ingenious way of circumventing the *Wade — Kirby* requirements of counsel at post-indictment lineups. Rather than conduct the lineup with the eyewitness present, they simply photograph or even videotape it and then show the photograph or videotape to the witness. Thus the identification procedure is conveniently transposed from a lineup to a photographic display. There is, of course, no right to counsel at a photographic display, whether before or after indictment.[41]

The constitutionality of this apparent circumvention of rights was addressed by the Supreme Court of California in *People v. Lawrence.*[42] In that case the 4-3 majority held:

> We are involved only with a photograph of a *simulated* lineup and we see no distinction in this respect between such identifications and identifications made from mug shots or other types of photographic displays. . . . [T]he showing of photographs of the accused to a witness is not a confrontation or exhibition as those words are used in *Wade* and *Gilbert.*[43]

The Court recognized, however, that "it appears that better police procedures could well have been employed by conducting a true lineup with counsel for defendant and the witness present."[44]

The dissenting opinion in *Lawrence* recognized "that this case involves a deliberate and conscious evasion of the rules of *Wade* and *Gilbert,*" and displayed considerable foresight in predicting "that law enforcement officers henceforth will decide that they can safely hold *all* their lineups without the

41. United States v. Ask, 413 U.S. 300, 93 S. Ct. 2568, 37 L. Ed. 2d 619 (1973).

42. 4 Cal. 3d 273, 481 P.2d 212 (1971).

43. 481 P.2d at 215.

44. 481 P.2d at 215.

bothersome presence of counsel if they utilize what will soon be known simply as a 'Lawrence lineup.' "[45]

Since the *Lawrence* decision, the few cases in other jurisdictions addressing the issue appear to have concurred in the majority opinion;[46] one of these even involved the showing of a videotape of a lineup.[47]

---

45. 481 P.2d at 219.

46. *E.g.*, People v. Davis, 88 Misc. 2d 774, 388 N.Y.S.2d 816 (1976); United States v. King, 461 F.2d 152 (D.C. Cir. 1972).

47. McMillian v. State, 265 N.W.2d 553 (Wis. (1978).

§ 8. Due Process: Fairness of Identification Procedures.

> "It is a piece of idle sentimentality that truth, merely as truth, has any inherent power denied to error of prevailing against the dungeon and the state."
>
> John Stuart Mill

The denial of counsel to a defendant in a post-indictment lineup can constitute grounds for suppression of the pre-trial identification as well as of the subsequent in-court identification. But is there any guarantee against suggestive procedures being employed simply because defense counsel is present? What remedy is available if a *pre*-indictment identification procedure is conducted in an unfair manner?

The Supreme Court addressed the issue of the fairness of pretrial identification proceedings in the *Stovall* segment of the *Wade — Gilbert — Stovall* trilogy. The Court set forth a general standard to be applied, the violation of which would constitute an "unfair" identification procedure or, in constitutional language, a violation of due process. As with *Wade — Kirby,* however, it was not long before the Court was to place a new interpretation on its own definition.

§ 8-1. Evolution of the Reliability Test: Stovall — Biggers.

The Supreme Court in *Stovall v. Denno* [1] addressed the

1. 388 U.S. 293, 87 S. Ct. 1967, 18 L. Ed. 2d 199 (1967).

issue of the constitutional validity of a hospital showup (the eyewitness was hospitalized the previous day after her husband's murderer shot and seriously wounded her). The Court initially noted that "[t]he practice of showing suspects singly to persons for the purpose of identification, and not as part of a lineup, has been widely condemned",[2] but then concluded that the hospital showup was not "so unnecessarily suggestive and conducive to irreparable mistaken identification that [the defendant] was denied due process of law." [3] The Court then expressed its vague but often repeated standard of fairness for pretrial identification proceedings: "[A] claimed violation of due process of law in the conduct of a confrontation depends on the totality of the circumstances surrounding it. . . ." [4]

Thus, the "totality of circumstances" standard was applied to determining whether pretrial identification procedures had been conducted "fairly." Each case must be independently assessed on its own facts, and a decision made as to whether all of the attendant details added up to constitute an unfair identification confrontation. Apparently, the exigency of the circumstances was a factor to be considered: If there is an urgent reason for the police to conduct a lineup or showup in a suggestive manner — such as in *Stovall* where the eyewitness is hospitalized and unable to attend a formal lineup — then the standards to be applied will be relaxed somewhat. The contrary, of course, also holds true: Absent compelling circumstances, the police will be hard-pressed to justify a suggestive confrontation.

The standard was reiterated by the Supreme Court one year later, although interestingly couched in different language. Dealing with a photographic display situation, the

---

2. *Id.* at 302.

3. *Id.*

4. *Id.*

Court in *Simmons v. United States* [5] held that "each case must be considered on its own facts, and that convictions based on eyewitness identification at trial following a pretrial identification by photograph will be set aside on that ground only if the photographic identification procedure was so impermissibly suggestive as to give rise to a very substantial likelihood of irreparable identification." [6] The Court then added: "This standard accords with our resolution of a similar issue in *Stovall v. Denno.*" [7]

This vague standard was subsequently analyzed and broken down into identifiable requirements by Judge Friendly in *United States ex rel. Phipps v. Follette:*

> [T]he required inquiry is two-pronged. The first question is whether the initial identification procedure was "unnecessarily" [*Stovall*] or "impermissibly" [*Simmons*] suggestive. If it is found to have been so, the court must then proceed to the question whether the procedure found to have been "unnecessarily" or "impermissibly" suggestive was so "conducive to irreparable mistaken identification" [*Stovall*] or had such a tendency "to give rise to a very substantial likelihood of irreparable misidentification" [*Simmons*] that allowing the witness to make an in-court identification would be a denial of due process. . . .
>
> The instruction that resolution of this issue "depends on the totality of the circumstances" [*Stovall*], although probably as good a start as could have been made, does not instruct very much . . . . The effort must be to determine whether, before the imprint arising from the unlawful identification procedure, there was already such a definite image in the witness' mind that he is able to rely on it at trial without much, if any, assistance from its successor.[8]

---

5. 390 U.S. 377, 88 S. Ct. 967, 19 L. Ed. 2d 1247 (1968).

6. *Id.* at 384.

7. *Id.*

8. 428 F.2d at 914-15 (2d Cir. 1970).

Thus, the "totality of circumstances" includes an analysis of such *external* factors as the witness' opportunity and motivation for observation, the lapse of time from observation to identification, and the amount and quality of independent incriminating evidence — factors relevant to determining the existence of an "independent source" for the in-court identification. The emphasis by Judge Friendly in his application of the *Stovall — Simmons* standards was on the reliability or probable *accuracy* of the identification.

In 1972, the Supreme Court changed the standards it had set forth in *Stovall* and *Simmons,* adopting instead a standard more closely approximating that suggested by Judge Friendly. In *Neil v. Biggers,*[9] the Court determined that external factors should be considered in deciding whether an identification, though tainted by suggestive identification procedures, was nevertheless "reliable."

> It is the likelihood of misidentification which violates a defendant's right to due process. . . .
>
> We turn, then, to the central questions, whether under the "totality of circumstances" the identification *was reliable even though the confrontation procedure was suggestive.* As indicated by our cases, the factors to be considered in evaluating the likelihood of misidentification include the opportunity of the witness to view the criminal at the time of the crime, the witness' degree of attention, the accuracy of the witness' prior description of the criminal, the level of certainty demonstrated by the witness at the confrontation, and the length of time between the crime and the confrontation. (Emphasis added.) [10]

Despite language by the Court that the decision was consistent with *Stovall* and *Simmons,* the emphasis had clearly shifted from a vague inquiry into whether the police iden-

---

9. 409 U.S. 188, 93 S. Ct. 375, 34 L. Ed. 2d 401 (1972).
10. *Id.* at 198-200.

tification procedure was "unnecessarily suggestive" and was "conducive to irreparable mistaken identification" to one simply of reliability. The sole inquiry now was one of probable accuracy: Was the identification reliable despite the suggestive procedures?

Under *Biggers,* no longer is the trial court to be concerned with the question of whether there has been a denial of fundamental fairness. Rather, the sole question is whether the identification is reliable — regardless of how suggestive the police conduct at pretrial identification proceedings is. This is analogous to a Supreme Court ruling that a confession is admissible if it is deemed truthful — regardless of the fact that it has been beaten out of the defendant.

§ 8-2. Admissibility of Suggestive Pretrial Identifications: Gilbert — Brathwaite.

The adoption of the "reliability" test by *Biggers* soon resulted in some confusion as to certain attendant issues. If an identification is considered by the trial court to be reliable despite suggestive police procedures, for example, is the fact of the pretrial identification admissible in evidence to bolster the witness' in-court identification?

Prior to *Biggers,* trial courts had applied the per se exclusionary rule enunciated by the Court in *Gilbert v. California.*[11] In essence, this rule stated that if the prosecution introduced evidence concerning an illegal pretrial identification as part of its case, any conviction would be automatically reversed and a new trial ordered. Nor would the establishment by the prosecution of an independent source be to any avail.

The question posed as to this issue was answered by the Supreme Court in *Manson v. Brathwaite.*[12] In that case, the

11. 388 U.S. 263, 87 S. Ct. 1951, 18 L. Ed. 2d 1178 (1967).

12. 432 U.S. 98, 97 S. Ct. 2243, 53 L. Ed. 2d 140 (1977).

Court considered a situation involving the introduction into evidence of a pretrial photographic identification, and concluded that the per se exclusionary rule did not apply to suggestive pretrial identification procedures. The sole standard to be applied to any identification issue was that of *Biggers:* Was the pretrial identification reliable despite being tainted by suggestive procedures?

The practical effect of this rejection of the per se exclusionary rule is, as Justice Marshall in his *Brathwaite* dissenting opinion said, to "dismantle the protections against mistaken eyewitness testimony erected a decade ago in (*Wade — Gilbert — Stovall*)" and to "allow seriously unreliable and misleading evidence to be put before juries."[13] Nevertheless, the courts have followed the *Brathwaite* decision: The due process test and sanctions for pretrial identifications have been abandoned, to be replaced by the test of reliability used in assessing the admissibility of in-court identifications. In other words, evidence of suggestive out-of-court identifications will be admitted as long as they are shown to be reliable.

Some courts have adopted a two-pronged approach in applying *Brathwaite* to pretrial identifications.[14] First, the trial court determines whether the identification was the result of suggestive police procedures. If it was, the court then proceeds to determine whether the tainted out-of-court identification was nevertheless reliable by applying the factors suggested in the *Brathwaite* decision.

Legal scholars and commentators have been critical of the *Brathwaite* decision[15] and there is some indication that

---

13. *Id.* at 128.

14. *See, e.g.,* United States v. Williams, 594 F.2d 1258 (9th Cir. 1979); State v. Gullick, 411 A.2d 1113 (N.H. 1980); State v. Hicks, 277 N.W.2d 889 (Iowa 1979).

15. *See, e.g.,* Comment, 26 Kan. L. Rev. 464 (1978); 9 Loy. U. L.J. 355 (1978).

a few jurisdictions will not be bound by *Brathwaite* and will continue to exclude evidence of suggestive pretrial identifications despite their reliability.[16] Nevertheless, the reliability test is now generally applied when the prosecution offers evidence of a tainted out-of-court identification.

As to what exactly constitutes a "reliable" or "fair" identification procedure, there is little agreement. One expert on the subject, Judge Nathan R. Sobel, has compiled a list which represents a composite of factors considered relevant to fairness and reliability by various courts, commentators and legal scholars.[17] As to lineups, Judge Sobel recommends ensuring fairness and reliability by adopting the following procedures:

1. The lineup should be composed of at least six persons including the suspect.
2. All participants should be the same approximate height, age, coloration of hair and skin, weight and body type.
3. The manner of dress of the participants should generally be the same.
4. Verbal statements (voice identification) should only be required when requested by the witness; if requested, all participants shall be required to say the same words.
5. When there are two or more identifying witnesses, each shall be required to view the lineup separately and each required to make the identification out of the presence of the other.
6. A written record of the composition of the lineup should be made and a large color photo taken for introduction in evidence at the suppression hearing.
7. Counsel at the lineup should be permitted to make suggestions concerning the composition of the lineup. An exception by counsel should be noted on the record.

---

16. *See, e.g.,* Harris v. State, 373 N.E.2d 149 (Ind. 1978); Commonwealth v. Venios, 389 N.E.2d 395 (Mass. 1979).

17. Sobel, N., *Eye-Witness Identification* (Clark Boardman 1972).

8. Prior to viewing the lineup each witness shall be required to give a description of the perpetrator in writing to the police and a copy made available to defense counsel.
9. Counsel should be present at pre-arraignment lineups to insure compliance with due process, even though *Kirby v. Illinois* has eliminated the Sixth Amendment right to counsel at pre-arraignment lineups.
10. No one-way mirrors which obstruct the suspect's view of the witness should be used at showups or lineups where counsel is not present.
11. The prosecutor, rather than the police, should conduct all lineup identifications.

While most of these procedures were recommended prior to the shifting of standards from "fairness" to "reliability," they would appear relevant to either. It should certainly be argued that the absence of any of these recommended safeguards would probably affect the reliability of any resultant identification. A similar list of factors affecting the fairness and reliability of photographic identification procedures will be found in the next section.

§ 8-3. Photographic Identification Standards: Simmons — Brathwaite.

The use of photographic displays by the police is, of course, a very common practice. It is considerably easier to simply show a series of photographs to an eyewitness than to go to the trouble of arranging a cumbersome and time-consuming lineup.

The employment of photographic identification procedures is understandable when the suspect has not yet been arrested. If he cannot be located, or if there is insufficient evidence to justify arresting him and placing him in a lineup, the police have little recourse but to use photographs. The problem, however, is that once a witness has seen a photograph and under the suggestive influences of the police identified it, he becomes committed. In future corporeal identifications the witness will tend to identify the person he saw in the photograph, not the one he saw at the crime scene. Any subsequent lineups become heavily influenced by the photographic identification, regardless of how fairly the lineup itself is conducted. Yet this procedure continues to be routinely followed by the police and condoned by the courts.

Certainly, however, it would seem that there is little justification for using the photographic technique once the suspect is in custody. The lineup becomes an available procedure, and the courts have repeatedly emphasized their preference for the lineup over the photographic display. Despite judicial disapproval, the police continue to utilize the procedure, employing photographic identification methods when lineups are available. Even worse, the courts have proven reluctant to apply meaningful sanctions, preferring instead to simply criticize the practice.[18]

The Supreme Court in *Simmons v. United States* specifically held that "convictions based on eyewitness identification at trial following a pretrial identification by photograph will be set aside ... only if the photographic identification procedure was so impermissibly suggestive as to give rise to a very substantial likelihood of irreparable misidentification."[19] Evidence of the pretrial photographic identification itself would fall along with the tainted in-court identification. However, the Supreme Court in *Manson v. Brathwaite*[20] changed this (see § 8-2). Dealing

18. *See, e.g.,* United States v. Marson, 408 F.2d 644 (4th Cir. 1968), *cert. denied,* 393 U.S. 1056 (1969); United States v. Williams, 436 F.2d 1166 (9th Cir. 1970); People v. Holiday, 47 Ill. 2d 300, 265 N.E.2d 634 (1970); State v. Sickels, 275 N.W.2d 809 (Minn. 1979).

19. 390 U.S. at 384, 88 S. Ct. 1967, 19 L. Ed. 2d 1247 (1968).

20. 432 U.S. 98, 97 S. Ct. 2243, 53 L. Ed. 2d 140 (1977).

with a case involving evidence of a suggestive pretrial photographic identification, the Court held that the *Biggers* reliability test applied. Thus, evidence of the out-of-court identification of the defendant's photograph can be placed before the jury if the "totality of the circumstances" indicate the identification was reliable.

In view of *Biggers — Brathwaite,* defense counsel will encounter considerable difficulty in attempting to suppress evidence of either suggestive pretrial photographic identifications or in-court identifications tainted by earlier photographic identifications. There are numerous decisions reflecting examples of exactly what the various courts consider to be an "unreliable" photographic identification procedure. Where the defendant, for example, was shown in a photographic display as the only one wearing a sweater described as stolen, evidence of the pretrial identification was suppressed.[21] Similarly, the photographic identification was excluded where a witness who had initially selected an individual other than the defendant was advised by the police that she might have picked the wrong man.[22] Where a witness was shown only a single photo — both before the defendant's arrest and on the day of trial — a court concluded that due process had been violated and evidence of the identification was suppressed.[23] Telling the witness that the suspect is in one of the pictures, together with the fact that only the defendant was shown wearing a beard like that described by the robbery victim, constituted grounds for exclusion.[24]

---

21. United States v. Baykowski, 583 F.2d 1046 (8th Cir. 1978).
22. United States v. Russell, 532 F.2d 1063 (6th Cir. 1976).
23. United States v. Workman, 470 F.2d 151 (4th Cir. 1972).
24. State v. LaRue, 271 S.C. 256, 246 S.E.2d 890 (1978).

A second objectionable use of photographic identification involves the showing of a photo of the defendant to the eyewitness just before he is to testify at a trial or preliminary hearing. This practice of prompting the witness at a critical time is referred to by police and prosecutors as "preparing" him. Whether called prompting or preparing, the practice is unquestionably suggestive and objectionable, and perhaps even a violation of the prosecutor's ethical obligations. There can be no other imaginable reason for showing a witness a photograph of the defendant just before he is to be asked on the stand to identify the culprit than to influence him to point to the defendant. Yet the courts have readily criticized the practice but generally been reluctant to go further in view of *Biggers* and *Brathwaite*. There are, however, examples available of courts excluding such out-of-court identifications.[25]

What factors should be considered by the courts in determining the fairness or reliability of a photographic identification procedure? A recognized expert in the area, Judge Nathan R. Sobel, has compiled the following list of procedures deemed relevant by various legal scholars and commentators:[26]

1. A series of at least ten photos, only one of which shall be of the suspect, shall be presented to the witness. As far as practicable the photos shall be unmarked and of the same size and nature.
2. All the photos should be of persons of approximately the same height, age and color of hair and skin.
3. If there are two or more suspects, no two shall be presented together in a single group photo.
4. Where there are two or more witnesses, each should be required to view the photos separately and to make identification separately out of the presence and hearing of one another.

---

25. *E.g.*, United States v. Dailey, 524 F.2d 911 (8th Cir. 1975); United States v. Workman, 470 F.2d 151 (4th Cir. 1972).

26. Sobel, N., *Eye-Witness Identification* (Clark Boardman 1972).

5. A police notation should be made of each photo of the group viewed and the group kept available for reconstruction and examination at the trial.
6. The police officer in charge shall make a contemporaneous notation of all remarks made by the witness upon the identification of any photo; also of failure to identify or mistakes in identification.
7. Mug shots should not be used in conjunction with other types of photographs for identification.
8. The witness should not be repeatedly exposed to photo displays containing the same picture which has been previously identified.
9. Use of photographs taken during the actual crime serves the useful purpose of refreshing the recollection of the witnesses.

While most of these procedures were recommended prior to the shifting of standards from those of "fairness" to those of "reliability," they would appear relevant to either. It should certainly be argued that the absence of any of these recommended safeguards would probably affect the reliability of any resultant identification.

§ 9. Pretrial Defense Procedures.

> "A lawyer is an artist whether he likes it or or not. The medium in which he works is the law. The question is not whether he is an artist, for in this he has no choice, but rather how good an artist he is going to be."
>
> Sokol, *Language and Litigation*

The defense counsel in a case involving eyewitness evidence often makes the mistake of waiting until trial before challenging the identification of his client. Cross-examination of the witness is, of course, the procedure used for directly attacking the identification. But the attack and a defense can be considerably more effective if counsel prepares for the confrontation long before trial. Through the use of proper discovery procedures, for example, he can obtain ammunition to use in his cross-examination, as well as information which may lead to presentation of eyewitness testimony for the defense. He may be able to confront the prosecution's eyewitness before trial, thus discovering potential weaknesses and at the same time committing the witness to a set of facts. Counsel may even be able to counter police identification evidence in trial by conducting his own corporeal or photographic pretrial identification proceedings.

§ 9-1. Discovery of Eyewitness Evidence.

Counsel should attempt to obtain certain information concerning eyewitness identification at the earliest available opportunity. This information relates to the location of the witness or witnesses, the circumstances surrounding any identification procedures, and most importantly, any statements they have made relative to identification of the client or other persons.

It should be recognized at the outset that criminal law has traditionally permitted only very limited pretrial discovery. The usual argument in support of this position is that permitting a defendant to review the prosecutor's evidence accomplishes two things: It subjects prosecution's witnesses to harassment or even intimidation, and it encourages the defendant to commit perjury or suborn perjury in others. The old "combat" or "sport" view of criminal litigation — not without its adherents — discourages discovery also. All of these arguments, however, overlook the primary tenets of our Anglo-Saxon system of justice: fairness ("due process") and the seeking of truth. Quite simply, keeping both parties to a criminal action in the dark until trial may make for a sporting contest, but such an approach is simply not designed to maximize the opportunities for establishing the truth.

Nor is such an approach fair. Defense counsel should perhaps consider reminding the trial court in his discovery argument that the accused stands alone with his attorney before the court; he has limited financial resources, and almost no power or influence. The prosecutor, on the other hand, has the almost unlimited resources of the federal, state and/or local government behind him, including police officers, lawyers, criminalistics laboratories, computerized records centers and so on.

The defense lawyer usually has only the information supplied to him by his client — and this is often misleading because of the client's ignorance or fear of divulging incriminating matters. When the defense lawyer attempts to interview witnesses, he finds that they are much more reluctant to talk to him than to a police officer or prosecutor.

Counsel should emphasize to the trial court that discovery is essential to the preparation of a defense. Without it, or even with curtailed discovery, the defendant is so handicapped that the trial becomes a one-sided contest: The defendant, kept in the dark and without anything near the prosecutor's resources, is in effect denied due process of law.

Fortunately, the general trend over recent years has been toward increased discovery in criminal cases. In some jurisdictions, the issue has at least initially been resolved by statute; in others, case law has established an increasingly liberal policy. In almost all jurisdictions, the trial judge is granted a broad range of discretion in determining exactly what information may be given the defense before trial. Because of this discretionary power, counsel should always invest considerable effort in his discovery affidavits and/or arguments even where the discovery being sought is not specifically authorized by statute or precedent.

What information should defense counsel be seeking in an eyewitness case? First, counsel should attempt to discover the names and addresses of all witnesses known to the police — both of those identifying the defendant as well as of those unable to identify him. If the prosecutor or the court permits discovery of identifying witnesses, counsel may be able to question them prior to trial; conduct investigations as to their sensory abilities, character, reputation for truthfulness, etc.; take a written statement differing from the police version of their identification; or even conduct a defense lineup or photographic display. It must be recognized, however, that the trial courts are generally given broad discretion in this area of discovery, and many are reluctant to release the names of prosecution witnesses for fear that there may be attempts to intimidate them.

The names and addresses of witnesses who have failed to identify the defendant — particularly of those who have stated that the defendant is *not* the individual observed at the scene of the crime — should be a different matter. If an eyewitness was unable to identify the defendant in a lineup, showup or photographic display, he could well become a valuable witness for the defense. Thus the defense' need for demonstrably relevant and perhaps even critical evidence should outweigh any interests the prosecution has in protecting eyewitnesses. The argument that a witness could be intimidated loses much of its validity where that witness' testimony is favorable to the defense.

Secondly, counsel should make appropriate demand for any and all statements — oral or written — made at any time by any eyewitness. This would include statements made to investigating officers at the scene of the crime, as well as those made before, during, or after pretrial identification procedures. The most important information concerning statements at the scene involve descriptions of the perpetrator. Police almost always try to obtain as detailed descriptions as possible in order to help them locate the suspect. Obviously, these descriptions can be of great use to the defense particularly where, for example, a witness describes a tall, dark man and then picks the fair-skinned defendant of medium height out of the lineup. A contradictory description given when the witness' memory was fresh can be a very effective weapon on cross-examination.

Similarly, counsel should look for statements made at the scene that indicate doubt on the part of the witness as to his ability to describe or later identify the suspect. Comments such as "I didn't really get a good look," "I don't think I'd recognize him if I saw him again," or "It all happened so fast" are typical of statements made by witnesses to investigators or to other witnesses. These statements are often in stark contrast to the confident witness on the stand who has been carefully groomed through pretrial identification procedures.

Statements made at or near the time of the lineup, showup or photographic display should also be discovered. Expressions of doubt or reluctance must be carefully noted for use in cross-examination. The positive identification in trial is all too often made by the same witness who, at the lineup, used such phrases as "It *might* be him," "I'm not sure," or "They all look the same." Certainly any failure to identify the defendant, or an identification of another individual, would be very relevant.

Third, counsel must attempt to reconstruct the circumstances surrounding the pretrial identification procedure or procedures. Whether through obtaining police investigator's reports, questioning police officers, or interviewing the witnesses involved, the defense should be entitled to know exactly how the lineup, showup or photographic display was conducted. Without this knowledge the defendant is in no position to question the fairness or reliability of the procedure. If it was a lineup, the defendant is usually unaware of what is happening around him — especially if the lineup involves a one-way mirror or a lit stage in a darkened auditorium. In any event, the defendant's testimony is usually discounted. If the identification involved a photographic display, the defendant would not be present. Only the police and witnesses are percipient to what happens at the procedure, and often the witnesses are not fully aware of suggestive police conduct. Nor are there any significant countervailing interests to be protected by withholding such information from the defense. The trial court and prosecutor alike should be concerned with determining whether a suggestive identification proceeding contributed significantly to a critical identification.

Finally, counsel should attempt to find out whether any of the witnesses have criminal records, or whether any of them have been given special consideration by the police or prosecutor.

As previously discussed, the degree to which the different states permit discovery of such matters varies. Traditionally, a defendant was considered to have no absolute right to inspection or prosecution evidence. This rule has been changed substantially, however, and today almost all states at least vaguely recognize broad discretionary power vested in the trial courts to grant inspection of evidence in the possession of the prosecution,[1] particularly where that evidence appears to be relevant and material to the case. Outright suppression of exculpatory evidence by the prosecution is usually viewed as constituting a violation of due process.[2]

The states differ, however, in their decisions as to exactly what type of evidence is discoverable and under what circumstances. In dealing with the discovery of statements made by prosecution witnesses, for example, the states fall roughly into two categories: those recognizing explicitly or impliedly the right of a defendant to inspect such statements before trial for the purpose of cross-examining or impeaching the witness in trial,[3] and those which do not recognize such a right.[4] In those states granting the right of discovery under such circumstances, failure to produce witness' statements may well provide grounds for later reversal.[5]

1. *E.g.*, Hill v. Superior Court, 10 Cal. 3d 812, 518 P.2d 1353 (1974); State v. Isley, 195 Neb. 539, 239 N.W.2d 262 (1976); State v. Taylor, 112 Ariz. 68, 537 P.2d 938 (1975).

2. *E.g.*, Lowe v. Commonwealth, 239 S.E.2d 112 (Va. 1977); State v. Spears, 350 So. 2d 603 (La. 1977); State v. Fowler, 101 Ariz. 561, 422 P.2d 125 (1967).

3. *See, e.g.*, State v. Harrison, 118 N.J. Super. 299, 287 A.2d 229 (1972); People v. Nicolini, 75 Misc. 2d 47, 349 N.Y.S.2d 971 (1973); People v. Estrada, 54 Cal. 2d 713, 355 P.2d 641 (1960).

4. *See, e.g.*, State v. Jones, 202 Kan. 31, 446 P.2d 851 (1968); Green v. State, 25 Md. 679, 337 A.2d 729 (1975); State v. Hutchins, 51 Del. 100, 138 A.2d 342 (1957).

5. *See, e.g.*, State v. Curtis, 399 A.2d 1330 (Me. 1979).

In many cases, counsel will find a paucity of statutory or case law on discovery in state criminal prosecutions; the position often taken is that this is simply a matter of judicial discretion. In such situations, the argument must be forcefully made that fairness — if not constitutional due process — requires disclosure so that the defendant can defend himself, and federal or foreign state authority cited in support.

In order to be permitted inspection of witness' statements or of any evidence in the prosecution's control, counsel must make his request in a timely and proper manner. It is usually incumbent upon the defense to show facts justifying the granting of a discovery motion, such as the existence of contradictory statements by an eyewitness or evidence of a suggestive lineup. Rarely will a trial court grant a vague, comprehensive discovery motion just so defense counsel can go on a "fishing expedition." The motion must indicate what counsel wants to discover and how it is relevant to the defense.

In federal courts the question of discovery of statements and reports of government witnesses is determined by the so-called Jencks Act.[6] That statute basically provides that written or recorded statements of prosecution witnesses must be produced for the defense — but only after that witness has testified in trial, and only statements relating to the subject matter about which the witness testified.

As to other materials in a federal case, Rule 16(b) of the Federal Rules of Criminal Procedure provides that upon a showing of reasonableness and materiality to the defense, the trial court may require the prosecution to make available for inspection and photocopying all documents, papers, physical objects and other materials it possesses or controls.

6. 18 U.S.C. § 3500.

In other words, the defense is now free to review any material the government has which may be relevant to the defense, and this is possible without the old rule that the defense specify exactly what item of evidence it wished to see. Further, discovery under Rule 16(b) now encompasses both material which may be used by the defense as well as that which may be part of the government's case.[7] It is not necessary to make any showing of reasonableness or materiality to the defense, as was previously the case; the right to the information is an absolute one.[8] Finally, it has now been clearly established by case law that the prosecution in a federal case must supply defense counsel with a list of all individuals whose testimony could possibly be of assistance in the preparation of the defendant's case.[9]

§ 9-2. Deposing the Eyewitness.

At common law, a criminal defendant had no right to take the deposition of an eyewitness. As a part of the general trend toward more liberal policies on discovery, however, several jurisdictions have enacted statutes authorizing such pretrial depositions under certain circumstances; these include Rule 15(a) of the Federal Rules of Criminal Procedure. As the deposition statutes of each of these jurisdictions vary widely, counsel should thoroughly familiarize himself with the appropriate authority before engaging in the deposing of witnesses.

Generally speaking, statutory and case authority envision the use of pretrial depositions in criminal cases not for the purpose of discovery, but rather for the purpose of perpetuating the testimony of a witness. Thus defense counsel may be hard pressed to justify a request to depose the prosecution's eyewitness — unless, of course, he can

7. United States v. Aadal, 280 F. Supp. 859 (S.D.N.Y. 1968).

8. United States v. Rosenfeld, 264 F. Supp. 760 (N.D. Ill. 1967).

9. United States ex rel. Meersu v. Wilkins, 326 F.2d 135 (2d Cir. 1964).

convince the court that the witness may have evidence favorable to the defense and therefore constitute at least arguably a potential defense witness.

Again generally speaking, there are two different kinds of depositions in criminal cases, each with its own purpose and procedure. The first of these is the *examination on commission.* It is employed where the witness lives outside of the jurisdiction and it appears reasonably unlikely that he will be available for trial. Such a deposition normally requires that notice be given to opposing counsel, along with an opportunity to attend and cross-examine. In some jurisdictions, the examination of the out-of-state witness can be conducted in the form of written interrogatories, in which case a set of questions is agreed upon by both defense counsel and the prosecutor.

The second type of deposition in a criminal case is the *conditional examination.* This is used where there is a reasonable possibility that the witness will not be able to appear at trial — either because of absence from the jurisdiction, medical incapacity, or for other good cause. As with the examination on commission, the opposing counsel usually has a right to be present at the deposition and to cross-examine.

Evidentiary objections during either procedure are normally withheld until trial. Either counsel can then make his usual objections as the deposition is read into evidence, much as would be done if the witness were present on the stand. Because he is *not* present, however, counsel should ask a potentially objectionable question in various ways at the deposition; the chances of a question being ruled proper at trial are thus increased.

It should be noted that in a few jurisdictions the relevant statutes grant the right to depose only to the defendant. Under such a statute, however, the prosecution is also granted the right once the defendant has availed himself of its provisions. Thus defense counsel in such a jurisdiction should consider the tactical considerations in deciding to depose an eyewitness: He may be opening the door to the perpetuation of an unavailable adverse witness' testimony by the prosecutor.

The motion or application for a deposition must be made in accordance with the requirements of the jurisdiction. This usually means that it must be timely; that affidavits must clearly establish in detail that the evidence is both material and necessary; and that the future unavailability of the witness must be shown to be reasonably probable. Proof of notice to the prosecution must be included.

The deposition itself will most often be taken before the judge who signed the order authorizing the deposition. In federal court, however, it will take place before the court clerk.

Criminal depositions in federal courts are governed by Rule 15(a) of the Federal Rules of Criminal Procedure. This statute as amended in 1975 provides in relevant part as follows:

> Whenever due to exceptional circumstances of the case it is in the interest of justice that the testimony of a prospective witness of a party be taken and preserved for use at trial, the court may upon motion of such party and notice to the parties order that testimony of such witnesses be taken by deposition and that any designated book, paper, document, record, recording, or other material not privileged, be produced at the same time and place. . . .

Thus vaguely worded, the courts have held that a defendant's right to take the depositions of prospective witnesses before trial is a matter for determination by the trial court "in the exercise of its sound discretion." The few decisions on point, however, make it clear that the purpose of such depositions is not discovery but rather the perpetuation of testimony.

§ 9-3. Conducting a Defense Lineup or Photographic Display.

Generally speaking, the few cases on point have made it clear that a defense request for a lineup soon after the crime has taken place should be granted. The question becomes somewhat greyer as the request becomes more remote in time from the date of the offense. In any event, the cases are also clear that a denial of such a request, whenever made, will not normally be considered a denial of a constitutional right. In other words, the decision of whether to permit the defendant to have a lineup rests within the discretion of the court.

There have been decisions, however, that have reversed convictions where a denial of a defense request for a pretrial lineup was held to constitute an abuse of the trial court's discretion.[10] Other decisions have expressed a strong preference for the granting of lineup requests, although falling short of holding a denial to be reversible error.[11] Thus, for example, one federal appellate decision specifically advised magistrates to favor defense requests for pretrial lineups.[12] In *People v. Evans,* the Supreme Court of California recognized a constitutional right of discovery:

> We conclude . . . that due process requires in an appropriate case that an accused, upon timely request therefore, be afforded a pretrial lineup in which witnesses to the alleged criminal conduct can participate. The right to a lineup arises, however, only when eyewitness identification is shown to be in material issue and and there exists a reasonable likelihood of a mistaken identification which a lineup would tend to resolve.[13]

---

10. *E.g.,* Commonwealth v. Sexton, 400 A.2d 1289 (Pa. 1979).

11. *E.g.,* State v. Boettcher, 338 So. 2d 1356 (La. 1976).

12. United States v. Smith, 473 F.2d 1148 (D.C. Cir. 1972).

13. 11 Cal. 3d at 625, 522 P.2d 681 (1974).

The *Evans* Court then went on to note that the defendant "has neither the facilities nor the experience to conduct an impartial lineup" and that "the burden on the police is a nominal one"; on the other hand, "motions which are not made until shortly before trial should, unless good cause is clearly demonstrated, be denied in most instances by reason of such delay."

What are the factors that a court should consider in determining whether to grant a defense request for a lineup, or whether to suppress identification evidence because of a police denial of such a request? Judge Friendly summarized some of those considerations in his oft-quoted decision in *United States v. Ravich:*

> Without any attempt at being exhaustive, we think some relevant factors are the length of time between the crime or arrest and the request, the possibility that the defendant may have altered his appearance (as was at least attempted here), the extent of inconvenience to prosecution witnesses, the possibility that revealing the identity of the prosecution witnesses will subject them to intimidation, the propriety of other identification procedures used by the prosecution, and the degree of doubt concerning the identification.[14]

Thus, for example, counsel would be in a relatively strong position to demand a lineup if the request was made soon after his client's arrest, the witnesses are available without unreasonable inconvenience, and there has been some doubt as to identity expressed by one or more of them during the initial investigation.

There is little to prevent defense counsel from attempting to conduct a lineup on his own. Care should be taken, obviously, to avoid any suggestion of witness tampering; advising the prosecuting attorney of the intention to

14. 421 F.2d at 1203 (2d Cir. 1970).

approach witnesses may be advisable. In any event, the chief problem will be one of reluctance on the part of the witness or witnesses. Most witnesses will be suspicious of defense lawyers, and there is always the matter of time and inconvenience. If a lineup can be arranged, certainly counsel should take every step to ensure that the results are not tainted by the very flaws commonly encountered in police lineups and discussed in detail in § 5 in this text.

Finally, counsel should consider the use of photographic displays. Such identification presentations to eyewitnesses are considerably easier than attempting to conduct a lineup, and there is almost no inconvenience to the witness. As with a lineup, however, every effort should be made to prevent the presentation from being so flawed that the prosecutor can attack any favorable results in court. Certainly, any displays should be preserved. Counsel should also strongly consider using an investigator or other individual in presenting the photographic display; if testimony concerning the circumstances of the identification or lack of it becomes necessary, counsel will not find himself in the conflict situation of having himself as his own witness.

PART THREE

IDENTIFICATION IN TRIAL

§ 10. Suppression of In-Court Identification.

> "A London theatre hoping to drum up interest in a film starring Charlie Chaplin decided to run a Charlie Chaplin look-alike contest. Charlie Chaplin entered himself as a contestant. He placed third."
>
> News item

The most effective method of dealing with an adverse witness who will identify the client during the course of trial is, of course, to prevent him from making such an identification in the first place. In appropriate cases this can be accomplished by making a timely motion to suppress any evidence of identification resulting from objectionable police practices. If, for example, the client was not advised of his right to counsel at a post-indictment lineup and an identification was made by the eyewitness at that lineup, a motion should be made to suppress not only any evidence of the identification at the lineup, but also any testimony relating to an identification in court of the defendant; the in-court identification, it should be argued, is a direct result of the identification at the lineup and is therefore "tainted" by the failure to advise the suspect of his right to counsel. Similarly, if due process standards of fairness were not met at a photographic showup, for example, counsel should attempt to suppress evidence of the pretrial photographic identification as well as of the more critical in-court identification. In many cases suppression of identification evidence proves dispositive of the case: Without any identification of the defendant, the prosecutor is simply unable to proceed.

§ 10-1. Issues, Burdens and Procedures.

The questions of whether due process ("fairness"), right to counsel, or search and seizure standards have been violated are questions of law, not of fact. As such, these are issues to be determined not by the jury but rather by the court outside of the presence of the jury. Conversely, the accuracy of an eyewitness' identification is a question of fact and thus a matter for the jury; it is not an issue at the hearing to suppress, and any evidence of accuracy should not be admitted at the hearing. There may, however, be evidence as to reliability or "independent source" which will be relevant to both the judge's determination of admissibility and the jury's later deliberation as to accuracy.

The broad issues at a suppression hearing, then, should be roughly limited to one or more of the following:

1. Was the pretrial identification procedure unfairly suggestive?
2. Was the defendant denied effective representation by counsel at a post-indictment lineup?
3. Was the pretrial identification the result of an unlawful search and/or seizure?
4. As the result of any improper police conduct at pretrial identification procedures, would any in-court identification be tainted?
5. If tainted, is there an untainted "independent source" for the in-court identification?

6. If tainted, is the in-court identification nevertheless sufficiently reliable to be admissible?

As to the burden of proof, the defendant always bears the responsibility for establishing a violation of such rights as due process. However, that burden is initially met if the defendant can establish a *prima facie* case by showing, for example, that the eyewitness was shown only one photograph or that the defendant was the only Black in the lineup. The burden of proof then shifts to the prosecution to establish that the identification procedure was not suggestive, that exigent circumstances existed which excused the suggestiveness, that the in-court identification has an independent source, or that it is nevertheless sufficiently reliable to be admitted into evidence. This prosecutorial burden must be met by "clear and convincing evidence." [1]

The preferable procedure for counsel to take in requesting that identification issues be resolved is to make a formal motion well before trial for a pretrial hearing. In fact, the majority of jurisdictions today have mandatory provisions *requiring* any such issues to be resolved before trial by means of a motion to suppress; failure to attack an identification before trial may well constitute a waiver as to the issue. Where, however, the prosecution has failed to provide identification information to the defense as required, a motion to suppress may be heard during the course of trial. Thus, for example, in New York the prosecution has an affirmative duty to give prior notice to the defense of its intention to use identification testimony; failure to give such notice will give defense counsel the right to challenge the suggestiveness of identification procedures during trial. [2]

---

1. United States v. Wade, 388 U.S. at 240, n. 31, 87 S. Ct. 1926, 18 L. Ed. 2d 1149 (1967). *See also* People v. Fowler, 1 Cal. 3d 335, 461 P.2d 643 (1969); State v. Cefalo, 396 A. 2d 233 (Me. 1979); Powell v. State, 86 Wis. 2d 51, 271 N.W.2d 610 (1978).

2. People v. Hand, 74 A.D.2d 989, 425 N.Y.S.2d 851 (1980).

It should be noted that there is no constitutional right as such to a hearing as to the admissibility of identification testimony outside of the hearing of the jury.[3] However, there is a right to an independent determination by the trial judge after hearing evidence.[4] It is clearly improper to permit a jury to hear or decide any issues relating to the admissibility of possibly tainted evidence of identification.[5]

Whether a defendant has a right to a separate hearing outside the jury's presence is a matter of some disagreement among the jurisdictions. The majority appears to hold that such a hearing is a right where the defendant has made a *prima facie* case that the identification may be tainted by improper pretrial procedures.[6] The failure to grant such a hearing may later constitute grounds for reversal.[7] However, the courts are often prone to find such a denial "harmless error" where there is substantial evidence of the defendant's guilt or of the reliability of the identification.[8] In such situations, counsel should bear in mind the Supreme Court's admonition in *Chapman v. California* that "before a federal constitutional error can be held harmless, the court must be able to declare a belief that it was harmless beyond a reasonable doubt."[9]

The courts are much less reluctant to find a *waiver* of the identification issue. If defense counsel fails to make a

---

3. *See* United States v. Poe, 462 F.2d 195 (5th Cir. 1972), *cert. denied,* 414 U.S. 845 (1973).

4. *See* Summit v. Bordenkircher, 608 F.2d 247 (6th Cir. 1979).

5. *See, e.g.,* People v. Hicks, 40 A.D.2d 836, 337 N.Y.S.2d 346 (1972).

6. *See, e.g.,* People v. Reynolds, 93 Mich. App. 516, 286 N.W.2d 898 (1979); State v. Porraro, 404 A.2d 465 (R.I. 1979).

7. *See, e.g.,* Green v. State, 281 Md. 483, 380 A.2d 43 (1977); People v. Chillis, 60 A.D.2d 761, 401 N.Y.S.2d 612 (1978).

8. *See, e.g.,* People v. Oliver, 359 N.Y.S.2d 112, 316 N.E.2d 578 (1974); People v. Leftwich, 82 Misc. 2d 993, 372 N.Y.S.2d 888 (1975).

9. 386 U.S. 18, 24, 87 S. Ct. 824, 17 L. Ed. 2d 705 (1967).

timely motion to suppress the identification evidence, most jurisdictions will hold that the right to challenge the evidence has been waived.[10] This does not mean that defense counsel cannot cross-examine the eyewitness as to the identification issue, but he will be precluded from attacking its admissibility.

§ 10-2. The Prosecutor's Duty to Disclose: Agurs.

Criminal defense counsel should be aware that the prosecutor in an eyewitness case is bound by a two-fold duty. First, he may not introduce identification evidence which he knows to be false. Second, he must disclose to the defense any exculpatory matter bearing on the issue of identification, whether requested by defense counsel or not. Violation of either of these duties may constitute grounds for reversal.

In *Miller v. Pate,*[11] the United States Supreme Court dealt with a murder case in which the prosecution represented to the jury that reddish-brown stains found on clothing were of human blood; the prosecutor knew, in fact, that the stains were from paint. The Court unanimously reversed the conviction, holding that the state had violated the defendant's rights under the Fourteenth Amendment by convicting him through the knowing use of false evidence.

It would appear at least arguable, then, that a prosecutor cannot offer the testimony of an eyewitness who identifies the defendant when he has substantial reason to believe the eyewitness has no credibility. If, for example, the prosecutor is aware of the fact that the witness has recanted an earlier identification, or has flatly stated that the defendant is definitely not the person observed at the crime scene or that he cannot identify him, it would seem that *Pate* precludes him

10. *See, e.g.,* People v. Mann, 89 Mich. App. 511, 280 N.W.2d 577 (1979); State v. Watie, 223 Kan. 337, 574 P.2d 1368 (1978); United States v. Thornton, 462 F.2d 307 (D.C. Cir. 1972).

11. 386 U.S. 1, 87 S. Ct. 785, 17 L. Ed. 2d 690 (1967).

from offering contradictory testimony from that witness to the effect that the defendant is definitely the culprit. It must be recognized, however, that this seemingly logical extension of the Supreme Court's position has not been recognized; to date, the issue has simply not been presented.

It is clear, however, that the prosecution in such a case has an affirmative duty to advise the defense of the previous failures of the eyewitness to identify the defendant. In fact, the prosecution is obligated to volunteer any exculpatory material to the defense without the need for a defense motion or even informal request.

In its landmark decision in *United States v. Agurs,*[12] the Supreme Court clearly imposed a new standard for prosecutorial disclosure. It held that a prosecutor must disclose any exculpatory evidence which was material to the defense, and that this was an affirmative duty independent of any defense motion for "all *Brady* material" or for "anything exculpatory." Although dealing with a federal case, the Court expressly applied its ruling to the states through the Fourteenth Amendment.

Certain questions immediately present themselves. First, is a prosecutor's good faith ignorance of the existence of such evidence an excuse? Second, what is the standard for determining what evidence is "material"? Third, what is the standard for determining whether the error is reversible?

The Court addressed the first issue by stating:

> Nor do we believe the constitutional obligation is measured by the moral culpability, or the willfulness, of the prosecutor. If evidence highly probative of innocence is in his file, he should be *presumed* to recognize its significance even if he has actually overlooked it . . . . If the suppression of evidence results in constitutional error, it is because of the character of the evidence, not the character of the prosecutor.[13] (Emphasis added.)

12. 427 U.S. 97, 96 S. Ct. 2392, 49 L. Ed. 2d 342 (1976).

13. *Id.* at 109.

Apparently the Court has imposed a heavy standard upon the prosecutor: He will be held responsible for the disclosure of any exculpatory evidence which he *should* have known about under the circumstances. Failure to disclose such evidence may constitute reversible error.

Addressing next the questions of the materiality of the exculpatory evidence and the standards for determining reversible error, the Court held:

> The proper standard of materiality must reflect our overriding concern with the justice of the finding of guilt. Such a finding is permissible only if supported by evidence establishing guilt beyond a reasonable doubt. It necessarily follows that if the omitted evidence creates a reasonable doubt that did not otherwise exist, constitutional error has been committed. This means that the omission must be evaluated in the context of the entire record. If there is no reasonable doubt about guilt whether or not the additional evidence is considered, there is no justification for a new trial. On the other hand, if the verdict is already of questionable validity, additional evidence of relatively minor importance might be sufficient to create a reasonable doubt.[14]

In eyewitness identification cases, then, the prosecutor is required to voluntarily supply to defense counsel any material evidence which tends to exculpate the defendant. This would seem to cover any inconsistent statements made by a prosecution witness, any failures in making an identification, and any earlier contradictory identifications. It would include the existence of witnesses whom the prosecution will not call and whom either failed to identify the defendant or identified another individual. Failure by the prosecutor to disclose such information without request may be deemed reversible error if it appears that the evidence may have raised a reasonable doubt in the jury's mind.

---

14. *Id.* at 112-13.

The standards are admittedly difficult for a prosecutor to assess before trial. In recognizing this, the Court offered the following advise:

> Because we are dealing with an inevitably imprecise standard, and because the significance of an item of evidence can seldom be predicted accurately until the entire record is complete, the prudent prosecutor will resolve doubtful questions in favor of disclosure.[15]

Although *Agurs* did not specifically deal with a question of eyewitness identification evidence, the lower courts were quick to apply its reasoning to such cases. One year after *Agurs,* the Fifth Circuit reversed a murder conviction because the state prosecutor failed to disclose to the defense attorney the existence of an eyewitness who positively identified the culprit as someone other than the defendant.[16] The Louisiana Supreme Court followed this with another *Agurs* reversal where the prosecution failed to disclose to the defense the fact that two of the state's eyewitnesses who had identified the defendant in court had earlier made a mistaken identification.[17] Other courts have followed suit.

§ 10-3. Due Process: Effect of Suggestive Pretrial Identification on In-Court Identification.

Assuming that an eyewitness has identified the defendant during a suggestive lineup, showup, or photographic display, defense counsel will certainly make a motion to suppress any evidence of that pretrial identification. In other words, counsel will attempt to prevent the prosecutor from letting the jury know — through testimony of the eyewitness or of a police officer present at the pretrial identification — that the witness has successfully identified the defendant on an earlier occasion. But what effect does the

15. *Id.* at 108.

16. Cannon v. Alabama, 558 F.2d 1211 (5th Cir. 1977).

17. State v. Falkins, 356 So. 2d 415 (La. 1978).

tainted pretrial identification have on the admissibility of an in-court identification? Knowing that an in-court identification is usually nothing more than a formality, a mechanical repetition of the much more critical pretrial identification, can defense counsel move to suppress any in-court identification by the witness on the grounds that it is tainted by the suggestive pretrial identification?

§ 10-3.1. Fairness vs. Reliability.

In understanding whether a given in-court identification will be suppressed or not on the grounds that it has been unfairly influenced by a suggestive pretrial identification procedure, it will prove helpful to briefly review the recent development of legal standards to be applied (covered in greater detail in § 8, *supra*).

§ 10-3.2. The "Independent Source" Rule.

Assuming that defense counsel can establish that a pretrial identification proceeding was so unconstitutionally suggestive as to render the pretrial identification unfair and "unreliable," or that a post-indictment lineup was held without counsel, he will move to suppress any evidence of that pretrial identification. Counsel will further argue that the procedures will "taint" an in-court identification as well, and therefore any in-court identification should also be suppressed. In so doing, however, he may be confronted by an argument made by the prosecutor to the effect that the in-court identification has a source independent from the showup, lineup, or mug shot display.

The Supreme Court in *Wade* specifically dealt with the question of whether the in-court identification must be suppressed in every case where there was a violation of a basic constitutional right at the pretrial identification proceeding.

> [T]he proper test to be applied in these situations is that quoted in *Wong Sun v. United States,* 371 U.S.

> 471, 488 . . . . "Whether, granting establishment of the primary illegality, the evidence to which instant objection is made has been come at by exploitation of that illegality or instead by means sufficiently distinguishable to be purged of the primary taint. . . ." On the record before us we cannot make the determination whether the in-court identifications had an independent origin.[18]

The standard to be applied, then, is the "fruit of the poisonous tree" doctrine: If the in-court identification can be shown to be a direct result of the pretrial identification procedure, then the in-court identification is tainted and must be suppressed. To put it another way, the in-court identification may be permitted if the prosecution can show that it has an independent origin or source.

But what factors should the trial court consider in determining whether the identification of the defendant before the jury has a source independent of the lineup, showup, or mug shot display? The *Wade* court set forth some suggested guidelines:

> Application of this test in the present context requires consideration of various factors: for example, the prior opportunity to observe the alleged criminal act, the existence of any discrepancy between any pre-lineup description and the defendant's actual description, any identification prior to lineup of another person, the identification by picture of the defendant prior to the lineup, failure to identify the defendant on a prior occasion, and the lapse of time between the alleged act and the lineup identification. It is also relevant to consider those facts which, despite the absence of counsel, are disclosed concerning the conduct of the lineup.[19]

What about *Neal v. Biggers?*[20] As was discussed in

18. 388 U.S. at 241-42, 87 S. Ct. 1926, 18 L. Ed. 2d 1149 (1967).

19. *Id.* at 241.

20. 409 U.S. 188, 93 S. Ct. 375, 34 L. Ed. 2d 401 (1972).

§ 10-3.1 *supra,* the Supreme Court in the 1972 case altered the *Stoval — Simmons* due process standard of "fairness" to one of "reliability." Thus, where a pretrial identification proceeding was challenged on due process grounds (*Biggers* does not apply to denial of counsel cases), the trial court is to determine not whether the proceedings and identification are "fair" but whether they are reliable — by which the Court appears to have meant "accurate." The Court set forth suggested guidelines for determining whether the identification is reliable:

> (1) the opportunity of the witness to view the criminal at the time of the crime, (2) the witness' degree of attention, (3) the accuracy of of the witness' prior description of the criminal, (4) the level of certainty demonstrated by the witness at the confrontation, (5) the length of time between the crime and the confrontation.[21]

Counsel should note the similarity between the *Wade* and *Biggers* guidelines: Both appear to apply external factors not known to the witness at the time of observing the suspect at the scene of the crime, and both appear primarily concerned with reliability or accuracy — not fairness. In other words, the differences between "independent source" and "reliability" seem minimal. Understandably, then, the courts have been somewhat confused in their applications.

There are important differences, however, and they should be clearly understood. First, the "independent source" rule applies to both due process and denial of counsel issues; the "reliability" standard applies only to due process issues. Second, the "reliability" test applies to evidence of pretrial identifications; "independent source"

---

21. *Id.* at 199.

refers to in-court identification. Third, the "independent source" rule is only to be applied to the circumstances attending the commission of the crime; the *Biggers* "reliability" test applies only to the circumstances attending the pretrial identification procedure. Fourth, the defendant has the burden of proving a violation of due process (*i.e.,* lack of reliability); the prosecution bears the burden of establishing "independent source" by "clear and convincing evidence."

Nevertheless, the courts today appear unwilling to distinguish between the in-court identification "independent source" standard and the pretrial identification "reliability" standard. At least one court has expressly stated that the two "are essentially the same."[22]

§ 10-4. Denial of Counsel at Post-Indictment Lineup.

As has been discussed at length in an earlier section (§ 7 *supra*), the Supreme Court in *United States v. Wade*[23] clearly established the right of a suspect to have counsel at a lineup identification proceeding. However, this requirement was later modified by the *Kirby v. Illinois*[24] decision to apply only to *post-indictment* lineup situations. Currently, therefore, all defendants who are placed in lineups after having been indicted or otherwise formally charged have an absolute right to have counsel present. This right was extended in *Moore v. Illinois* to preliminary hearings and to any proceeding after the "initiation of adversary judicial criminal proceedings."[25]

22. Patterson v. United States, 384 A.2d at 666, n. 2. *See also* Thacker v. South Carolina, 438 F. Supp. 447 (D.S.C. 1977); Commonwealth v. Gordon, 374 N.E.2d 1228 (Mass. 1978); United States v. Mann, 557 F.2d 1211 (5th Cir. 1977).

23. 388 U.S. 218, 87 S. Ct. 1926, 18 L. Ed. 2d 1149 (1967).

24. 406 U.S. 682, 92 S. Ct. 1877, 32 L. Ed. 2d 411.

25. 434 U.S. at 229 (1977).

Evidence of any pretrial identification occurring at a post-indictment lineup would be clearly inadmissible where there was a denial of the *Wade* right to counsel. Just as obvious, however, the Supreme Court has held that the sanction for denial of counsel at a post-indictment lineup is the exclusion of any in-court identification.

> Since counsel's presence at the lineup would equip him to attack not only the lineup identification but the courtroom identification as well, limiting the impact of violation of the right to counsel to exclusion of evidence only of identification at the lineup itself disregards a critical element of that right.[26]

This was reasserted by the Court in *Gilbert v. California,* in referring to its decision in *Wade:*

> We there held that a post-indictment pretrial lineup at which the accused is exhibited to identifying witnesses is a critical stage of the criminal prosecution; that police conduct of such a lineup without notice to and in the absence of his counsel denies the accused his Sixth Amendment right to counsel and calls in question the admissibility at trial of the in-court identifications of the accused by witnesses who attended the lineup.[27]

The remedy of exclusion is not automatic, however. In-court identification testimony will be permitted despite the denial of counsel if the prosecution can show either that the in-court identification has an "independent source" (see § 10-3.2 *supra*) or, on appeal, that their introduction into evidence constituted only "harmless error" under the *Chapman* doctrine.[28] The prosecution must establish the former by "clear and convincing evidence," and the latter "beyond a reasonable doubt."

---

26. United States v. Wade, 388 U.S. at 241.

27. 388 U.S. at 272, 87 S. Ct. 1951, 18 L. Ed. 2d 1178 (1967).

28. Chapman v. California, 386 U.S. 18, 87 S. Ct. 824, 17 L. Ed. 2d 705 (1966).

For a discussion concerning the issues of substitute counsel, waiver, etc., refer to § 7 *supra.*

§ 10-5. Identification Arising from Illegal Search or Arrest: Crews.

Occasionally, defense counsel will be presented with a situation where his client was arrested without probable cause and placed in a lineup. If an eyewitness identifies him in the lineup, counsel may have grounds for suppressing any evidence of the pretrial identification (see § 11-2.2.3 *infra*). Further, he may well be able to have any in-court identification resulting from that lineup identification excluded as "fruit of the poisonous tree."

Clearly, intangible evidence is as susceptible to suppression for Fourth Amendment violations as is physical evidence.[29] A number of cases have specifically suppressed in-court identifications resulting from unlawful arrest [30] or unnecessary delay in arraignment.[31] However, the various jurisdictions have disagreed on exactly what standards are to be applied and how to apply them. Some courts will permit an in-court identification where the taint of the unlawful arrest or search has been sufficiently "attenuated." Other courts will allow the eyewitness to identify the defendant in court where the prosecutor is able to show an "independent source" for the in-court identification. Still others have overruled motions to suppress on the theory that the defendant would have eventually been arrested anyway (the "inevitability" theory).

---

29. Mapp v. Ohio, 367 U.S. 643, 81 S. Ct. 1684, 6 L. Ed. 2d 1081 (1961); Wong Sun v. United States, 371 U.S. 471, 83 S. Ct. 407, 9 L. Ed. 2d 441 (1963).

30. *See, e.g.,* United States v. Barragan-Martinez, 504 F.2d 1155 (9th Cir. 1974); People v. Glover, 64 Ill. App. 3d 662, 351 N.E.2d 439 (1978).

31. *See, e.g.,* Adams v. United States, 399 F.2d 574 (D.C. Cir. 1968).

The confusion was somewhat clarified in 1980 by the Supreme Court in *United States v. Crews.*[32] In *Crews,* the defendant had been photographed by the police during an illegal detention; a witness later identified the photograph from a mug shot display. The Court affirmed the suppression of evidence of the pretrial identification, but reversed the lower court's reversal and held the in-court identification admissible. The Court then went on to hold in essence that the *Biggers — Brathwaite* test of "reliability" previously applied to due process and Sixth Amendment violations would also be applied to Fourth Amendment violations.

In its reasoning, the *Crews* court isolated the three suppressible elements of an in-court identification: the presence of the witness; the presence of the defendant; and the source of the witness' knowledge. In Crews' case, the witness was clearly present as the direct result of no unlawful police activity. The defendant's own presence was not relevant. The Court simply declared: "[Defendant] is not himself a suppressible 'fruit.' "[33] As for the witness' knowledge, she was able to identify the defendant in court based upon her observations at the scene of the crime — "the toxin in this case was injected only after the evidentiary bud had blossomed."[34] The Court then went on to say:

> This is not to say that the intervening photographic and lineup identifications — both of which are conceded to be suppressible fruits of the Fourth Amendment violation — could not under some circumstances affect the reliability of the in-court identification and render it inadmissible as well. Indeed, given the vagaries of

32. 445 U.S. 463, 100 S. Ct. 1244, 63 L. Ed. 2d 537 (1980).
33. *Id.* at 474.
34. *Id.* at 472.

> human memory and the inherent suggestibility of many identification procedures, just the opposite may be true. But in the present case the trial court expressly found that the witness' courtroom identification rested on an independent recollection of her initial encounter with the assailant, uninfluenced by the pretrial identifications. . . .[35]

Thus, the violation of the defendant's Fourth Amendment right does not result in automatic suppression of in-court identification. The witness' identification of the defendant before a jury will be permitted if it can be shown that it has an independent source. However, the language of the Court seems to suggest that by "independent source" it, in fact, means "reliability." Certainly, the factors which have been suggested by the Supreme Court to be considered as to each are very similar.[36]

In summary, defense counsel may be able to suppress in-court identification of his client where it stems from an earlier lineup, showup, or mug shot display which is tainted by an illegal search or seizure. It will not be suppressed, however, if the prosecution can establish that the facts indicate the witness' in-court identification is reliable independent of the lineup, showup, or mug shot spread.

For a discussion of suppression of pretrial identification evidence, refer to § 11-2.2.3 *infra.*

---

35. *Id.* at 473.

36. *See* Neal v. Biggers, 409 U.S. at 199, and United States v. Wade, 388 U.S. at 241.

§ 11. Corroboration of Identification Testimony.

> "[C]onvictions based solely on 'one eyewitness' identifications represent conceivably the greatest single threat to the achievement of our ideal that no innocent man shall be punished." [1]
>
> Senior Circuit Judge David L. Bazelon

Corroboration of an identification during trial by an eyewitness will generally take one of two forms: third party corroboration or corroboration through the witness' own prior identification. In the first, the in-court identification is reenforced through the testimony of other witnesses or through the introduction of other evidence to the effect that the defendant is, in fact, the guilty party. This can take the form of a second eyewitness; more commonly it consists of independent physical evidence such as fingerprints which tend to connect the defendant with the crime independent of the eyewitness identification.

The second form of corroboration is in the form of reenforcement from the eyewitness himself. This usually consists of introducing evidence of prior identification by the eyewitness — *i.e.,* evidence that the witness had on earlier occasions identified the defendant either in person or by photograph.

1. United States v. Butler, 636 F.2d at 732 (D.C. Cir. 1980).

§ 11-1. Third-Party Corroboration and the "One Witness" Rule.

It must be recognized at the outset that, at present, there are simply no American jurisdictions which require the identification testimony of an eyewitness to be corroborated, either by the identification testimony of a second eyewitness or by evidence tending to independently connect the defendant with the offense. Quite simply, the present state of the law almost universally recognizes that a conviction can stand upon the lone testimony of a single eyewitness; nothing more is required to sustain a conviction than the identification by one witness. This has come to be known — derisively by its many critics — as the "one witness" rule.

There are exceptions to be found to this general rule. However, these exceptions apply only to certain kinds of charged offenses. Thus, the Federal courts will require corroboration of a witness' testimony in cases involving "particular crimes, notably 'sex' offenses, where the urge to fantasize or motive to fabricate makes the risk of unjust conviction high." [2] Many state courts also have varying corroboration requirements where the complaint charges such sex-related offenses as rape, incest, abortion, fornication, adultery, breach of marital promise, and seduction. In addition, most states will require corroboration of the testimony of accomplices and of children.

For the most part, however, American jurisdictions continue to follow the "one-witness" rule allowing a case to be proven through the uncorroborated testimony of a single eyewitness. But the rule has drawn more than its share of fire from both scholarly commentators and from the courts, and it is reasonable to assume that this area of law rep-

2. United States v. Telfaire, 469 F.2d at 554 (D.C. Cir. 1972).

resents one which is ripe for change in the coming years. For this reason alone, trial counsel should make appropriate objections and motions to protect the record on appeal; in fact, many appellate courts today will examine the record of conviction resting upon uncorroborated testimony with particular scrutiny, and even reverse upon grounds which may not have normally been sufficient in the presence of corroborated testimony.

The "one witness" rule has long been a battleground for conflicting opinions by recognized commentators. As early as 1948, for example, a report by a New York Judicial Council on the problems of eyewitness identification concluded that such evidence "is perhaps of all classes of evidence the least to be relied upon, and therefore, unless supported by other facts, an unsafe basis for the verdict of a jury." [3] Yet Wigmore, in defending the existing rule, concluded in 1940 that

> our whole presumption should be against any specific rule requiring a number of witnesses, or corroboration of a single witness; that such arbitrary measurements are likely to be of little real efficacy and to introduce disadvantages greater than those which they purport to avoid . . . .
>
> The readiness of the modern American professional mind to cling to rules formally requiring corroboration is due mainly to the natural desire to protect the litigants from the unrestrained and inexperienced mental processes of the jury. But the true way to afford this protection is to empower the judge to comment on the testimony.[4]

On the other hand, one of the most prominent modern commentators on the topic of eyewitness identification, Patrick M. Wall, has argued that

3. "Fourteenth Annual Report of the Judicial Council, State of New York," pp. 229, 257-58 (1948).

4. 7 Wigmore § 2033 at 259 (3d ed. 1940).

> it is clear that those who are familiar with the administration of criminal justice realize that one of its greatest problems is that posed by evidence of eye-witness identification. It is upon this issue that there is the greatest danger of a miscarriage of justice. Surely, if corroboration is ever useful and necessary, it is useful and necessary with respect to this issue. Approximately half of the fifty states require corroboration of the testimony of an accomplice; none requires that identification evidence be corroborated. Yet surely there is greater danger of convicting an innocent man upon the latter testimony than upon the former. Granted that a witness who has participated in a crime may falsely accuse an innocent man, but is this as likely to happen as is an honest mistake in identification? Assuming that such a witness does falsely implicate another, his perjury is usually far more easily exposed, since it must be rather detailed, than is the honest mistake of a person who testifies as to identity. If experience and logic teach us anything, it is that identification evidence has a greater need for corroboration than any other kind of evidence.[5]

Wall is far from alone in his position. There appears to be a small but growing wave of modern opinion in support of the need for corroboration of eyewitness testimony. Houts, for example, concludes in his treatise on evidence that "no person should be convicted of a crime solely on the uncorroborated identification of eye witnesses unless it can be shown that the witnesses were previously acquainted with the accused." [6] In Great Britain, Lord Patrick Devlin's prestigious "Committee on Identification in Criminal Cases" concluded after a lengthy study of the problem that requiring corroboration "is the obvious remedy when the prosecution is relying upon a class of evidence that may have inherent defects." [7]

5. Wall, *Eyewitness Identification in Criminal Cases*, p. 187 (Charles C. Thomas 1965).

6. Houts, *From Evidence to Proof*, p. 26 (1956).

7. Devlin, "Report to the Secretary of State for the Home Department of the Departmental Committee on Identification in Criminal Cases," p.

In all probability, the "one witness" rule will not soon be abrogated, but like the hearsay rule, it is likely to experience an increasing number of exceptions to its general application. Existing exceptions as to certain types of offenses have already been noted, but it is probable that these exceptions will begin expanding beyond categorized offenses and into general situations.

A preview of this erosion of the "one witness" rule can perhaps be seen in (as has often been the case in the past) a dissenting opinion of Senior Circuit Judge David Bazelon of the District of Columbia Circuit Court of Appeals. In a 1980 case involving the uncorroborated testimony of a police undercover narcotics officer, Judge Bazelon suggested the need for an exception to the rule:

> One need not be versed in the extraordinary unreliability of eyewitness testimony to tremble at the spectre of policemen roaming the streets with warrants for the arrest of nameless citizens who will be plucked from the throng and convicted based upon the uncorroborated memory of the arresting officer. That this is standard procedure is appalling. That it is standard procedure in cases where corroborating evidence could be obtained with reasonable effort is unconscionable.
>
> To use the "one eyewitness" rule to support convictions where corroboration can be obtained with reasonable effort is to expand that rule far beyond its original justification. It may so inexcusably flirt with the danger of mistaken identification as to be a violation of due process.[8]

Judge Bazelon then went on to formulate his new exception to the "one witness rule":

> We need not entertain an across-the-board ban on convictions based upon uncorroborated eyewitness tes-

79 (London: Her Majesty's Stationery Office 1976), quoted in United States v. Butler at 735.

8. United States v. Butler, 636 F.2d at 735.

> timony to address the problem I have outlined. We already require corroborating evidence to support some "one eyewitness" testimony. I propose merely the additional requirement of a good faith effort on the part of police to obtain corroborating evidence for eyewitness testimony in cases where such evidence can be acquired with reasonable effort. In a case where the government desires to use such uncorroborated evidence, it would be required to show that it could not have reasonably acquired corroborating evidence. Fundamental fairness demands this much.[9]

It should perhaps be noted that although rejecting Judge Bazelon's exception to the "one-witness" rule, the majority opinion cautioned trial judges to screen eyewitness cases, advising them that "[i]n deciding whether a one-witness case should go to the jury it is incumbent upon the trial judge to consider a number of factors relating to the period of identification and to determine whether the totality of circumstances gives rise to a very substantial likelihood of irreparable misidentification." [10]

In view of the current wave of recognition of the general unreliability of eyewitness identification, it is probable that Judge Bazelon's exception — as well as others — will be adopted in the near future. Both trial and appellate counsel should protect their clients' rights accordingly.

§ 11-2. Evidence of Prior Identifications: "Bolstering."

The identification of the defendant by the eyewitness during trial is, in most cases, no more than a technicality. The prosecutor is, of course, required by law to have the defendant identified in court as the guilty party, but this process is usually nothing but a well-rehearsed play in

9. *Id.*

10. *Id.* at 729.

which the actor-witness is repeating his earlier performance at pretrial police identification procedures. Dramatic though it may be, and impressive to the jury as it may appear, the in-court identification is usually a pointless exercise — the real issue is the original identification and the possibly suggestive conditions under which it was made. If there is ever any doubt in the witness' mind as to who is the culprit, he has only to look where so many television courtroom dramas have taught him to look: defense counsel's table.

Despite all this, eyewitnesses do occasionally have difficulty in identifying the defendant; they may prove forgetful or, more probably, appear hesitant or make a reluctant or inconclusive in-court identification. The prosecutor will then attempt to reenforce or "bolster" the witness' shaky testimony with evidence of earlier identifications by the witness in which he picked out the defendant with considerably more confidence. He may attempt this through asking the witness himself about his earlier statements when confronted either with the defendant or a photograph of him. If the witness is still unhelpful, the prosecutor may try to resort to third party bolstering — calling the investigating officer, for example, and having him testify to the earlier identification or identifications, as well as to the circumstances under which they were made.

In some instances, the prosecutor will rely upon bolstering techniques even where the eyewitness confidently identifies the defendant in trial. The theory here is that if one identification by the witness is good, evidence of two or three is even better: The jury is shown that the in-court identification was not just a charade, and that the witness has consistently identified the defendant all along.

In most identification cases, defense counsel will *want* evidence of prior identification received by the court. He will want to attack the in-court identification by showing that it is nothing but a reenactment of the identification at the police station lineups, for example, and that that identification was tainted by suggestive procedures. Defense counsel will want, in other words, to focus the jury's attention on the real issue in the case: the validity of the original identification. Therefore, he will not object to the bolstering tactics of the prosecutor. The catch, of course, is that the prosecutor will probably not resort to bolstering unless the in-court identification is less than positive. If the in-court identification is subject to some doubt, it is obviously in defense counsel's interests to prevent the prosecutor from introducing evidence of any earlier, more positive identifications. The focus in the next section will be upon the general admissibility of prior identifications as well as upon grounds for suppressing such evidence.

§ 11-2.1. Admissibility Generally: Hearsay.

The law as to the admissibility of evidence of prior identifications varies considerably from jurisdiction to jurisdiction, often depending upon the circumstances under which it is offered — *i.e.,* whether by the witness or by a third party, whether on direct or on redirect examination to corroborate discredited testimony and so forth. Very generally speaking, however, most state jurisdictions will permit bolstering by the eyewitness himself. The Federal Rules of Evidence [11] expressly permit a witness to testify about his own or an eyewitness' earlier identifications. As to third party bolstering, a majority of states also permit other individuals to testify as to earlier identifications made by the eyewitness, at least where the eyewitness' testimony has been discredited on cross-examination.[12]

11. Fed. R. Evid. 801(d)(1)(C).

12. *See generally* 72 A.L.R.2d 449.

At one time, bolstering of any type was completely prohibited in trial. The theory was that evidence of prior identifications was self-serving, of no probative value, and constituted an out-of-court statement offered for the truth of the matter stated — *i.e.*, hearsay. However, a number of commentators criticized this position for denying jury access to highly probative evidence. Patrick Wall, for example, strenuously argued that:

> The rule excluding evidence of prior corporeal identifications is without doubt the most senseless evidentiary rule in the area of eye-witness identification. It is no more than a mechanical application of the hearsay rule or the rule prohibiting evidence of prior consistent statements to a type of testimony which creates few of the dangers against which those rules were intended to guard. It distorts the facts by preventing the introduction of evidence which may be highly probative and of great assistance to a jury which has been delegated the responsibility of solving what is often a difficult identification problem. It should be discarded.[13]

The legislatures and courts of most jurisdictions as a result now permit bolstering, at least, by the eyewitness himself. California, for example, amended its Evidence Code to permit prior consistent statements as an exception to the hearsay rule where the witness has been impeached on cross-examination with a prior inconsistent statement or a charge of bias or other improper motive.[14] Other states have imposed no such restrictions, however, and permit unlimited bolstering by the eyewitness;[15] there is no need to wait for discrediting cross-examination to introduce evidence of earlier identifications.

A slightly different situation presents itself when evidence of the prior identification is in the form of testimony

13. Wall, *Eyewitness Identification in Criminal Cases*, p. 140 (Charles C. Thomas 1965).

14. Cal. Evid. Code §§ 791 and 1236.

15. *See, e.g.*, New York C.P.L. §§ 60.25 and 60.30.

from a police officer or other person — *i.e.*, third party bolstering. Where the evidence of prior identification is not from the eyewitness himself, many states prohibit its introduction.[16] New York, for example, which permits unrestricted bolstering from the lips of the eyewitness, denies the prosecutor the right to present such evidence from other witnesses;[17] additionally, New York prohibits any reference to prior photographic identifications by *any* witness, partly because of the fear that reference to police photos will indicate that the defendant has a criminal record. Illinois considers third party bolstering error even where the in-court identification was weak.[18] California, on the other hand, expressly legislated an exception to the hearsay rule to permit third party bolstering under limited conditions. The statute is illustrative of the approach of other jurisdictions as well:

> Evidence of a statement previously made by a witness is not made inadmissible by the hearsay rule if the statement would have been admissible if made by him while testifying (author's note: this requires under § 791 that the witness has been impeached during his testimony) and:
>
> (a) The statement is an identification of a party or another as a person who participated in a crime or other occurrence;
>
> (b) The statement was made at a time when the crime or other occurrence was fresh in the witness' memory; and
>
> (c) The evidence of the statement is offered after the witness testifies that he made the identification and that it was a true reflection of his opinion at that time.[19]

16. *E.g.*, Towning v. State, 521 P.2d 415 (Okla. 1974); State v. Degraffenreid, 477 S.W.2d 57 (Mo. 1972); Lyons v. State, 388 S.W.2d 950 (Tex. 1965).

17. *E.g.*, People v. Malloy, 22 N.Y.2d 559, 240 N.E.2d 37, 293 N.Y.S.2d 542 (1968); People v. Burgess, 66 A.D.2d 667, 410 N.Y.S.2d 837 (1978).

18. People v. Simpson, 39 Ill. App. 3d 318, 349 N.E.2d 441 (1976).

19. Cal. Evid. Code § 1238.

In attempting to prevent the prosecutor from introducing evidence of the eyewitness' earlier identifications, then, counsel must first determine what kind of bolstering is involved. Is it being offered through the eyewitness' own testimony, or through a third party? Does it involve a prior corporeal or photographic identification? Is it being offered as cumulative evidence or is its purpose to rehabilitate a discredited eyewitness? Once the nature of the attempted bolstering has been characterized, counsel must then determine whether the relevant law of the jurisdiction permits its introduction into evidence and under what conditions. If the law is vague or unsettled, a forceful argument should certainly be made that the evidence, whether from the eyewitness or a third party, constitutes inadmissible hearsay and is, additionally, both self-serving and lacking in the probative value represented by an in-court identification. Failing in that, counsel must look for grounds by which he can move to suppress evidence of pretrial identification on constitutional grounds.

§ 11-2.2. Suppressing Evidence of Prior Identification.

A suspect who is subjected to pretrial identification procedures has certain constitutional rights. Violation by the police authorities of those rights can result in suppression of evidence of an eyewitness' identification at a lineup, showup, photographic lineup or, possibly, of the actual identification in court. The courts have fluctuated as to what rights are to be granted a suspect and as to what types of identification procedures are to be used. Generally, there has been a de-emphasis in applying the right against self-incrimination, while the right to counsel and the fairness of identification proceedings have, to a limited degree, been stressed. Similarly, a suspect's constitutional rights have been extended primarily to the lineup and showup situations, to the relative exclusion of mug shot displays, voice identification procedures, and the use of composites.

If the suspect has been significantly denied a constitutional right in a manner that could affect the identification process, there would be two primary remedies: (1) suppression of evidence of the pretrial identification; and (2) suppression of any in-court identification. The next section will deal with attacking the introduction of evidence of pretrial identification.

Preferably, defense counsel should move to suppress any evidence of a pretrial identification before the commencement of trial. Upon the assertion of a denial of a constitutional right, the prosecution will have the burden of showing that the defendant was, for example, advised of his right to counsel prior to the post-indictment lineup. In the alternative, an objection during trial should be interposed before the jury hears of the nature of the offered evidence, and testimony taken on the issue out of the jurors' presence. Care should be taken that the suppression motion is made as early as possible; an objection at trial may be overruled as untimely where defense counsel was — or should have been — aware of the constitutional defect before trial.

§ 11-2.2.1. Due Process and the Per Se Exclusionary Rule: Gilbert — Brathwaite.

The primary avenue of constitutional attack on a pretrial identification involves the due process argument: The procedure used by the police to have the eyewitness make an identification was so suggestive that inherent standards of fairness were violated. What constitutes an "unfair" identification procedure? What sanctions, if any, may be imposed? These two topics are the subject of a string of sometimes confusing and contradictory Supreme Court decisions. (See § 8-1.)

§ 11-2.2.2. Denial of Counsel at Post-Indictment Lineup.

As was discussed in some detail in § 7 ("The Right to Counsel at Identification Proceedings"), the Supreme Court in *United States v. Wade*[20] recognized the dangers to a suspect inherent in police pretrial identification proceedings and therefore granted him the right to counsel at this critical stage:

> Since it appears that there is grave potential for prejudice, intentional or not, in the pretrial lineup, which may not be capable of reconstruction at trial, and since presence of counsel itself can often avert prejudice and assure a meaningful confrontation at trial, there can be little doubt that for Wade the post-indictment lineup was a critical stage of the prosecution at which he was "as much entitled to aid (of counsel) . . . as at the trial itself" (cite). Thus, both Wade and his counsel should have been notified of the impending lineup, and counsel's presence should have been a prerequisite to conduct of the lineup, absent an "intelligent waiver" (cite).[21]

The holding was clear: A suspect in a pretrial identification proceeding had a constitutional right to have counsel present. The standard for determining suppression was made equally clear by the Court in quoting from *Wong Sun v. United States:*

> [W]hether, granting establishment of the primary illegality, the evidence to which instant objection is made has been come at by exploitation of that illegality by means sufficiently distinguishable to be purged of the primary taint.[22]

The *Wade* Court further held that where counsel is denied to a lineup suspect, evidence of the resulting lineup identifi-

20. 388 U.S. 218, 87 S. Ct. 1926, 18 L. Ed. 1149 (1967).

21. *Id.* at 236-37.

22. 371 U.S. at 488, 83 S. Ct. 407, 9 L. Ed. 2d 441 (1963).

cation is inadmissible in trial. Further, any in-court identification resulting from the pretrial identification would also be suppressed if the prosecution could not establish by clear and convincing evidence that the in-court identification was not based upon the tainted pretrial identifications.

Five years later the Supreme Court severely limited the application of *Wade*. In *Kirby v. Illinois*,[23] the Court held that the right to counsel was only to be applied to *post-indictment* situations. Despite extensive criticism, the law has emerged requiring counsel to be afforded a suspect only if he is required to take part in a post-indictment lineup or showup.

For most practical purposes, the right established by *Wade* has been effectively emasculated by *Kirby*. By limiting the right to counsel to post-indictment proceedings, the *Kirby* court eliminated the presence of counsel at almost all identification proceedings in which identification is a critical issue. A post-indictment lineup takes place only after a suspect has been formally charged — *i.e.*, after the police *already* have sufficient evidence to prosecute. The pre-indictment lineup, on the other hand, usually is necessary because there is insufficient evidence to justify the filing of charges. In other words, *Kirby* grants the suspect the right to counsel when he least needs it.

Many state courts have been openly critical in reluctantly applying *Kirby*,[24] and a number of them have flatly refused to impose the watered-down version of *Wade*, electing instead to extend the right to counsel to pretrial identification situations occurring prior to indictment or

---

23. 406 U.S. 682, 92 S. Ct. 1877, 32 L. Ed. 2d 411 (1972).

24. *See, e.g.*, People v. Chojnacky, 8 Cal. 3d 759, 505 P.2d 530 (1973); State v. Gray, 503 S.W.2d 457 (Mo. 1973).

arraignment.[25] The Michigan Supreme Court has held that since *Kirby* was not binding upon the states, it was free to require that counsel be available to a suspect at any lineup or showup conducted after his arrest.[26] In Tennessee, the right to counsel at pretrial identification procedures attaches when an arrest warrant has been issued.[27] In New York, Louisiana and Alabama, a suspect must be permitted to have previously retained counsel present at the pre-indictment lineup or showup.[28]

Perhaps reacting to rather widespread criticism of the *Kirby* decision, the Supreme Court in 1977 made certain rather obvious concessions. In *Moore v. Illinois,*[29] the Court conceded that a defendant in a preliminary hearing or other pretrial judicial proceeding where an identification is made has a right to counsel even though no formal indictment has been filed. Further, the Court confirmed that the post-indictment right to counsel applied to showups as well as lineups. But the *Kirby* version of *Wade* remains: A suspect has a right to counsel at pretrial identification proceedings only after an indictment/information has been filed. If he is denied this right, any resulting identification may be suppressed as "fruit of the poisonous tree."

§ 11-2.2.3. Identification Tainted by Illegal Search or Arrest.

Can evidence of a pretrial identification be suppressed at

25. *See, e.g.,* Blue v. State, 558 P.2d 636 (Alaska 1977); Commonwealth v. Richman, 458 Pa. 167, 320 A.2d 351 (1974); State v. Kiraly, 56 Ohio App. 2d 37, 381 N.E.2d 649 (1977).

26. People v. Anderson, 389 Mich. 155, 205 N.W.2d 461 (1973); People v. Jackson, 391 Mich. 323, 217 N.W.2d 22 (1974).

27. State v. Mitchell, 593 S.W.2d 280 (Tenn. 1980).

28. People v. Blake, 35 N.Y.2d 331, 320 N.E. 625 (1974); State v. Vaughn, 378 So. 2d 905 (1979); Sparks v. State, 376 So. 2d 834 (Ala. 1979).

29. 434 U.S. 220, 98 S. Ct. 458, 54 L. Ed. 2d 424 (1977).

trial on the grounds that it was the result of an unlawful arrest of the defendant? In other words, does an arrest without probable cause invalidate a subsequent pretrial eyewitness identification?

Assuming that the defendant has been arrested unlawfully — *i.e.,* there has been a "seizure" of his person without probable cause — the Fourth Amendment makes inadmissible not only any physical evidence obtained as a result of the arrest, but also any intangible evidence.[30] As with a confession, a pretrial identification would appear to constitute such intangible evidence. It would seem that the question involves a simple determination of whether the pretrial identification "has been come at by exploitation of that illegality or instead by means sufficiently distinguishable to be purged of the primary taint."[31] Yet, as always, there has been some confusion when it comes to applying the concept to given facts.

In 1980 the Supreme Court in *United States v. Crews*[32] addressed the issue of suppression of an *in*-court identification; prior to trial, and after his illegal arrest, the defendant had been identified by photographs and then in a court-ordered lineup. The Court concluded that the in-court identifications were admissible, but concurred with the lower court's suppression of the *pretrial* identification. The identified photographs of the defendant were "fruit of the poisonous tree" as was the lineup, and therefore the identifications resulting from both should be suppressed. Yet the Court failed to spell this reasoning out, preferring instead to address itself to the in-court identification issue alone (see § 10-5 *supra*), leaving the suppression of the

30. Mapp v. Ohio, 367 U.S. 643, 81 S. Ct. 1684, 6 L. Ed. 2d 1081 (1961); Wong Sun v. United States, 371 U.S. 471, 83 S. Ct. 407, 9 L. Ed. 2d 441 (1963).

31. 371 U.S. at 487-88.

32. 445 U.S. 463 (1980).

pretrial identification stand by recognizing that "the intervening photographic and lineup identifications . . . are conceded to be suppressible fruits of the Fourth Amendment violation." [33]

It would appear clear that an arrest of the defendant without probable cause, followed by a lineup, showup, or photographic identification, would result in suppression of any evidence of the pretrial identification. But what if the defendant was lawfully arrested but the identification took place during an illegally long pre-arraignment delay? What if a witness identifies a mug shot of the defendant which had been obtained as the result of an unlawful arrest? What would be the result where the *identifying witness* is found by an illegal search and subsequently identifies the defendant?

In *Adams v. United States* [34] a Federal court addressed the issue of a defendant who had been legally arrested but whose arraignment was unnecessarily delayed; it was during the delay that he was identified in a lineup as the perpetrator of another offense altogether. The court reversed the conviction, ruling that the defendant had, in effect, been arrested without probable cause on the second offense and that this tainted the lineup identification. Then — Justice Warren Burger concurred with the result, but only because the identification was made during an unnecessary delay. He argued that an illegal arrest does not *necessarily* taint a pretrial identification; if a suspect is already legally in custody, an additional "arrest on probable cause would be totally superfluous — a sheer ritual serving no legitimate protective function." [35]

Chief Justice Burger's reasoning has been followed in at least two state cases where police arrested the defendant

33. *Id.* at 472.

34. 399 F.2d 574 (D.C. Cir. 1968).

35. *Id.* at 581.

illegally and then discovered he was involved with another crime.[36] In those cases, the courts ruled that the subsequent identifications as to the second crimes were attenuated sufficiently to permit their introduction into evidence.

It would seem to follow from the "fruit of the poisonous tree" doctrine that evidence of an identification of a mug shot taken by the police affer an illegal arrest should be suppressed. Although this reasoning has been followed,[37] there is at least one case admitting evidence of the photographic identification on the theory that the photograph could have been obtained by the police by other means.[38]

A different situation is presented where the identifying witness is the person who has been unlawfully obtained by the police. If the subsequent identification is the direct result of the police finding the witness during an illegal search, the identification should be suppressed.[39] On the other hand, if the defendant was found and placed in a lineup as the result of the illegal confession of another, the identification may be permissible.[40]

The courts are particularly reluctant to suppress identification evidence as the result of unlawful searches or arrests. Consequently, a number of ingenious exceptions to the exclusionary rule have been formulated. The first of these is the "independent source" exception: The taint of an illegal arrest or search can be eliminated where an independent source for the identification can be established.[41] The

36. People v. Teresinski, 26 Cal. 3d 457, 605 P.2d 874 (1980); People v. Ramsey, 77 Ill. App. 3d 294, 395 N.E.2d 973 (1979).

37. *See, e.g.,* Jones v. Commonwealth, 556 S.W.2d 918 (Ky. 1977).

38. United States v. Jarvis, 560 F.2d 494 (2d Cir. 1977).

39. *See, e.g.,* People v. Stoner, 65 Cal. 2d 595, 422 P.2d 585 (1967); People v. Albea, 2 Ill. 2d 317, 118 N.E.2d 277 (1954).

40. *See, e.g.,* Gissendanner v. Wainwright, 482 F.2d 1293 (5th Cir. 1973).

41. *See, e.g.,* Commonwealth v. Davis, 400 A.2d 199 (Pa. 1979); Wright

second is the "inevitable discovery" rule: If the defendant would have eventually been arrested anyway, then the fact of an illegal arrest does not taint the identification sufficiently to justify suppression.[42] The third is the attenuation doctrine: The taint of the illegal conduct has been sufficiently attenuated by intervening time and/or events to justify admission of evidence of the identification. This is, of course, a general doctrine used in any discussion of tainted evidence, but it can be applied very liberally by a court determined to justify admission of identification evidence. A fourth means used to avoid the exclusion mandate is denial of causation. One state court has simply held that the mere fact of an illegal arrest "furnished only the occasion for the identification; it did not suggest or influence it." [43] Perhaps the most direct theory for avoidance was adopted by North Carolina in simply ruling that "the Constitution protects no citizen from being viewed by the police or other citizens at the invitation of the police." [44] Despite the evasive efforts of many courts, however, the law remains: Pretrial identifications directly resulting from an unlawful search or arrest must be suppressed as tainted evidence.

§ 11-3. The Cautionary Jury Instruction: Telfaire.

There is an increasing recognition by the appellate courts of the general unreliability of eyewitness identification, accompanied by a judicial mistrust of the jury's disturbing reliance upon eyewitness testimony. Yet the courts are understandably reluctant to comment directly upon the credibility of such witnesses.

---

v. State, 528 S.W.2d 905 (Ark. 1975); People v. Hunter, 607 P.2d 1026 (Colo. 1979).

42. *See, e.g.,* Commonwealth v. Regan, 253 Pa. Super. 92, 384 A.2d 1243 (Pa. 1978).

43. State v. Brown, 50 Wisc. 565, 185 N.W.2d at 326 (1971).

44. State v. Matthews, 295 N.C. 265, 245 S.E.2d at 737, *cert. denied,* 439 U.S. 1128 (1979).

This problem was directly addressed in a series of decisions by Federal circuit courts which established the need for cautionary instructions to be given juries in criminal prosecutions relying heavily upon eyewitness identification. The first of these was *United States v. Barber,* a 1971 Third Circuit case in which the court stated that

> while we endorse the wide latitude to be accorded the trial courts in the area of jury instructions, we recognize a compelling need for guidelines which will obviate skeletal, pattern instructions and assure the essential particularity demanded by the facts surrounding each identification. Accordingly, we approve for use in this circuit the approach taken by the Pennsylvania courts concerning jury instructions on identification, and require, for prospective application only, that such instructions satisfy the following:[45]

The *Barber* court then set forth its mandate respecting instructions to be given in eyewitness identification cases.

> In any case raising the question whether the defendant was in fact the criminal actor, the jury will be instructed to resolve any conflict or uncertainty on the issue of identification. The jury will be instructed that identification may be made through the perception of any of the witness' senses, and that it is not essential that the witness himself be free from doubt as to the correctness of his opinion. The identification testimony may be treated by the jury as a statement of fact by the witness: (1) if the witness had the opportunity to observe the accused; (2) if the witness is positive in his identification; (3) if the witness' identification testimony is not weakened by prior failure to identify or by prior inconsistent identification; *and* (4) if, after cross-examination, his testimony remains positive and unqualified. In the absence of *any one* of these four conditions, however, the jury will be admonished by the court that the witness' testimony as to identity *must be received with caution and scrutinized with care.* The

45. United States v. Barber, 442 F.2d at 528 (3d Cir. 1971).

> burden of proof on the prosecution extends to every element of the crime charged, including the burden of proving beyond a reasonable doubt the identity of the defendant as the perpetrator of the crime for which he stands charged. (Emphasis added).

This ruling was followed one year later by the decision of the District of Columbia Circuit in *United States v. Telfaire.*[46] In this landmark case, the court reluctantly recognized the existence of the "one witness rule" (see § 11-1 *supra*), but then strongly suggested that cautionary instructions be given in cases where "the minds of the jury were plainly focused on the need for finding the identification of the defendant as the offender proved beyond a reasonable doubt."[47] The court took notice of the recent *Barber* decision, then clearly set forth the following directive:

> To further the administration of justice in the District of Columbia the Appendix contains a model instruction, using material from *Barber* to some extent, which trial judges can use to focus on the identification issue — with revision and adaptation to suit the proof and contentions of a particular case. It is not being set forth in terms of compulsion, but *failure to use this model, with appropriate adaptations, would constitute a risk in future cases that should not be ignored* unless there is strong reason in the particular case.[48] (Emphasis added.)

After this strong language, the court then set forth in an appendix what has become known as the *Telfaire* instruction:

> *Model Special Instructions on Identification.*
>
> One of the most important issues in this case is the identification of the defendant as the perpetrator of the crime. The Government has the burden of providing

46. United States v. Telfaire, 469 F.2d 552 (D.C. Cir. 1972).
47. *Id.* at 556.
48. *Id.* at 557.

(sic) identity beyond a reasonable doubt. It is not essential that the witness himself be free from doubt as to the correctness of his statement. However, you, the jury, must be satisfied beyond a reasonable doubt of the accuracy of the identification of the defendant before you may convict him. If you are not convinced beyond a reasonable doubt that the defendant was the person who committed the crime, you must find the defendant not guilty.

Identification testimony is an expression of belief or impression by the witness. Its value depends on the opportunity the witness had to observe the offender at the time of the offense and to make a reliable identification later.

In appraising the identification testimony of a witness, you should consider the following:

(1) Are you convinced that the witness had the capacity and an adequate opportunity to observe the offender?

Whether the witness had an adequate opportunity to observe the offender at the time of the offense will be affected by such matters as how long or short a time was available, how far or close the witness was, how good were lighting conditions, whether the witness had had occasion to see or know the person in the past.

[In general, a witness bases any identification he makes on his perception through the use of his senses. Usually the witness identifies an offender by the sense of sight — but this is not necessarily so, and he may use other senses.] *

(2) Are you satisfied that the identification made by the witness subsequent to the offense was the product of his own recollection? You may take into account both the strength of the identification, and the circumstances under which the identification was made.

If the identification by the witness may have been influenced by the circumstances under which the defendant was presented to him for identification, you should scrutinize the identification with great care. You may also consider the length of time that lapsed between the occurrence of the crime and the next opportunity of the witness to see defendant, as a factor bearing on the reliability of the identification.

[You may also take into account that an identification made by picking the defendant out of a group of similar individuals is generally more reliable than one which results from the presentation of the defendant alone to the witness.]

[(3) You may take into account any occasions in which the witness failed to make an identification of defendant, or made an identification that was inconsistent with his identification at trial.]

(4) Finally, you must consider the credibility of each identification witness in the same way as any other witness, consider whether he is truthful, and consider whether he had the capacity and opportunity to make a reliable observation on the matter covered in his testimony.

I again emphasize that the burden of proof on the prosecutor extends to every element of the crime charged, and this specifically includes the burden of proving beyond a reasonable doubt the identity of the defendant as the perpetrator of the crime with which he stands charged. If after examining the testimony, you have a reasonable doubt as to the accuracy of the identification, you must find the defendant not guilty.

* Sentences in brackets to be used only if appropriate. Instructions to be inserted or modified as appropriate to the proof and contentions.[49]

The *Telfaire* Court thus created a model instruction which advised the jury to consider eyewitness testimony with a cautious eye and while not actually *requiring* the

49. *Id.* at 558.

courts in the District of Columbia to give such an instruction in an appropriate situation, the Court did strongly suggest that "failure to use this model, with appropriate adaptations, would constitute a risk." [50]

Since *Telfaire,* the other circuits have taken varying positions concerning adoption of such an instruction. Some have been reluctant to require the instruction, feeling that it amounts to a commentary on the evidence by the trial judge and thus invades the province of the jury. The Ninth Circuit, for example, has noted that "the giving of jury instructions on identification rests largely within the discretion of the trial judge," adding that "this court has repeatedly declined to require the use of the *Telfaire* instruction." [51] However, even that court made note of the fact that there was no abuse of this discretion since the trial court had instructed the jury that eyewitness identification testimony "should be considered with great caution and weighed with great care." [52]

Another reluctant approach to the problem has been to limit the requirement of a cautionary instruction to the narrowest circumstances. The Tenth Circuit Court in 1980 decided "that it is not error to refuse to give a *Telfaire* instruction where the Government's case does not hang on a single eyewitness, and where there is in fact corroborating evidence." [53] The Second Circuit has held that reversal for failure to give a cautionary instruction was not necessary where the identification was not "dubious" and the conviction did not rest alone on eyewitness testimony.[54] The First Circuit has expressed similar limitations, recognizing the appropriateness of a *Telfaire* instruction but refusing to

---

50. *Id.* at 557.

51. United States v. Collins, 559 F.2d at 566 (9th Cir. 1977).

52. *Id.* at 566.

53. United States v. Cueto, 628 F.2d 1273 (10th Cir. 1980).

54. United States v. Montelbano, 605 F.2d 56 (2d Cir. 1979).

reverse for failure to give it where the court's remaining instructions covered much of the requested instruction and where, in any event, the case "did not hinge on possibly mistaken identification testimony alone. . . . Independent evidence connected the defendants with the crime."[55] The court went on to say:

> We are tempted to join the majority of other circuits by announcing that in the future the preferred practice in this circuit will be to give a particularized identification charge at the request of counsel when the evidence establishes a factual basis for it. But, for the present at least, we resist the temptation. . . . We are confident that district courts will, in situations where misidentification is a real risk, remind jurors of their critical task of assessment.[56]

As stated, however, the majority of federal jurisdictions today have expressed at least a preference that an instruction of the *Telfaire* type be given — though often couching it in terms of strong suggestion rather than outright requirement. The Eighth Circuit Court has stated that "although we do not specifically adopt the *Telfaire* model instruction today, we will view with grave concern the failure to give specific and detailed instructions on identification in future cases where identification of the defendant is based solely or substantially on eyewitness testimony."[57] The court backed this up three years later in reversing a conviction based upon eyewitness identification because a cautionary instruction had not been given.[58] In remanding the case for a new trial, the court commented:

> It has traditionally been recognized that identification testimony presents special problems of reliability because the in-court testimony of an eyewitness can be

55. United States v. Kavenaugh, 572 F.2d at 12-13 (1st Cir. 1978).

56. *Id.* at 13.

57. United States v. Dodge, 538 F.2d at 774 (8th Cir. 1976).

58. United States v. Greene, 519 F.2d 471 (8th Cir. 1979).

> devastatingly persuasive (Cites). Therefore, it is essential that a jury be aware of the conditions under which the observation was made, the physical ability of the witness to observe the defendant, and any possible problems which could distort the witness' observation powers and judgment.[59]

The court noted that a cautionary instruction must be given in an appropriate case where "the eyewitness testimony is essential to support a conviction."[60]

A number of states have also expressed a preference for — though not mandating — the giving of a cautionary instruction when appropriate. One of the earliest and most cited of these is a 1954 case where the Supreme Court of Pennsylvania[61] held that such an instruction would not be necessary if the following conditions prevailed: (1) there was a good opportunity for positive identification; (2) the witness is positive in his identification; (3) the identification is not weakened by prior failure to identify; and (4) the witness remains positive as to the identification even after cross-examination. However, the court went on to say that

> where the witness is not in a position to clearly observe the assailant, or he is not positive as to identity, or his positive statements as to identity are weakened by qualification or by failure to identify defendant on one or more prior occasions, the accuracy of the identification is so doubtful the Court should warn the jury that the testimony as to identity must be received with caution.[62]

This decision has been cited with approval by courts in a number of states.

---

59. *Id.* at 475.

60. *Id.* at 475.

61. Commonwealth v. Kloiber, 378 Pa. 412, 106 A.2d 820, *cert. denied,* 348 U.S. 875 (1954).

62. *Id.* at 826-27.

It must be recognized, however, that the majority of state jurisdictions view the cautionary instruction in an eyewitness case as a matter left to the sound discretion of the trial judge. Nevertheless, it must always be recognized that an appropriate case may present facts sufficient to establish grounds for reversal for abuse of discretion in refusing a *Telfaire*-style instruction. In any event, trial counsel should never fail to submit such a cautionary instruction where appropriate.

The trend appears to be toward a recognition of the unreliability of eyewitness identification testimony by requiring some type of limiting instruction on the order of the *Telfaire* model. Just where this trend may lead us might perhaps be gleaned from a study done in England. Appointed by the Home Secretary to investigate a disturbing series of erroneous eyewitness identifications, a committee headed by the respected Lord Patrick Devlin studied the problem and concluded in a 1976 report:

> We do, however, wish to ensure that in ordinary cases prosecutions are not brought on eyewitness evidence only and that, if brought, they will fail. We think they ought to fail, since in our opinion it is only in exceptional cases that identification evidence is by itself sufficiently reliable to exclude a reasonable doubt about guilt. We recommend that the trial judge should be required by statute
>
> (a) to direct the jury that it is not safe to convict upon eyewitness evidence unless the circumstances of the identification are exceptional or the eyewitness evidence is supported by substantial evidence of another sort; and (b) to indicate to the jury the circumstances, if any, which they might regard as exceptional and the evidence, if any, which they might regard as supporting the identification; and (c) if he is unable to indicate either such circumstances or such evidence, to direct the jury to return a verdict of not guilty.[63]

63. Devlin, "Report to the Secretary of State for the Home Department of the Departmental Committee on Evidence of Identification in Criminal Cases." (London: Her Majesty's Stationery Office 1976).

§ 12. Cross-Examination.

"Truth has a way of shifting under pressure."

Curtis Bok

The testimony of an eyewitness is almost uniquely subject to effective cross-examination. In nearly any type of identification case, the areas for inquiry will be limited only by counsel's experience and imagination.

In dealing with the eyewitness, counsel should organize a multi-pronged attack. These areas of questioning may include the following:

1. Witness' physical disabilities (hearing, eyesight, etc.)
2. Perception
3. Conditions at scene (lighting, distance, time, etc.)
4. Memory
5. Suggestive effect of police procedures (police statements, lineups, photos, etc.)
6. Inconsistent statements, descriptions, and/or identifications

7. Motive, bias and/or prejudice

In addition, of course, counsel will want to consider the possibility of suppressing evidence of any pretrial identifications as well as of an in-court identification.

§ 12-1. General Considerations.

Most defense counsel will conduct an extensive but conventional cross-examination of the eyewitness, and in this he will be given extensive latitude by the trial judge. However, counsel may also choose to employ more innovative techniques such as conducting experiments, lineups, or demonstrations in court, requesting a jury view of the crime scene, or employing psychologists as expert witnesses. In these and other areas he may encounter resistance from the trial judge.

§ 12-1.1. In-Court Lineups, Experiments, Demonstrations and the Use of Psychological Testimony.

Defense counsel may consider the possibility of conducting an in-court lineup — *i.e.,* a lineup held during the course of the trial and before a jury — or of seating his client in the audience during the eyewitness' testimony. The effect of an inability on the part of the witness to select the defendant out of an in-court lineup should have a devastating effect on the prosecution's case. But the in-court lineup is a terrible gamble: An identification of the defendant in a lineup is equally devastating. Obviously, counsel should give long and hard thought to the question of whether to ask for an in-court lineup.

Similar considerations apply to the conduct of experiments and demonstrations before the jury. For example, the eyewitness may have testified that he was able to see the defendant's facial features in a dark room because of the flash of light when he fired his revolver. In such a case, defense counsel may wish to conduct an experiment in which the witness is to observe an individual in the darkened courtroom as he fires a revolver loaded with blanks, and subsequently attempt to pick him out of an in-court lineup. Counsel may wish to demonstrate the inability of the eyewitness to perform certain psychological tests concerning memory and/or perception. Again, however, the risks of a "backfire" must be weighed against the possibility of beneficial results.

The proper procedures for the conduct of an effective lineup have been discussed elsewhere in this text, and the range of possible experiments and demonstrations is almost endless. Our concern here will be with the admissibility of such procedures.

Generally speaking, the granting or denial of permission to conduct in-court lineups lies within the "sound discretion" of the trial court, and a refusal to permit such a lineup will not constitute grounds for reversal. The currently prevailing attitude is best summarized in the following federal decision:

> [S]ome trial judges have granted defense requests to place the defendant in an in-court lineup, or to seat the defendant in the courtroom audience, before and during the testimony of the prosecution identification witness. (Cites.) Such arrangements are desirable efforts to ensure fair trials. But we cannot find any support for the assertion that a defendant has a right to such an arrangement whenever he requests it. Like the seating arrangement for prospective witnesses (cites), the procedure for in-court eyewitness identification is left to the trial judge's discretion. Absent abuse of that discretion resulting in procedure "so unnecessarily suggestive and conducive to irreparable mistaken identification" as to amount to a denial of due process of law (cites), we should not question the trial judge's ruling.[1]

---

1. United States v. Williams, 436 F.2d at 1168 (9th Cir. 1970).

There are a number of decisions specifically stating that such lineups may be permitted or prohibited according to the trial court's discretion.[2] Yet, the desirability of an in-court lineup under certain circumstances cannot be denied, and in the right situation a refusal by the trial judge to permit such a procedure may, at least arguably, amount to an abuse of discretion. As the same federal court quoted above stated:

> [W]here the question of guilt or innocence hangs entirely on the reliability and accuracy of an in-court identification, the identification procedure should be as lacking in inherent suggestiveness as possible. Yet that is often not the case. When asked to point to the robber, an identification witness — particularly if he has some familiarity with courtroom procedure — is quite likely to look immediately at the counsel table, where the defendant is conspicuously seated in relative isolation. Thus the usual physical setting of a trial may itself provide a suggestive setting for an eyewitness identification. . . .
>
> [In-court lineups] are desirable efforts to ensure fair trials. . . .[3]

For a discussion of pretrial lineups conducted by the defense and the right thereto, refer to § 9-3 *supra*.

Turning to the admissibility of experiments and demonstrations, again the universal position taken by the courts is that the trial judge has discretion to permit such procedures or not. Absent a very difficult to prove abuse of that discretion, denial of permission to conduct an in-court demonstration or experiment will not constitute grounds for reversal.

Finally, the admissibility of the testimony of experts, such as clinical psychologists on the issue of perception,

---

2. *See, e.g.*, Boyd v. State, 50 Tex. Crim. 138, 94 S.W. 1053 (1906); Green v. State, 223 Ind. 614, 63 N.E.2d 292 (1945).

3. 436 F.2d at 1168.

memory or out-of-court experiments, is also a matter left to the court's discretion. There does, however, appear to be greater room here for a finding of an abuse of that discretion.[4] An increasing number of commentators are advocating the use of experts on perception and memory. One such widely-recognized expert in the field, Patrick M. Wall,[5] points out that the psychological factors affecting a witness' identification can rarely be brought out for a jury by even the most skilled of lawyers on cross-examination. He advocates a solution, once suggested by Judge Jerome Frank,[6] that the trial judge himself call "testimonial experts" such as psychologists to testify as to the problems inherent in eyewitness identification. These "testimonial experts" could listen to the witness testify, perhaps administer psychological test(s) before trial, and then render an opinion as to the ability of the witness to perceive and remember. Wall then considers the current objections to such a procedure:

> First, it has been stated that the use of testimonial experts with respect to each witness would unduly prolong the trial. Judge Frank himself recognized this difficulty. But the suggestion here is limited to identification witnesses, and could be further limited, if necessary, to apply only to trial for serious crimes. Moreover, there seems to be no need for such experts to testify as extensively as do psychiatric experts in cases where insanity is a defense. Second, the objection has been made that these test results reflect only a general capacity on the part of the witness, while it is only his accuracy in the particular case which is of importance; one who has observed accurately may score low on the tests, while one who is completely in error may score high. This is no doubt true; test results may lead to

4. *See, e.g.,* State v. Hedgepath, 230 N.C. 33, 51 S.E.2d 914 (1949); Richardson v. State, 90 Md. 109, 44 A. 999 (1899).

5. Wall, Patrick M., *Eye-Witness Identification in Criminal Cases,* p. 212 (Charles C. Thomas 1965).

6. Frank, J., *Courts on Trial* (1949).

> error in any given case. But it is submitted that if a test has psychological validity, its use will prove of great value in the long run. Finally, it has been argued that when experts are allowed to give opinion as to the reliability of particular witnesses, they are "trespassing on the province of the jury." But the jury can well use all the help it can get in this area, and it may accept or reject the expert testimony as it wishes. It is submitted, therefore, that the objection based upon the "province of the jury" is no more than a shibboleth which, if accepted, would deprive the jury of important information useful and perhaps necessary for a proper decision on a difficult issue.[7]

There are any number of scientifically accepted psychological tests which will give indications as to the witness' relative ability to perceive and/or remember what he perceives. One of the most interesting and certainly relevant of these tests has been described by Dr. Robert Buckhout, Professor of Psychology and Director of the Center for Responsive Psychology at the Brooklyn College of the City University of New York. See § 4-3.2.

§ 12-1.2. Restriction by Trial Judge of Cross-Examination: Denial of Confrontation.

The Sixth Amendment grants to the defendant in a criminal case the right to confront witnesses testifying against him. Implicit in this right of confrontation is the right to cross-examination of those witnesses.[8] This right extends beyond a mere technical opportunity to cross-examine; it envisions the opportunity to *effectively* conduct a thorough cross-examination. Thus, if the trial judge unreasonably

---

7. Wall at 212.

8. Pointer v. Texas, 380 U.S. 400, 85 S. Ct. 1065, 13 L. Ed. 2d 923 (1965); Douglas v. Alabama, 380 U.S. 415, 85 S. Ct. 1074, 13 L. Ed. 2d 934 (1965); Barber v. Page, 390 U.S. 719, 88 S. Ct. 1318, 20 L. Ed. 2d 255 (1968).

restricts defense counsel's cross-examination of a prosecution eyewitness, grounds for reversal due to a denial of the right of confrontation may well be established.

The Supreme Court of the United States specifically addressed the issue of restrictions on cross-examination in *Smith v. Illinois.*[9] In that sale of narcotics case, the prosecution's informant admitted on cross-examination that the name he had given as his own on direct examination was not, in fact, his real name. When the witness was asked what his true name was, the trial judge sustained the prosecutor's objection; another prosecutorial objection was sustained when the defense attorney asked the witness where he lived. The Court reversed the conviction, then quoted from a forty-year-old Supreme Court decision.[10]

> "It is the essence of a fair trial that reasonable latitude be given the cross-examination, even though he is unable to state to the court what facts a reasonable cross-examination might develop. Prejudice ensues from a denial of the opportunity to place the witness in his proper setting and put the weight of his testimony and his credibility to a test, without which the jury cannot fairly appraise them. . . . To say that prejudice can be established only by showing that the cross-examination, if pursued, would necessarily have brought out facts tending to discredit the testimony in chief, is to deny a substantial right and withdraw one of the safeguards essential to a fair trial. . . ."[11]

§ 12-2. Establishing Suggestiveness of Pretrial Identification Procedures: Illustrative Cross-Examination.

The first avenue of attack in an eyewitness identification case is to attempt to suppress the in-court identification on

---

9. 390 U.S. 129, 88 S. Ct. 748, 19 L. Ed. 2d 956 (1968).

10. Alford v. United States, 282 U.S. 687, 51 S. Ct. 218, 75 L. Ed. 624 (1931).

11. 390 U.S. at 132.

constitutional grounds, as well as any evidence of pretrial identifications. This is normally done by properly noticing a pretrial motion to suppress, at which defense counsel can conduct examination of the police officer conducting the lineup, showups or mug shot display in question, and/or of the eyewitness himself. The purpose of questioning the officer is to establish noncompliance with constitutional requirements — due process, right to counsel, etc.; questioning the witness can also establish this (in fact, it is more likely to), but it can also indicate the effect on the witness of the suggestive procedures.

It should be recognized that the sample cross-examinations reproduced here need not be limited to motions to suppress. Most of the questions would be relevant to examination in trial to persuade the jury of the unreliable nature of the identification.

§ 12-2.1. Cross-Examination at Hearing of Police Officer Supervising Lineup.

The following represents an illustrative cross-examination hearing of an investigating officer who personally supervised the conduct of a lineup.

Advisement of rights.

Q. Officer Wilson, did you inform my client, Mr. Mendoza, of his constitutional rights?
A. I did.
Q. This was done by yourself?
A. By myself.
Q. Did you recite his rights from a Miranda card?
A. No. I recited them from memory.
Q. And what was the substance of the rights you recited to him?
A. That he had a right to remain silent; that if he gave up that right, anything he said could be used against him; that he had a right to have an attorney present.

Q. You've done some investigation into Mr. Mendoza's background, have you not?
A. A cursory investigation, yes.
Q. Mr. Mendoza comes from an economically poor community, from the barrio, doesn't he?
A. Yes.
Q. And you know that he has no job and receives disability compensation?
A. That's what I understand.
Q. Did you feel that Mr. Mendoza could afford to hire an attorney?
A. I didn't think about it; that's really not my concern.
Q. Well, you apparently didn't advise Mr. Mendoza that if he could not afford an attorney, one would be appointed free of charge.
A. I don't recall; I may have.
Q. Can you testify, under oath, that you definitely advised him that an attorney would be appointed if he could not afford one?
A. I'm not sure. But it didn't matter — he waived his rights.
Q. What exactly did he say?
A. I asked him if he understood the rights I had recited and if he wished to waive them. He then nodded affirmatively.
Q. Mr. Mendoza's primary language is Spanish, is it not?
A. I believe so.
Q. In fact, isn't his grasp of the English language rather poor?
A. He understands enough.
Q. You were aware he spoke English poorly?
A. That's obvious.
Q. Yet you recited his rights in English?
A. I don't speak Spanish.

Q. Did you attempt to obtain the services of a Spanish-speaking officer?
A. No.
Q. Can you testify that he understood those rights when you read them?
A. Like I said, he nodded.
Q. And you concluded that he was communicating an understanding and a waiver?
A. Yes.
Q. Were there any witnesses to this waiver?
A. No.
Q. Did you attempt to get the waiver in writing?
A. No.

Probable cause to arrest and place in lineup.

Q. How was it that Mr. Mendoza came to be in the lineup?
A. He was arrested by patrol officers.
Q. For what offense?
A. Suspicion of robbery. The lineup was for that robbery.
Q. What was the probable cause for the arrest?
A. He fit the description given us by the witnesses.
Q. What was that description?
A. Male, Latin, 20 to 30 years, wearing a T-shirt.
Q. Doesn't that description fit thousands of young men in the community?
A. Maybe. But he was found in the area of the robbery.
Q. How soon after the robbery took place?
A. About three, maybe four hours.

Suggestiveness of circumstances prior to lineup.

Q. Officer Wilson, when did this lineup take place?
A. November 2, about 1:30 p.m.
Q. This was the day after the robbery took place?

A. That's right.
Q. During that one day interval, was the witness confronted with Mr. Mendoza in a showup?
A. No, he was not.
Q. Was the witness, Mr. Johnson, shown any photographs, sketches, or composites during this period?
A. Yes, photos.
Q. By yourself?
A. Yes; I was the investigating officer.
Q. Was Mr. Mendoza in one of the photos?
A. He was.
Q. Were the photos shown one at a time or in strips?
A. Strips. Five to a strip.
Q. And how many strips?
A. Two.
Q. Were any of the persons in the first strip repeated in the second strip?
A. I believe so.
Q. Who was that?
A. The defendant.
Q. You are saying that Mr. Mendoza's photograph was the only one shown to the witness twice?
A. That's correct.
Q. Where did you get these photographs?
A. Mr. Mendoza's came from booking. Some of the others were from personnel, some from central index.
Q. Would you please explain?
A. Well, Mendoza's picture was from the booking procedure, a mug shot. Some were from police personnel files, photos of police department employees. Others came from our files on known criminals.
Q. As to Mr. Mendoza's mug shot, I presume there

were booking numbers under his face?
A. Yes.
Q. Were there any such numbers on the personnel photos?
A. No.
Q. Were there any numbers on the index photos?
A. No.
Q. Then a witness viewing those photos would immediately realize that only Mr. Mendoza's photo was definitely of a prisoner?
A. I wouldn't know what was in a witness' mind.
Q. I presume Mr. Johnson selected my client from these photographs?
A. He did.
Q. Did he choose any others?
A. No, only your client.
Q. When were these strips shown to Mr. Johnson?
A. About noon, November 2.
Q. One and a half hours before the lineup?
A. Yes.
Q. For how long was he allowed to study the two photographs of Mr. Mendoza before he selected him from the lineup?
A. He didn't study them; he just picked them out from the strips.
Q. Did Mr. Johnson appear to think for a while before selecting Mr. Mendoza's photo?
A. He appeared to give it thought, yes.
Q. Then he did not appear to immediately recognize Mr. Mendoza in the strip?
A. Not immediately, no.
Q. I must assume that other individuals represented in the photo displays were placed in the lineup?
A. No.
Q. Mr. Mendoza was the only one shown to the wit-

ness who appeared again in the lineup?
A. That's correct.
Q. Did any officers talk to the witnesses before the lineup?
A. Yes. I did.
Q. This took place at the police station?
A. Yes.
Q. Were you wearing a uniform and a gun at the time?
A. Yes.
Q. I assume you told them that the robbery suspect may not be in the lineup.
A. I don't believe so.
Q. You did not?
A. No.
Q. Who, then, did you tell them would be in the lineup?
A. Well, I don't think I told them anyone. That would be improper.
Q. I see. Had you told any of the witnesses that you had arrested a suspect?
A. Well, sure. That's what they were at the lineup for.
Q. You mean you told them that the suspect would be in the lineup?
A. I assumed they knew that.
Q. As the investigating officer, you informed them, in essence, that the person you believed was guilty would appear in the lineup?
A. Not in those words.
Q. What else did you tell the witnesses?
A. To think about it before making a choice.
Q. Did you tell them how expensive and time-consuming the lineup had been?
A. No.

Q. Or that it was important that they make an identification?
A. No. Well, I mentioned that it would be very helpful.
Q. Helpful?
A. To the case. It would be very helpful — to the case.
Q. You told the victims that an identification would help convict and punish the person who had terrorized them?
A. You're putting words in my mouth.
Q. Just before the lineup began, did you or did you not tell Mr. Johnson that if he could pick someone out it would be very helpful to you?
A. Words to that effect, yes.

Suggestiveness during conduct of lineup.

Q. What is a "blank lineup"?
A. A blank lineup is one where the person suspected of the crime is not included. He'd be put in a second lineup.
Q. And what is the purpose of a blank lineup?
A. I guess the theory is that it's a protection of sorts against the witnesses picking someone out just to pick them out.
Q. It tends to eliminate the propensity of a witness to make a selection regardless; is that correct?
A. That's the theory.
Q. And, of course, you used a blank lineup?
A. I did not. I don't hold with that theory.
Q. Is it an accepted police practice?
A. Accepted by some police, maybe. Not by me.
Q. Just how many lineups were shown to the witnesses?
A. One. The defendant was picked out by all the witnesses. There was no need for a second lineup.

Q. Isn't it possible some of the witnesses would have picked out others in a second lineup?
A. I doubt it.
Q. You do not know?
A. I don't know.
Q. How many men were in that lineup?
A. Six, including Mendoza.
Q. And where did you get them from?
A. Two were from patrol, one from vice.
Q. Police officers?
A. Yes. Three of them. But they weren't in uniform, of course.
Q. What were they wearing?
A. I don't recall exactly.
Q. Was a photograph taken of the lineup?
A. No.
Q. Were the officers either reporting to or leaving work?
A. Probably, yes.
Q. Then presumably they were in their casual street clothes?
A. Yes, I believe they were.
Q. The police department has standards for how officers must report to and from work, doesn't it?
A. Yes.
Q. Can I assume, then, that these three officers were dressed in clean, neat, and relatively conservative clothing?
A. I suppose so.
Q. And in what was Mr. Mendoza clothed at the lineup?
A. He wasn't in jail uniform, if that's what you're driving at.
Q. What was he wearing?
A. We gave him back the clothing he was arrested in.

He put them on for the lineup.
Q. As I recall, that clothing was wrinkled and soiled.
A. That's right. He got into a little scuffle with the patrolmen that arrested him.
Q. And there was blood on the front of the shirt.
A. From the scuffle.
Q. And so this man, in bloodied and soiled garments, was lined up next to the officers in their departmentally approved clothing?
A. Well, yes. And the other two men in the lineup.
Q. Who were the other two men?
A. They were from the holding cell. One was arrested on a drunk charge; I think the other was in for suspicion of rape. And they were both dressed pretty grubby, just like your client.
Q. Please describe the two men.
A. The rape suspect was tall with big shoulders.
Q. His race?
A. Black.
Q. And the other — the drunk?
A. Chicano, like Mendoza.
Q. Height? Weight?
A. Short, squat.
Q. Quite short and quite fat, wasn't he?
A. Yes.
Q. And about 49 and semi-bald?
A. I think that's about right.
Q. Mr. Mendoza is about 25, tall, slender, and with a full head of hair; is that a fair description?
A. I'd say so.
Q. Would you mistake Mr. Mendoza for being black?
A. No.
Q. And of what racial group were the three officers in the lineup?

A. I believe two were white, one black.

Q. You had obtained a physical description of the robber from the witnesses, had you not?

A. Yes.

Q. And what was that description?

A. Male, latin, 20 to 30 years, wearing a T-shirt.

Q. Did anyone in that lineup match that description, other than Mr. Mendoza?

A. No.

Q. Were you in charge of composing the lineup?

A. I was supervising.

Q. And, knowing the physical description, you put in only one person matching it?

A. I didn't actually choose the five men; I think the desk sergeant did.

Q. In the lineup that you supervised, the witnesses were shown only one man who came within their description of Mr. Mendoza; is that correct?

A. That's right.

Q. Why did you use police officers in the lineup?

A. They were available and were about the same age and height.

Q. Were there other officers present in the room during the lineup?

A. Probably.

Q. Isn't there a danger that there will be signs of recognition between the officers in the room and the witnesses and officers in the lineup?

A. No. The lighting is toward the stage. The men in the lineup cannot see into the rest of the room.

Q. Nevertheless, the three officers are not likely to appear nervous or afraid, are they?

A. I don't see why they would.

Q. Would you expect a person who had been in a fight with police officers, booked and jailed, and paraded before witnesses on a robbery charge to be nervous and frightened?

A. Not unless he was guilty.

Q. How many people are normally found in the county jail at one time?

A. Oh, maybe 60 or 70.

Q. And the court's holding cell?

A. A dozen, give or take.

Q. And, on an average, how many of them would be Chicano?

Q. I don't know. Ten or 20 maybe.

Q. Mostly young?

A. Yes.

Q. Then you had a ready source of men to put in the lineup, men who would come within the witnesses' descriptions?

A. I suppose so.

Q. Didn't you mention that the witnesses had described the robber as wearing a T-shirt?

A. Yes.

Q. Did any of the three officers in the lineup come to work wearing a T-shirt that day?

A. Of course not.

Q. Was the drunk wearing a T-shirt?

A. No.

Q. The rape suspect?

A. No.

Q. Then Mr. Mendoza was the only man shown to the witnesses who was wearing a T-shirt?

A. That's right.

Q. How many officers in the room during the lineup knew which of the six men was the suspect?

A. Well, some of the officers were coming and going. Only Sergeant Billings was there with me all the time.

Q. You and Sergeant Billings knew which was the

suspect, of course. And I presume the other officers were familiar with the three officers in the lineup?
A. I suppose so.
Q. Isn't there a possibility the witnesses may notice you or Sergeant Billings looking at Mr. Mendoza?
A. I doubt it.
Q. Or notice the other officers in the room smiling at their fellow officers in the lineup?
A. I doubt it.
Q. Were any of the participants standing in the lineup asked to speak or move?
A. Yes.
Q. Which ones?
A. All of them spoke. And your client was asked to point.
Q. Let's take that one at a time. What were all of them asked to speak?
A. Each one was told to say, "Lie down and don't say nothing."
Q. Mr. Mendoza spoke in a heavy Spanish accent?
A. Yes.
Q. Did any of the others in the lineup speak with an accent?
A. The guy arrested for drunkenness had a Spanish accent, too.
Q. Had the witnesses told you earlier that this was a phrase the robber had used?
A. That's right.
Q. And that it was said with a strong Spanish accent?
A. Yes.
Q. Were any participants in the lineup asked to say anything else?
A. Yes. Your client was told to repeat, "Any of you move, you're dead."
Q. Only Mr. Mendoza?

A. That was not my idea. Mr. Johnson asked me to have him say something else.
Q. Why didn't you use a neutral phrase?
A. I didn't really think about it.
Q. What is a neutral phrase?
A. Well, just some ordinary words that are unrelated to the incident.
Q. Why is it used?
A. Assuming it is used, I suppose the reason is that it won't trigger an emotional reaction in the witness.
Q. You mean a reaction to the words rather than to the voice?
A. Yes, something like that.
Q. But you had Mr. Mendoza use the exact words used at the scene.
A. That seems the proper procedure.
Q. Mr. Johnson had a loaded gun pointed at his head the last time he heard those words, hadn't he?
A. Yes.
Q. Now, you said Mr. Mendoza was asked to move?
A. Yes. I asked him to stand sideways and point his arm at Mr. Johnson. I asked Mr. Johnson to walk up to the stage, about five feet from the defendant.
Q. Was this to simulate an action that took place during the robbery?
A. Yes.
Q. Was it Mr. Johnson's idea to confront the man again?
A. No, it was mine. But only after Mendoza's voice had been identified.
Q. So Mr. Johnson was made to relive this traumatic incident in his life, with Mr. Mendoza playing the role of the robber?
A. If you want to look at it that way.
Q. No one else in the lineup was made to do this?

A. No.
Q. And after acting out this terrifying incident with Mr. Mendoza, Mr. Johnson identified him as the robber?
A. He did.

§ 12-2.2. Cross-Examination at Hearing of Eyewitness at Lineup.

The following is an example of cross-examination of an eyewitness at a hearing who had identified a suspect from out of a suggestive lineup.

Contrasting conditions at scene and at lineup.

Q. Now, Mr. Johnson, how was the lighting at the police lineup?
A. It was fine.
Q. And you had plenty of time to view the man?
A. Yes.
Q. Were you distracted?
A. No.
Q. Or frightened?
A. No.
Q. In other words, the conditions at the lineup were totally different from those at the scene of the robbery, weren't they?
A. Yes, I guess so.

Effect of suggestive police conduct.

Q. I understand you were shown some photographs by Officer Wilson shortly before the lineup?
A. Yes, the officer showed me two sets of photographs.
Q. Was there anything unusual about any of those photographs?
A. I don't think so. They were just photographs of faces.

Q. Did any of them have any names or numbers on them?
Q. Yes. In fact, the one I picked out had numbers.
Q. Were these numbers across the chest of the person in the photograph?
A. Yes.
Q. What were the numbers for, do you know?
Q. My understanding is that they're for identification when a person is arrested and thrown in jail.
Q. Then that person apparently had been, or was, in jail for some charge?
A. It would seem so.
Q. Did any of the other persons in the other photos appear to have been in jail?
A. No, I don't think so. At least, I couldn't tell from the photographs.
Q. How many men of Latin descent were in those photographs?
A. I don't recall.
Q. After you picked out Mr. Mendoza's photograph, did Officer Wilson say anything?
A. No. He just nodded quietly. I think he may have smiled.
Q. Why do you think he did that?
A. I don't know. I guess he was pleased with the results.
Q. He felt you picked out the right man?
A. I suppose so. That's what it seemed like, anyway.
Q. At the lineup, did Officer Wilson tell you that you didn't have to pick out anyone?
A. No, but he didn't tell us we had to, either. He just said it would be real helpful if we could.
Q. What did you think he meant by "real helpful"?
A. Well, obviously, if I could identify the man, then the case against him would be stronger than if I didn't.

Q. Then did you feel they already had a case against one of the men in the lineup, and it was a question of whether you could be of any help or not?
A. Sort of, yes.
Q. You wanted to be of help in that lineup, didn't you?
A. Of course.
Q. Did anyone say anything to you after you identified Mr. Mendoza?
A. Ms. Jones said something like, "It took long enough."
Q. Did any police officers talk with you?
A. Officer Wilson did; he just said they'd be in touch. I'd get a subpoena. You know, that kind of thing. And he thanked me, of course.
Q. Thanked you?
A. Sure. He said I'd done a service to the community, something like that.
Q. Officer Wilson told you that your selection of Mr. Mendoza was a service to the community?
A. Yes, words to that effect.
Q. Did he say anything else?
A. No, just that I'd picked the right man. And that they'd been trying to nail him for six months.
Q. Then Officer Wilson informed you that Mr. Mendoza was, in fact, the man who had committed the robbery?
A. In effect, yes.
Q. How did you think he knew Mr. Mendoza was guilty?
A. I didn't really think about it. Maybe Mendoza confessed.
Q. What did you think he meant when he said he'd been trying to nail Mr. Mendoza for six months?
A. That's obvious, isn't it? Mendoza must have pulled

a number of other robberies before he got to us.

Effect of suggestive lineup procedures.

Q. What did you expect to see in the lineup, Mr. Johnson?
A. Expect? I expected to see a bunch of men, like in the TV shows, standing next to each other.
Q. Why?
A. So I could pick out the man who robbed us.
Q. Then you assumed the man would be in the lineup?
A. Well, I never really thought about it. Yes, I guess I expected to see the man. Why else were we down there?
Q. You saw only one lineup; is that correct?
A. That's right.
Q. And how many men of Latin descent were in that lineup?
A. Two , I think.
Q. Were both of them young men?
A. No, only one. The defendant.
Q. Without looking at him, would you please describe him?
A. Medium height to tall, 20 to 30 years old, slender, and Mexican.
Q. Is that essentially the same description you originally gave the police?
A. Yes, I guess so.
Q. Can't you supply any greater detail now that you've seen him a number of times?
A. I don't understand your question.
Q. What about his hair, his facial structure, his speech patterns?
A. Well, like I said, he's Mexican.
Q. You mean his face is Mexican?
A. Well, you know, there's a lot of similarity among them.

Q. Most men of Mexican descent have similar features?
A. Somewhat, I guess. Yes.
Q. How did Mr. Mendoza differ from other men of his age and size, men of Mexican descent?
A. I don't know. It's hard to say. I'd have to see them, one next to another.
Q. But this was not done in the lineup, was it?
A. No.
Q. Nor in the photographic display you were shown?
A. No.
Q. Did you see anyone in the lineup wearing clothes that you recognized?
A. Sure. The defendant had on the same T-shirt he was wearing at the robbery.
Q. How do you know it was the same one?
A. Well, it looked the same.
Q. How was it different than any other T-shirt?
A. No different, I guess. A white T-shirt.
Q. Had there been blood on the shirt you saw at the robbery?
A. No.
Q. But there was blood on Mr. Mendoza's shirt in the lineup?
A. Yes. I guess he must have put up a fight when he was arrested.
Q. Is that what you thought when you saw him in the lineup?
A. I thought that maybe that was the reason for the blood.
Q. How many witnesses were there in the room watching the lineup?
A. Three: myself, Ms. Jones, and Mr. Smith.
Q. Where were you all seated with relation to one another?

A. We were seated a few feet apart.
Q. Did Mr. Smith or Ms. Jones select anyone from the lineup?
A. Yes. They both chose the defendant, same as me.
Q. Who picked him out first?
A. Ms. Jones. She was sure, right off the bat.
Q. And who was second?
A. Mr. Smith was second.
Q. You were third.
A. Yes. I wanted to be sure, so I took my time.
Q. I see. How was it that you knew Ms. Jones was first and Mr. Smith second?
A. Well, they told Officer Wilson.
Q. And you could hear?
A. Of course. We were only a few feet apart. Ms. Jones pointed to the defendant right off, and said "That's the man, that's him."
Q. This was before you had decided?
A. Yes.
Q. What did Mr. Smith say?
A. Well, I think he waited a few seconds. Then he kind of mumbled something like, "Yeah, it looks like him."
Q. And this was while you were still studying the men in the lineup and trying to decide if you recognized the man who had robbed you?
A. Yes.
Q. At this point, you were the only one of the witnesses who hadn't identified Mr. Mendoza, weren't you?
A. That's right. Like I said, I wanted to be sure.
Q. I suppose everyone's attention was focused on you then?
A. I don't know.

Q. Didn't you feel a bit like a "holdout"?
A. I never really thought about it.
Q. Did anyone say anything to you after the other two witnesses had identified Mr. Mendoza?
A. Yeah. Ms. Jones said something like, "It's obvious."
Q. Did Officer Wilson say anything to you?
A. No. Only that it was important, and I should try harder.
Q. When you didn't immediately agree with the other two witnesses, Officer Wilson told you to try harder?
A. Yes.
Q. Mr. Mendoza was asked to speak some phrases in the lineup, was he not?
A. That's right.
Q. And he speaks with a very strong Spanish accent?
A. Yes, I could barely understand him. It was the same accent I heard at the robbery.
Q. How did it differ from other Spanish accents?-
A. I don't know. It was a Spanish accent. They all sound the same to me.
Q. Then you couldn't differentiate Mr. Mendoza's accent from any other Spanish accent?
A. I don't know. Maybe.
Q. Did you hear Mr. Mendoza say at the lineup, "Any of you move, you're dead"?
A. Yes.
Q. He was the only one asked to say that?
A. Yes.
Q. When was the last time you had heard that phrase?
A. At the robbery.
Q. And that was also in a Spanish accent?
A. It was.

Q. When you heard it again, at the lineup, with the accent, did it remind you of the robbery?
A. It sure did. Sent a shiver up my spine. I could see that gun pointed at me.

§ 12-3. Establishing Unreliability of Identification: Illustrative Cross-Examination.

In most eyewitness identification cases, the verdict will largely depend upon defense counsel's ability to cross-examine the witness. Again, however, the benefits from calling the officer in charge of the investigative lineup, showup, or mug shot display as an adverse witness should not be overlooked; he may be able to establish suggestive police conduct of which the witness was not aware or which he does not recall.

§ 12-3.1. Cross-Examination at Trial of Eyewitness.

The following represents an illustrative cross-examination of an eyewitness in the most common of identification cases, a robbery:

Eyesight.

Q. Mr. Hilgard, I see you are wearing glasses today.
A. Yes.
Q. And were you wearing them at the time you saw the man at the scene?
A. Well, no. But I don't need them; I only use them for reading.
Q. They are bifocals, are they not?
A. Yes.
Q. And what are the upper halves of the lenses for?
A. My doctor seemed to think I needed them for astigmatism, but I don't.
Q. Astigmatism? You mean, to assist you in seeing objects and people?

A. I suppose so. But I find I don't need them, except for reading.
Q. What is your vision today, uncorrected?
A. Uh, well, I don't know.
Q. What was it when your optometrist last examined you?
A. I don't recall.
Q. Was it 20/20?
A. No, it wasn't 20/20.
Q. It was less than that?
A. I guess so.
Q. According to your optometrist, then, your vision is impaired?
A. That's what he says. But I can see fine.
Q. When was the last time you saw your optometrist?
A. Well, about two years ago, I think.
Q. Two years. And you have no corrective treatment since then?
A. No.
Q. Astigmatism is often degenerative; that is, it tends to get worse if not corrected, does it not?
A. I don't know. I think that's what the doctor told me.
Q. Do you have a current driver's license?
A. Sure.
Q. Does the license specify that you are required to wear corrective glasses when you drive?
A. Yes, it does.

Emotional condition at scene.

Q. When you saw the man coming out of the store with a gun in his hand, where were you?
A. I was across the street, maybe 30 or 40 feet from him. I could see him clearly.
Q. And you said the gun was a revolver, not an automatic?

A. That's right.
Q. You're sure of that? Were you able to see the gun clearly?
A. I sure could.
Q. Why was your attention directed to the gun?
A. I thought he might use it!
Q. On you?
A. Sure.
Q. Then you were afraid he was going to shoot at you?
A. Sure.
Q. Was the gun pointed directly at you?
A. Well, for a second, I think. But mostly it was being waved around.
Q. What went through your mind when it was pointed directly at you?
A. I don't know. I guess I was scared—real scared. I thought he'd kill me.
Q. And you watched the gun as it was being waved around?
A. Yes.
Q. Then your attention was primarily on the gun?
A. Well, that and other things.
Q. For how long did you stare at the gun?
A. I don't know—maybe ten seconds.
Q. Why didn't you drop to the ground?
A. I guess I was frozen. I mean, I couldn't move; I was scared.
Q. Did you see the gun as soon as you saw the man?
A. Yes. He was waving it around.
Q. Did you see the gun when he left?
A. Yes. He was still waving it.
Q. You were still afraid as he was leaving?
A. Sure.
Q. I assume you were still carefully watching what he

did with the gun.
A. I guess so.
Q. It must be pretty nerve-racking to experience a robbery such as that.
A. It sure is.
Q. Did you find your hands shaking afterward?
A. Some, yes.
Q. Heart pounding?
A. Some.
Q. Perspiration?
A. Yes, some.
Q. Do you have high blood pressure?
A. No.
Q. So your reaction was just normal nervousness or excitment?
A. I suppose so.
Q. When was the last time you were that nervous?
A. I don't know. I can't remember.
Q. You can't remember ever being that scared and nervous?
A. Not right off, no.

Conditions at scene of incident.

Q. You were across the street from this man with a gun, is that correct?
A. Yes.
Q. Were there cars passing along the street?
A. I guess so.
Q. And cars parked along the street?
A. I think so, yes.
Q. These moving and stationary cars were between you and this man when you saw him?
A. I suppose so. But I could still see him.
Q. And was he moving as well?
A. Yes.

Q. Then you were observing a moving man, partially blocked by moving cars and parked cars?
A. That's right.
Q. Now, you said you were carrying a bag of groceries when you first saw him?
A. That's what I said.
Q. And you dropped them to the pavement?
A. Yes.
Q. Did you later find anything broken?
A. Some eggs and a bottle of something.
Q. Did you hear them break when they hit?
A. The bottle, yes.
Q. I assume you looked down at the bag when you heard the bottle break?
A. Yes, I think I did. But just for a second.
Q. You were distracted only briefly then?
A. Yes. Briefly.
Q. How many seconds passed from the time you dropped the sack to the time the man left your sight?
A. Oh, five or ten seconds, maybe.
Q. Did it seem like a long time to you?
A. It sure did.
Q. In actual time, then, I assume it may have been less than five seconds?
A. I don't know. I wasn't timing it.
Q. And you dropped the sack right after you saw the man?
A. Yes.
Q. A second later?
A. Maybe.
Q. So you observed the man for a total of perhaps five seconds, perhaps less?
A. I don't know. Maybe. It seemed like a long time.

Q. All right. Now, this incident occurred at about nine o'clock in the evening, is that right?
A. About that. It was dark.
Q. And there are overhead lamps on the streets there, aren't there?
A. Yes.
Q. On the corners?
A. I think so.
Q. But none between the corners?
A. I'm not sure. But I think that's right.
Q. Was the store you saw him coming out of well lit?
A. Yes. Plenty of light to see him.
Q. And this store was a third of the way from the closest corner?
A. I think so, yes.
Q. So the only direct light was from the store.
A. Probably. Enough to light him up good.
Q. The light was coming from behind him, was it not?
A. What?
Q. He was coming out of the store, on the street in front of the store, when you saw him?
A. Yes.
Q. And he was facing you across the street?
A. Yes.
Q. Then the lighting was from the store behind him?
A. Well, yes, I guess that's right.
Q. Then he was outlined by the light?
A. Well, sort of, I guess. But I could see him.
Q. There was no direct light on his face?
A. I guess not.
Q. Did you see Mrs. Tafoya, the elderly lady in the blue dress, when she fainted?
A. Yes. I remember that. She was right next to me.
Q. Did you watch her fall?

A. Yes. But I couldn't move. I was afraid he'd shoot if I moved.
Q. Let me see. You observed the man for a total of perhaps five seconds?
A. Something like that.
Q. It was dark; he was outlined from the back; and there was no light directly on his face?
A. I guess that's right.
Q. Your view was somewhat blocked by a number of cars?
A. Partly. Only partly.
Q. And during the five seconds or less, your attention was diverted twice, once by the spilled bag and once by Mrs. Tafoya?
A. That's right.
Q. And during the undiverted three seconds or so, your attention was riveted to the gun.
A. Well, not riveted. I saw the man, too.

Witness' description of suspect at scene.

Q. You gave a description of this man to the police soon after the incident?
A. Yes.
Q. While it was still fresh in your mind?
A. That's right.
Q. Was it fresher in your mind then than it is today?
A. I suppose so.
Q. Showing you this report, and specifically directing your attention to page four, is that the description you gave to the police?
A. It looks like it.
Q. Would you please read it to the jury?
A. "Male Latin, approximately 25 to 30 years, 5 feet 10 inches, 160 to 170 pounds, long black hair, large moustache, white T-shirt, black jacket, black pants."

Q. Now, take a good look at my client [asking him to stand]. Would it surprise you to learn that he is 5 feet 6 inches tall?
A. Well, I guess he could be.
Q. And 145 pounds.
A. Maybe.
Q. How old does he appear to be?
A. Oh, I don't know.
Q. If I tell you he is 21, would that surprise you?
A. I suppose he could be 21.
Q. Would you call that moustache "large"?
A. Medium, I guess.
Q. What was my client wearing when you selected him from the police lineup?
A. Blue jeans, I think. And a denim jacket.
Q. Would it surprise you to learn that's what he was wearing when he was arrested a few minutes after the robbery occurred?
A. Well, the jeans were dark.
Q. The fact is, my client is not the same height, weight, or age of the man you saw, is he?
A. He's the man I saw.
Q. And he wasn't wearing the same clothes you described?
A. They're similar.
Q. And his moustache is not the same?
A. But he has a moustache.
Q. Aside from the white T-shirt and long black hair, is there anything about my client that fits your description?
A. He's a male Mexican.
Q. Does he appear to be of Spanish or Indian descent?
A. I don't know. They all look pretty much the same. But I know he's the one.

Pretrial identification.

Q. How many other witnesses were present at the lineup?
A. One other, Mrs. Tafoya.
Q. So this lineup was all for your benefit, you and Mrs. Tafoya.
A. I guess so.
Q. You realized, did you not, that the police had gone to a lot of trouble to arrange this lineup for you?
A. Yes.
Q. A lot of time and expense?
A. Yes.
Q. If you hadn't picked anyone out, it would have all been for nothing, wouldn't it?
A. I guess so.
Q. For how long did you look at the men in the lineup?
A. Oh, for about five minutes, I think.
Q. And of that, you spent most of the time studying my client, isn't that so?
A. Well, a lot of time, yes. I wanted to make sure.
Q. The lighting was good?
A. Yes, it was perfect.
Q. Better than where the robbery took place?
A. Yes.
Q. And you were only a few feet from the lineup?
A. That's right.
Q. Closer than you were to the man at the robbery?
A. Yes.
Q. And you had more time to view him — five minutes rather than five seconds?
A. That's right.
Q. And there were no distractions?
A. No.
Q. And you were not afraid, not nervous?
A. No. I guess not. Well, maybe a little nervous.

Q. And in five minutes, under those ideal conditions, you were able to memorize my client's face, to burn him in your memory, were you not?
A. Well, I remember him pretty good, yes.
Q. Were you convinced after studying the man at the lineup that he was the man you had seen at the robbery?
A. Pretty sure, yes.
Q. *Pretty* sure?
A. I'm sure.
Q. Your memory of the man's features at the lineup is much clearer than your memory of the man at the robbery?
A. Sure. I told you that.
Q. But you are convinced they are the same man?
A. I am.
Q. And the man you have identified here in court today, my client, is the man you saw in the lineup?
A. That's right.
Q. Therefore, he must be the man you saw at the robbery?
A. Yes.
Q. Then you are identifying my client here today primarily because you saw him in the lineup?
A. Well, he's the one I saw both times.
Q. Of which event is your memory clearer, the robbery or the lineup?
A. The lineup, of course.
Q. Then it is mainly on the basis of the *lineup* that you today identified my client?
A. Well, on the basis of both times.
Q. You are absolutely sure that this man, my client, is the one you saw in the lineup?
A. Absolutely.
Q. But your observations at the scene of the robbery

lasted only about three seconds and were under poor conditions.

A. Well, sure, things were easier at the lineup.

Q. And more reliable?

A. I guess so.

Q. Then your identification today is based more on having seen my client at the lineup than on having seen him at the scene of the robbery?

A. I guess so.

Motive, bias.

Q. Was anyone injured during this robbery?

A. Yes, I believe Mrs. Tafoya was.

Q. Did you know her?

A. Yes.

Q. And you were friends with the victims in the robbery, were you not?

A. Yes. I knew them.

Q. How did you feel about this incident?

A. Feel?

Q. Yes, what was your emotional reaction?

A. Well, I was afraid, of course.

Q. And after it was over and the fear gone?

A. I guess I was upset, concerned.

Q. Angry?

A. Yes, I think I was angry.

Q. At the person who committed the robbery and endangered you and your friends?

A. Of course.

Q. Did you feel any desire to seek revenge against this person?

A. Well, maybe so.

Q. Then you felt you wanted to do something damaging to this person?

A. Well, not illegally, of course.

Q. Within the law?

A. Yes, within the law.
Q. Then you wanted to injure this person in court?
A. I wouldn't put it that way.
Q. You wanted to have revenge and you wanted to do it in a legal way . . . in a legal proceeding?
A. Well, I suppose so. In a legal way.
Q. Have you or any close relatives or friends ever been robbed?
A. Yes. I was held up two years ago, and our apartment was burglarized about five years ago. And my wife had her purse taken from her last year.
Q. You've been the victim of a number of crimes, then?
A. Yes.
Q. How many of the culprits were caught and sent to jail?
A. Only one, the purse-snatcher. But he was let go on probation.
Q. You mean that every time you or your wife have been assaulted, the criminal has gotten away or gotten off?
A. That's right.
Q. That must be frustrating.
A. Yes.
Q. But this time, with my client, you're going to make sure he doesn't get off?
A. That's up to the jury.
Q. I assume that if it ever happens to you again, you will be careful in your observations of the culprit to help the police as much as possible?
A. Of course.
Q. And you'll do everything you can — legally, of course — to see that he is punished?
A. I will.

Q. You want very much to see such a person punished, do you not?
A. I want to see justice, if that's what you mean.
Q. Have you ever testified in court before?
A. No.
Q. Ever taken part in a police investigation?
A. My wife has, but I haven't.
Q. Ever had your name on the front page of the newspaper before?
A. I don't think so.
Q. It must be pretty exciting being the star witness in such a case as this?
A. I never really thought about it.
Q. You never thought about how important you are in this case?
A. Well, I suppose so — a little.
Q. You're the star witness, the key to the whole case, are you not?
A. I'm not a lawyer, I don't know.
Q. But you do realize how important you are and how much your testimony means?
A. Yes, I guess so.
Q. How old was the individual who yanked your wife's purse from her?
A. He was 18, according to the police.
Q. And the man who robbed you two years ago?
A. I'd say he was 20 or so.
Q. And the man who burglarized your home. I realize you didn't see him, but do you think he was young or old?
A. I assume he was probably young, also.
Q. That's a pretty safe assumption, isn't it?
A. Yes.
Q. Why?
A. Why?

Q. Why is it safe to assume the burglar you didn't see was a young man?
A. Well, young people seem to commit all the crimes nowadays.
Q. So, if you read of a person committing a crime, you'd assume he was young?
A. Well, probably — I mean, the probabilities are he was.
Q. How old would you say my client is?
A. Oh, about 22, I guess.
Q. About the age of the person who robbed you two years ago?
A. About, yes.
Q. Are you nervous?
A. Well, a little, I guess.
Q. Well, that's understandable. There are a lot of people listening to your testimony. These trial proceedings must appear pretty formidable to you.
A. Yes, they do, to tell you the truth.
Q. I assume with all of this, you want to make sure you get your story straight, tell all the facts exactly the way they were.
A. Sure. That's what I'm here for.
Q. But suppose the police disagreed with part of your story?
A. I don't understand.
Q. Suppose the police records showed one fact but you thought that fact was wrong?
A. Yes?
Q. Would you feel you were right anyway?
A. I guess so.
Q. The police are the experts in this sort of thing, aren't they?
A. Yes.

Q. Wouldn't you have doubts about your version of the fact if the experts said you were wrong?
A. Maybe. Yes, I'd probably have doubts.
Q. The police are more likely to be right about a criminal matter than you are, aren't they?
A. Well, I guess so.
Q. Wouldn't you tend to reassess your version of the facts?
A. Yes, I probably would.
Q. Certainly before testifying in an important matter such as this trial, with reporters taking down every single word you say, you'd want to make sure your version of the facts was accurate?
A. Yes.
Q. You wouldn't want to make a mistake?
A. Of course not.
Q. And the police are the experts, aren't they?
A. Yes.

§ 12-3.2. Cross-Examination at Trial of Police Officer Conducting Lineup.

The following is an example of an examination before a jury of a police officer who supervised a lineup in a robbery case, conducted to illustrate for the jury the effect upon the eyewitness of suggestive police procedures. The witness should, of course, be called as a hostile witness so that leading questions may be asked.

[After introduction and identification of witness]

Q. Sergeant Tennyson, you conducted the lineup in which Mr. Sager identified my client as the robbery suspect, did you not?
A. That's correct.
Q. How many persons were placed in the lineup, exclusive of my client?

A. Five.
Q. And how many lineups were there?
A. One.
Q. You did not use a blank lineup first?
A. No. I didn't feel it was necessary.
Q. What is a blank lineup?
A. A lineup in which the suspect is left out.
Q. And what is its purpose?
A. The theory is that the witness tends to believe, before he even sees the lineup, that one of the persons in it must be the culprit, and thus is inclined to pick someone.
Q. But Mr. Sager was shown no blank lineup?
A. I didn't feel it necessary. And we were short of men.
Q. What men did you use?
A. Some vice officers and narcotics officers going off duty; they were in plain clothes.
Q. Isn't it true that police officers tend to have a different bearing, an attitude of confidence, that separates them from suspects in a lineup?
A. I don't know.
Q. Did the officers all know each other?
A. Yes.
Q. Then they all knew my client was the only non-officer in the lineup?
A. I suppose so.
Q. Were any of them looking at my client during the lineup viewing?
A. I don't recall.
Q. Weren't any inmates available for use in the lineup?
A. It was easier to use the officers.
Q. All five officers were male Latins?
A. Four of them were. The fifth was white.
Q. You had Mr. Sager's description of the suspect?
A. Yes.

Q. Then you knew he would not select the white man?
A. I didn't know what Mr. Sager would do.
Q. How many of the remaining four officers were within three inches and twenty pounds of my client?
A. Well, three of them were, I believe.
Q. And how many were within five years of my client's age?
A. One was.
Q. Did he have long, black hair?
A. Yes.
Q. Was he wearing a moustache?
A. I don't believe he was.
Q. Then, my client was the only one shown to Mr. Sager who matched the description given by him?
A. I suppose that would be correct.
Q. Was my client wearing a T-shirt and dark trousers and jacket?
A. Yes.
Q. Were any of the five officers wearing T-shirts with dark trousers and jackets?
A. I believe two of them had on T-shirts.
Q. Then my client was also the only one who was wearing clothing similar to that described?
A. Similar, yes.
Q. Did you tell my client to say anything while Mr. Sager was watching?
A. Yes. I instructed him to repeat, "Don't nobody move, or you're dead."
Q. Why these words?
A. That's what the robbery suspect said at the scene when he came out of the store.
Q. You are aware that many officers at lineups have the persons repeat neutral phrases rather than words used during the crime?
A. Yes.

Q. Why is that, Sergeant?
A. The theory, I suppose, is that hearing the words again has an emotional effect on the witness, triggers identification or something. I personally don't agree with this theory.
Q. And you did not use a neutral phrase.
A. I did not.
Q. When Mr. Sager arrived at the lineup, did you tell him who was in it?
A. Of course not. He didn't know five of the men were police officers.
Q. Did he know one of the men was a suspect?
A. I presume so.
Q. Did you tell him that?
A. I informed him that we had a man whom we believed to be involved in the robbery.
Q. And that he was one of the men in the lineup?
A. No. I never told him that.
Q. But that was the only lineup you showed him?
A. Yes.
Q. So he believed the man whom he had seen commit the robbery was one of the six men in the lineup?
A. I can't say what he believed.
Q. Isn't it normal procedure to inform the witness that the lineup doesn't necessarily contain the person seen, and that he is not to infer that any of the people in the lineup are suspects?
A. That is not my normal procedure.
Q. Now, Sergeant, what exactly did Mr. Sager say in picking out my client?
A. He said, "That's the man."
Q. Didn't he say, "I think that's the man."
A. Yes. Something like that.
Q. In fact, didn't he waver between my client and one of the other men in the lineup?

A. I believe he did initially consider one of the other men.
Q. Then Mr. Sager almost selected a police officer as the robbery suspect?
A. He considered him briefly.
Q. Were there any other witnesses at the lineup while Mr. Sager was there?
A. Yes, there was one.
Q. Did the other witness identify my client?
A. Yes.
Q. Did she do so before Mr. Sager selected my client?
A. Yes.
Q. How did she indicate her selection?
A. She pointed to your client and said, "He's the one — I'm sure of it."
Q. This is the woman who fainted a second after seeing the man with the gun?
A. Yes.
Q. And Mr. Sager saw her pick out my client?
A. I suppose so.
Q. And he then also picked him out — after he had seen her selection?
A. Yes.

BIBLIOGRAPHY

Books

Bailey, F. Lee, and Rothblatt, Henry B., *Cross-Examination in Criminal Trials* (Bancroft-Whitney/LCP, 1978).

Basinger, Louis F., *The Techniques of Observation and Learning Retention* (Charles C. Thomas 1973).

Bischof, L.J., *Adult Psychology* (Harper & Row, 1976).

Block, Eugene B., *Hyponosis* (David McKay, 1976).

Borchard, E.M., *Convicting the Innocent* (Archon, 1961).

Burtt, *Legal Psychology* (Prentice-Hall, 1931).

Cipes, *Criminal Defense Techniques* (Mathew Bender).

Fraisse, P., *The Psychology of Time* (Harper & Row, 1963).

Frank, J., *Courts on Trial* (Princeton, 1949).

Frankfurter, Felix, *The Case of Sacco and Vanzetti* (Little, Brown, 1927).

Freedman, J.L., et al., *Social Psychology* (Prentice-Hall, 1974).

Gibson, J.J., *The Perception of the Visual World* (Houghton Mifflin, 1950).

Houts, *From Evidence to Proof* (1956).

Inbau, Fred E., and Reid, J.E., *Lie Detection and Criminal Interrogation* (Williams and Wilkins, 1953).

James, W., *The Principles of Psychology* (Dover, 1950).

Kagan, J., and Havemann, E., *Psychology: An Introduction* (Harcourt Brace Jovanovich, 1972).

Klatzky, R.L., *Human Memory* (Freeman, 1975).

Liggett, J., *The Human Face* (London: Constable, 1974).

Loftus, Elizabeth F., *Eyewitness Testimony* (Harvard, 1979).

Loftus, Elizabeth F., *Memory* (Addison-Wesley, 1980).

Marshall, J., *Law and Psychology in Conflict* (Bobbs-Merrill, 1966).

McCarthy, *Psychology and the Law* (1960).

Neisser, U., *Cognitive Psychology* (Appleton, 1967).

Norman, D., *Memory and Attention* (Wiley, 1976).

Paivio, A., *Imagery and Verbal Processes* (Holt, Rinehart and Winston, 1971).

Rolph, *Personal Identity* (1957).

Sales, B.D. (Ed.), *Psychology in the Legal Process* (Spectrum, 1977).

Secord, P.F., and Backman, C.W., *Social Psychology* (McGraw-Hill, 1974).

Sobel, Nathan R., *Eye-Witness Identification* (Clark Boardman, 1972).

Thornwald, J., *Crime and Science* (Harcourt Brace Jovanovich, 1967).

Toch, H., *Legal and Criminal Psychology* (Holt, Rinehart and Winston, 1961).

Trankell, Arne, *Reliability of Evidence* (Beckmans, 1972).

Wall, Patrick M., *Eyewitness Identification in Criminal Cases* (Charles C. Thomas, 1965).

Wellman, Frances, *The Art of Cross-Examination* (1927).

Wicklegren, W.A., *Learning and Memory* (Prentice-Hall, 1977).

Wilder and Wentworth, *Personal Identification* (1918).

Yarmey, A. Daniel, *The Psychology of Eyewitness Testimony* (Free Press/Macmillan, 1979).

Zavala, Albert, and Paley, James J., *Personal Appearance Identification* (Charles C. Thomas 1972).

Articles

Baddeley, A.D., "Selective Attention and Performance in Dangerous Environments," 63 British J. Psychology 537 (1972).

Brigham, J.C., and Barkowitz, P., "Do They All Look Alike?," 8 J. Applied Psychology 306 (1978).

Brown, "An Experience in Identification Testimony," 25 J. Crim. L., C. and P.S. 621 (1934).

Brown, E., et al., "Memory for Faces and the Circumstances of Encounter," 62 J. Applied Psychology 311 (1977).

Buckhout, R., "Eyewitness Identification and Psychology in the Courtroom," 4 Crim. Defense 5 (1977).

Buckhout, R., "Eyewitness Testimony," 231 Sci. Amer. 23 (1974).

Buckhout, R., "Nearly 2000 Witnesses Can't Be Wrong," 2 Social Action and the L. 7 (1975).

Cady, H.M., "On the Psychology of Testimony," 35 Am. J. Psychology 110 (1924).

Chenowith, "Police Training Investigates the Fallibility of the Eye Witness," 51 J. Crim. L.C. and P.S. 378 (1960).

Clifford, B.R., and Scott, J., "Individual and Situational Factors in Eyewitness Testimony," 63 J. Applied Psychology 352 (1978).

Comment, "Defendant's Right to a Lineup as a Means of Discovery," 21 Wayne L. Rev. 991 (1975).

Comment, "*Manson v. Brathwaite,*" 26 Kan. L. Rev. 464 (1978).

Comment, "No Right to Counsel at Photographic Identification," 34 Ohio St. L.J. 928 (1973).

Doob, A.M., and Kirshenbarum, H.M., "Bias in Police Lineups — Partial Remebering," 1 J. Police Sci. and Admin. 287 (1973).

Eisenberg and Feustel, "Pretrial Identification: An Attempt to Articulate Constitutional Criteria," 58 Marq. L. Rev. 659 (1975).

Ellis, et al., "Experimental Studies of Face Identification," 3 Nat. J. Crim. Defense 219 (1977).

Feingold, G.A., "The Influence of Environment on Identification of Persons and Things," 5 J. Crim. L. and Criminology 39 (1914).

Fogelsong, "Control of Procedures for Identifying a Suspect," 12 J. Forensic Sci. 135 (1967).

Gardner, D.S., "The Perception and Memory of Witnesses," 18 Cornell L.Q. 391 (1933).

Grano, "*Kirby, Biggers* and *Ash:* Do Any Constitutional Safeguards Remain Against the Danger of Convicting the Innocent?," 72 Mich. L. Rev. 717 (1974).

Harmon, "The Recognition of Faces," 229 Sci. Amer. 70 (1973).

Hisko, "Are the Courts Listening to Voiceprints?," 12 Creighton L. Rev. 517 (1978-1979).

Kubie, "Implications for Legal Procedure of the Fallibility of Human Memory," 108 U. Pa. L. Rev. 59 (1959).

Laughery, K.R., et al., "Recognition of Human Faces," 55 J. Applied Psychology 477 (1971).

Lefcourt, "The Blank Lineup: An Aid to the Defense," 14 Crim. L. Bull. 428 (1978).

Leippie, M.R., et al., "Crime Seriousness as a Determinant of Accuracy in Eyewitness Identification," 63 J. Applied Psychology 345 (1978).

Lesgold, A.M., and Petrush, A.R., "Do Leading Questions Alter Memories?," unpublished (Univ. of Pittsburgh, 1977).

Levine, F.J., and Tapp, J.L., "The Psychology of Criminal Identification," 121 U. Penn. L. Rev. 1079 (1973).

Lipton, J.P., "On the Psychology of Eyewitness Testimony," 62 J. Applied Psychology 90 (1977).

Loftus, E.F., "Leading Questions and the Eyewitness Report," 7 Cognitive Psychology 560 (1975).

Loftus, E.F., "Unconscious Transference in Eyewitness Identification," 2 Law and Psychology Rev. 93 (1976).

Loftus, E.F., "Reconstructive Memory Processes in Eyewitness Testimony," in *Perspectives in Law and Psychology* (Plenum, 1978).

Loftus, E.F., "Reconstructive Memory: The Incredible Eyewitness," 62 J. Applied Pyschology 90 (1977).

Loftus, E.F., and Zanni, G., "Eyewitness Testimony: The Influence of the Wording of a Question," 5 Bull. Psychonomic Soc. 86 (1975).

Malpass, R.S., and Kravitz, J., "Recognition of Faces of Own and Other Races," 13 J. Personality and Social Psychology 330 (1969).

Marshall, "Evidence Psychology and the Trial: Some Challenges to Law," 63 Colum. L. Rev. 197 (1963).

Morris, "Convicting the Innocent," 37 J. Crim. L., C. & P.S. 408 (1947).

Murray, "The Criminal Lineup at Home and Abroad," Utah L. Rev. 610 (1966).

Nahstoll, "Observation and Memory of Witnesses," 48 ABA J. 68 (1962).

Note, "Did Your Eyes Deceive You? Expert Psychological Testimony on the Unreliability of Eyewitness Identification," 29 Stan. L. Rev. 969 (1977).

Note, "*Evans v. Superior Court:* A Discovery Dimension to the Pretrial Lineup," 12 Cal. Western L. Rev. 614 (1976).

Note, "Expert Testimony on Eyewitness Perception," 82 Dick. L. Rev. 465 (1978).

Note, "The Lineup's Lament — *Kirby v. Illinois,*" 22 DePaul L. Rev. 660 (1973).

Note, "Pretrial Identification Procedures: The Expanded Duty to Disclose Favorable Evidence," 50 Notre Dame Law. 508 (1975).

Note, "The Pretrial Right to Counsel," 26 Stan. L. Rev. 399 (1974).

Paul, "Identification of Accused Persons," 12 Austl. L.J. 42 (1938).

Pridgen, "*U.S. v. Crews:* Eyewitness Identification Under the Exclusionary Rule," 7 Search and Seizure L. Rep. (May 1980).

Pulacki, "*Neil v. Biggers:* The Supreme Court Dismantles the *Wade* Trilogy's Due Process Requirements," 26 Stan. L. Rev. 1097 (1974).

Redmount, "The Psychological Basis of Evidence Practices: Memory," 50 J. Crim. L. C. and P.S. 249 (1959).

Rouke, F.L., "Psychological Research on Problems of Testimony," 13 J. Social Issues 50 (1957).

Rouse, "Are We in Focus on Photo Identification?," 3 U.S.F.L. Rev. 419 (1973).

Ruffin, "Out on the Limb of the Poisonous Tree: The Tainted Witness," 15 U.C.L.A. L. Rev. 32 (1967).

Ryle and Mackbee, "Authentication and Identification," 49 Mississippi L.J. 151 (1978).

Siegel, J.M., and Loftus, E.R., "Impact of Anxiety and Life Stress Upon Eyewitness Testimony," 12 Bull. Psychonomic Soc. 479 (1978).

Snee, T.J., and Lush, D.E., "Interaction of the Narrative and Interrogative Methods of Obtaining Testimony," 11 J. Psychology 229 (1941).

Sobel, "Assailing the Impermissible Suggestion: Evolving Limitations on the Abuse of Pre-Trial Criminal Identification Methods," 38 Brooklyn L. Rev. 261 (1971).

Sommer, R., "The New Look on the Witness Stand," 8 Canadian Psychologist 94 (1959).

Stafford, C.F., "The Child as a Witness," 37 Wash. L. Rev. 303 (1962).

Thorson, G., and Hochhaus, L., "The Trained Observer: Effects of Prior Information on Eyewitness Reports," 10 Bull. Psychonomic Soc. 454 (1977).

Trovillo, "Scientific Proof of Credibility," 22 Tenn. L. Rev. 743 (1953).

Tyrrell and Cunningham, "Eyewitness Credibility: Adjusting the Sights of the Judiciary," 37 Ala. L. Rev. 563 (1976).

Wells, G.L., et al., "Accuracy, Confidence and Juror Perceptions in Eyewitness Identification," J. Applied Psychology (1979).

Vickery and Brooks, "Time-Spaced Reporting of a 'Crime' Witnessed by College Girls," 29 J. Crim. L., C. and P.S. 371 (1938).

Williams and Hammelmann, "Identification Parades," 1963 Crim. L. Rev. 479.

Zanni, G.R., and Offermann, J.T., "Eyewitness Testimony: An Exploration of Question Wording Upon Recall as a Function of Neuroticism," 46 Perceptual and Motor Skills 163 (1978).

INDEX

References are to page numbers.

A

B

C

D

E

F

G

H

I